ILLUSTRIOUS AMERICANS:

HENRY CLAY

*One of a series of books
about great men and women,
each studied in three ways*

BIOGRAPHY

PICTURE PORTFOLIO

HIS OWN WORDS

ILLUSTRIOUS AMERICANS:

HENRY CLAY

By Glyndon G. Van Deusen
and the Editors of Silver Burdett

Editor in Charge: Sam Welles

SILVER BURDETT COMPANY
A Division of General Learning Corporation
Morristown, New Jersey • Park Ridge, Ill. • Palo Alto • Dallas • Atlanta

CONTENTS

LIBRARY OF CONGRESS CATALOG CARD NUMBER: 66-24454
© 1967 GENERAL LEARNING CORPORATION
ALL RIGHTS RESERVED
PRINTED IN THE UNITED STATES OF AMERICA
PHILIPPINES COPYRIGHT 1967 BY GENERAL LEARNING CORPORATION
PUBLISHED SIMULTANEOUSLY IN CANADA

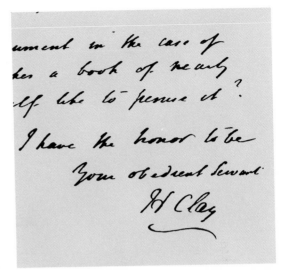

ACKNOWLEDGMENTS

The biography section of this book was written by Glyndon G. Van Deusen, Research Professor of History, Emeritus, at the University of Rochester, where he also served as Chairman of the History Department and Associate Dean for Graduate Studies of the College of Arts and Sciences. Dr. Van Deusen took his Ph.D. at Columbia and has taught in New Zealand and Europe. An authority on nineteenth-century American history, he has published several books dealing with the men and events of that period as well as some more general works written in collaboration with others.

The editors have prepared the boxed observations on Clay, selected the illustrations, and excerpted some 60,000 words that Clay himself wrote, with a commentary placing each passage in a meaningful context.

Excerpts from the following book have been used with permission: Abridged from pp. 9–10, 30, 48–49 of *America's Silver Age* by Gerald Johnson. Copyright 1939 by Harper & Brothers; renewed 1957 by Gerald W. Johnson. Reprinted by permission of Harper & Row, Publishers. The editors also wish to thank the following individuals and collections for permission to quote from documents in their possession: J. Winston Coleman, Jr., and Thomas D. Clark of Lexington, Kentucky; the University of Kentucky Library; and the National Archives. In addition, the compilation *The Papers of Henry Clay* edited by James F. Hopkins, University of Kentucky Press, was a valuable source.

Walter Kossmann was assistant editor for the volume. Henry Moscow wrote the text accompanying the Picture Portfolio. The text research was done by Denise Farrell and Mara Jayne Klein, and the picture research by Elizabeth Evans and Patricia Smalley. Elizabeth Roberts did the copy editing and Louella Still Culligan prepared the index.

Designer: Wayne Young

An elderly but determined Henry Clay faces a divided Senate to promote the 1850 Compromise, an apex in his career.

Chapter 1 **OUT OF THE SLASHES**

IN APRIL 1777, the American Revolution had been in progress for two years; Virginia, the Old Dominion (so-named by King Charles II when it demonstrated loyalty to the Stuarts while other dominions fell away during the Commonwealth era of Cromwell), was in the front ranks of the fight. A galaxy of Virginians—George Washington, Thomas Jefferson, Patrick Henry, James Madison, and others—were leaders in this struggle for independence. Many a planter and stout Virginia yeoman had volunteered for service in the Continental Army, and much Virginia blood had already been spilled in the cause of liberty. That same year, Benjamin Franklin was negotiating the all-important alliance with the French, and Jefferson was appealing to the consciences of Virginians by speaking out boldly for religious freedom and against the feudalistic laws (such as quitrent, entail, and primogeniture) that stood as a barrier to equal opportunity in landholding. Democracy was on the march.

About a year before Henry Clay was born on April 12, 1777, Jefferson had drafted the Declaration of Independence, laying down the basic principles of American democracy: that men are created equal and that they have an inalienable right to life, liberty, and the pursuit of happiness. To attain these principles, the American colonists had fired the shots at Concord Bridge signaling the beginning of their fight for independence from Great Britain. These were stirring times, manifested finally by an upheaval of political philosophy that would bring on the French Revolution and the eventual toppling of monarchs from their gilded thrones in much of Europe.

The fortunes of war were soon to turn against Great Britain, but the immediate prospects of the American cause seemed none too bright in early 1777. The army of the "rebels," as King George III called them, had been roughly used in the campaigns of the previous year, and had emerged from winter quarters at Morristown, New Jersey, in less than fighting trim. In Canada, a British expedition under the command of "Gentleman Johnny" Burgoyne—a debonair individual whose passion for gambling, as well as for literature and the arts, was greater than his military talent—had begun to muster, for an invasion of New York State.

Rumors that the Redcoats might next appear in Virginia were as plentiful there as the spring flowers, especially in Hanover County where the Reverend John Clay, a Baptist preacher and tobacco planter of modest means, had made his home. Sometimes called Sir John, though nobody knows just why, Clay and his wife, Elizabeth Hudson Clay, owned a few slaves and thus were considered people of some financial substance. They were also good Patriots, supporters of Thomas Jefferson and Patrick Henry in their opposition to the British king and his Tory minions.

Sir John died in June 1781. The day after his funeral Colonel Banastre Tarleton's dragoons raided Hanover County and pillaged the Clay homestead—etching a lasting image on the mind of a four-year-old boy who was to show in later years no consuming love for Great Britain. That fall when the war ended, for all practical purposes, with Lord Cornwallis' surrender at Yorktown, young Henry Clay undoubtedly added his childish treble to the general rejoicing among the Clays' friends and neighbors.

In later life, Clay often told how he, "an orphan boy," had been brought up in a condition of poverty and ignorance. One of the nicknames bestowed upon him by his followers was "The Millboy of the Slashes," a reference to the cutover area in which he was born (see pages 90–91). Actually, he lived moderately well during his childhood. Elizabeth Clay, his mother, married a second time, and Clay's stepfather, Henry Watkins, was a man of property, who took young Henry into his household and gave him such scanty opportunity for schooling as the place and times afforded. Henry Clay the statesman, however, found it politically expedient to expound on this legend of youthful poverty. Apparently unconscious of this exaggeration, Clay seems to have eventually convinced himself of an essence of truth in the fiction about his early environment.

Education and early politics

Virginia, in the years of struggle for American independence and evolution of a constitutional government, boasted its full share of Patriots and statesmen. Besides Washington, Jefferson, Henry, and Madison, there were John Marshall and the lawyer, George Wythe. Jurists, debaters, and legalists, these men must have provided inspiration for an ambitious Henry Clay. As a youngster, he heard Patrick Henry, also of Hanover County, argue a case so eloquently that the judge on the bench exclaimed in admiration, "Gracious God! He is an orator indeed!" The Virginia convention for the ratification of the federal constitution met in Richmond in 1788, and its debates were read and discussed throughout the state. Patriotism and oratory were two highly prized attributes in those days, and young Henry formed the habit of going out by himself into the fields or the barn and there practicing the art of public speaking. His adeptness at debate stemmed partly from this early self-training.

In 1792, Henry's mother, stepfather, and two of his brothers moved west to Kentucky, but they left Henry in Richmond, where a position had been found for him as a deputy clerk in the High Court of Chancery. There he came to the attention of beak-nosed, blue-eyed Chancellor George Wythe, who needed a transcriber with a clear and steady pen. For

Not only Clay's family (see page 9) but much of Revolutionary Virginia felt the brunt of Tarleton's forages. This old painting shows one such attack being rebuffed by Peter Francisco in Amelia County, not far south of the Clays' home.

four years the youth worked as Wythe's secretary. The Chancellor saw promise in the boy, gave him the run of his library, and finally took him on as a law student. Later Clay studied more intensively for a year in the law office of Robert Brooke, a former governor of Virginia.

During these formative years Henry joined a debating club, met other promising young men, and steadily broadened his intellectual horizon. By November 1797, when he was admitted to the bar, he had become an avid follower of Thomas Jefferson, a strong sympathizer with the French Revolution and the doctrine of the rights of man, and an orator of considerable skill.

His legal training had been rather superficial; his alert, ready mind quickly learned to skim, rather than go to the depths of a problem. But Clay did recognize his shortcomings. Writing to his son, Henry Clay, Jr., in 1829, he said: "I never studied half enough. I always relied too much upon the resources of my genius. If I had life to pass over again, and, with my present information, could control my movements, I would not appear at the Bar . . . until after two or three years, at the least, of close study." On the other hand, Clay had gained considerable knowledge of social usage and amenities, had earned the right to hang out his shingle as a lawyer, and was eager to make a name for himself.

His thoughts turned naturally to Kentucky, where his family had gone (see pages 92–95). Soon after receiving his license to practice law, Clay started out across the mountains by way of the Cumberland Gap and the Wilderness Road, which led to the heart of the Bluegrass region and the town of Lexington.

A metropolis expanding in the West

The town that Henry Clay had selected as his destination claimed a total of sixteen hundred inhabitants, twenty-four retail stores, and about two hundred houses, mostly log cabins. It was the political and economic center of the West, a frontier beehive where

A period engraving depicts a juvenile Henry Clay in the bucolic environment of "the slashes" in Hanover County.

tobacco and hemp planters, hunters, merchants dealing with the Indians, and slave traders bought and sold their wares. The neighboring forests were alive with squirrels, and it was thought nothing if five thousand were killed in a day. The Indians who lived in the surrounding areas were regarded by the settlers as nuisances, also—often more so than the squirrels.

As a rising western metropolis where frontier manufactures were already beginning to spring up, Lexington could proudly point to some outstanding citizens. There were lawyers such as John Breckinridge and James Brown, some very keen businessmen, and a printer, John Bradford, editor of the *Gazette*, who was referred to as the Kentucky Franklin. Young Clay not only had family connections in the region but also arrived armed with letters of introduction from Wythe and Brooke. He easily gained admittance to the Kentucky bar (as may be imagined, its standards of admission at that time were none too strict), joined a debating society known as the Junto, and dove into local politics.

Clay's first speech before the Junto was on a subject then much under discussion, the revision of the state constitution. He began it awkwardly enough, addressing the society members with a ringing "Gentlemen of the Jury!" But he quickly warmed to his topic, and before he had finished, his fellow club members knew that they had an orator among them. Shortly thereafter he ventured to take issue with some of the town's leading citizens, urging that the constitution be revised to curb the power of the state senate and to provide for the gradual emancipation of slaves (see pages 122–124).

Clay, and others who felt strongly about the need for constitutional revision, worked diligently toward this goal. Although there was no overwhelming vote for a new state constitution in the next general elections, there was enough voter support to convince the legislature that it should summon a constitutional convention. When it met in 1799, this convention established direct election of the state senate and of the governor but took no steps toward abolishing slavery. Slaveholders and conservatives in general were not impressed favorably with this foray by Clay into Kentucky politics but, fortunately for his political future, an issue had appeared in 1798 upon which both the conservative and liberal wings of the party could unite.

In the East a great battle was raging between the Jeffersonians, advocates of confining the powers of federal government and friendly to the French Revolution, and the Federalists led by John Adams and Alexander Hamilton, who felt that it was important to keep on good terms with the British government, distrusted France, and hoped to centralize more power in Washington. The same divisions of opinion were expressed in the Bluegrass region, with the Kentucky Jeffersonians even more violent in their opinions because the Eastern Federalists had not moved fast and far enough in freeing the Mississippi from Spanish control.

Then, in 1798, the Federalists in control of the national government passed the Alien and Sedition Acts, giving President John Adams the power to deport aliens, and curbing freedom of speech and of the press. These laws were in part an effort to discredit the Jeffersonian Republican party, and its adherents in Kentucky were much alarmed.

At a gathering in Lexington, so vehemently did Clay denounce the Federalists and their leanings toward what he and other Republicans regarded as despotism that the incensed crowd refused to listen to the following speaker, William Murray, a Federalist. The angry citizenry would have ridden Murray out of town on a rail if Clay and his companion orator, George Nicholas, had not intervened. When the Kentucky Resolutions

Fond of tracing law to its ancient sources, Virginia's Chancellor George Wythe employed Clay to copy Latin documents.

supporting Jefferson's agrarian, states'-rights position were sponsored later in the state legislature by his fellow Republican, John Breckinridge, Clay certainly must have given them his personal acclaim.

The Republicans in power

Before his twenty-fourth birthday, then, Henry Clay, the aspiring politician and lawyer, had played an active but minor part in "the revolution of 1800"—the defeat of the Federalists by Thomas Jefferson in the campaign for President of the United States. Clay had also made something of a name for himself in Kentucky as a liberal humanitarian who did not favor slavery. He was, however, ambitious to succeed in law and politics, and shrewd enough to see that in urging emancipation he would be fighting a losing cause. There were to be no more tilts over human bondage with such powerful conservative Republican leaders as John Breckinridge, who even referred some of his law practice clients to Clay when he went to Washington as a member of the Senate in 1801. Indeed, it would not be long before Henry Clay himself bought slaves.

Gaining repute both as an orator and as an ardent Republican was helpful in promoting Clay's social and economic status. So, too, were certain personal characteristics. Physically, he was an appealing man with attributes that attracted both men and women to him. His lanky six-foot frame was crowned with hair so blond as to be almost white, but his face was marred somewhat by a mouth so wide that, as he himself remarked, he could never learn to spit. However, he did have an engaging smile and his manners were courtly. He loved to play cards for money and he drank his share of Kentucky whiskey, habits that made for popularity especially among the males on the frontier.

The favorable regard of his contemporaries bred self-assurance, a quality that aided him in wooing and wedding eighteen-year-old Lucretia Hart, a daughter of Thomas Hart,

Henry Clay in his thirties

one of Lexington's leading and wealthiest citizens. Henry and Lucretia were married on April 11, 1799, and the groom subsequently focused his attentions on earning a livelihood for his bride and the family that soon began to increase in numbers. Lucretia, a woman gifted with discretion, the ability to manage, and devotion to motherhood, bore him eleven children and lived to celebrate with him a golden wedding anniversary.

Clay early gained a great reputation at the Kentucky bar, and Lexington, with its plentiful lawsuits, was a lucrative spot for setting up an office. Clever at spotting weaknesses in an opponent's argument, Clay, with his melodious voice, was easily able to capture the sympathies of the juries. He was phenomenally successful in criminal trials. "Ah, Willis, poor fellow," he said on one occasion to a murderer who had been accused of a particularly gruesome crime, "I fear I have saved too many like you, who ought to be hanged."

CELERITY OF ACTION, INTUITIVE GRASP

Clay's official biographer, Calvin Colton (see page 224), who knew him personally, described some of the initial stages of his long and notable career:

"He followed his mother to Kentucky in 1797. . . . A poor young man, without a penny in his pocket, he opened his office in Lexington. . . . In a speech delivered at Lexington . . . in 1842, he told the people then how much pleasure he had on receiving his first fee as a lawyer—15 shillings—for he was then in need of it. But he soon rushed into a lucrative practice. . . .

"His professional practice and its emoluments grew upon his hands with unexampled rapidity. His eloquence at the bar attracted crowds, and his influence with juries and with the Court was such that clients flocked to his office to commit their cause to his hands. In one instance, on the rehearing of a cause, he obtained a decision against the record of the Court, who, on being referred to it, said it could not be so. They had been persuaded against their own convictions, and their first decision was right. How then, could the second be right?

"A lawyer employed Mr. Clay to assist him in an important case where much was at stake, but in the meantime he became anxious about it, because he could not see that Mr. Clay was giving proper attention to it. On riding to court in another county, while in the saddle, Mr. Clay asked the lawyer to show the case by the file of papers belonging to it, which he did, one by one, to the end. 'That'll do,' said Mr. Clay, and the file of papers was restored to the saddlebags, and they rode on to the county seat where the cause was to be tried next day. As the lawyer thought, Mr. Clay appeared to pay no more attention to the subject, but was engaged in exciting company till the cause came on. The lawyer gave up the cause as lost. What was his astonishment when he found Mr. Clay possessed of every point in the case, and complete master of the argument! The cause was gained. 'How is this?' said the lawyer to Mr. Clay. 'I never could see when or how you studied the case, and I expected to lose it.' 'Why,' said Mr. Clay, 'if you ever want me to help you, you must let me have my own way.' This may, perhaps, serve to show the celerity of action and the intuitive grasp of Mr. Clay's mind. . . .

"Under his influence [the House of Representatives] became the all-potent power of the nation. . . . William H. Seward, in his eulogy on Mr. Clay . . . says that Mr. Clay 'became a perpetual tribune of the people,' and that . . . the House of Representatives under Mr. Clay as Speaker . . . was undoubtedly 'the active ruling power of the Republic.' "

Friendly toward his Negro clients, Clay often volunteered to defend slaves who tried to obtain their freedom legally. In only one instance was it ever recorded that he actually requested the death penalty, and that was for a Negro who had murdered his overseer in an unusually brutal manner. Yet, in the courts, Clay never attempted to prevent a Negro from winning his liberty.

His conduct of land suits and other civil cases was equally notable. This was true not only in Lexington but also when he was on circuit attending the sessions of local courts, where he widened his circle of personal acquaintances while increasing his legal reputation. A growing tendency to domineer over fellow lawyers, judges uncertain of the law, and illiterate juries was one of the consequences of this success. Yet within six years, all had to admit that Clay's warmth, friendliness, and personality, plus his victories in the courtroom, had made him a leader at the bar and one of Kentucky's most promising men.

Clay's achievements in the field of law, his growing contacts with influential friends and clients, and his never-resting ambition made it almost inevitable that he become a politician. Fayette County friends nominated him while he was out of town, and the electors sent him to the state legislature at Frankfort in 1803.

The first session that Clay attended was uninspiring. But then, a little earlier, it had appeared that he might never even have a political career, or at least that it would be interrupted by the excitement aroused in Kentucky when the port of New Orleans was closed to Americans by Spain. Even more inflamed when they discovered that Spain had ceded Louisiana to the French, whom they suspected would block their commercial outlet to the west, the Kentuckians began to mobilize in 1803. Clay was selected as an aide to General Samuel Hopkins and prepared to "go with the crowd to endeavor to share the glory of the expedition." Meanwhile, though, Jefferson completed the long-advocated trans-

The courthouse and public square in Lexington was a focal point of Clay's legal career in Kentucky. The "miserable building" (as Clay called it, because he disliked its design) was often crowded with spectators at major trials.

action with the French, purchasing the vast Louisiana territory, and the turmoil in Kentucky subsided.

During the next two sessions of the legislature, Clay was able to introduce some of his pet projects, such as the paving of streets in Lexington and the incorporation of the Ohio Canal Company. He also supported the legislation designed to uphold the establishment of the Kentucky Insurance Company, which was in reality a bank with vested interests for local businessmen. At the same time that he was serving as a legislator, he continued his legal practice, and, in 1806, acted as counsel in cases that became famous throughout the country (see pages 127–128).

Aaron Burr had come from New York across the mountains, restless with plans for carving a great western empire out of the territory held by Spain. An adventurer and intriguer, Burr had killed Alexander Hamilton in a duel and there was a price on his head in New Jersey, but this weighed lightly with Westerners. The United States district attorney at Frankfort, a Federalist, twice brought Burr before a jury as an enemy of the peace, accusing him of raising a military expedition to invade the Spanish territories to the west of Louisiana, and twice Clay was retained as one of his defense attorneys. Both times the prosecution was unable to produce evidence of his guilt, and Burr was acquitted amid great public jubilation. Clay had honestly believed that his client was innocent of wrongdoing and even had a letter from Burr guaranteeing his innocence. Later, however, shortly after the case was closed, when Clay was appointed to go to Washington to fill out an unexpired term in the United States Senate, President Jefferson showed him evidence that convinced him of Burr's guilt. In later years, political opponents claimed that Clay was involved in Burr's schemes, but there was no truth in this allegation.

15

In those early years of the nineteenth century, Washington, the capital, was still, as the Portuguese minister so aptly described it, "the city of magnificent distances." Avenues were not paved, and the streets were rutted in the winter, muddy in the spring, and dusty in the summer. Houses were sparse, pigs wandered through the parks, and quail could be hunted near the Capitol. The north wing of the building leaked, and the members were terrified that a wall would crumble the way the plaster often did from the ceiling.

Although Clay had no legal right to take his Senate seat, for he was only twenty-nine, no one took the trouble to challenge his appointment. Politically, he manifested a vigorous interest in the building of roads and canals at federal expense, an idea very popular in the West, but he also stated that he expected this congressional session to be a "tour of pleasure." He went to a great many parties and spent much time playing brag and poker, games in which he relied recklessly and often successfully on his luck. After his return to Kentucky, Clay's admiring constituents again elected him to the state legislature in 1807; he served two more years, some of the time as Speaker of the House.

The approach of war

During 1808 and 1809 the attention of the people in the western as well as the eastern part of the United States centered more and more on the conduct of foreign relations with Europe. A great duel raged there between Napoleon and Britain—the Tiger and the Shark—and because of this conflict the lot of neutral countries, such as the United States, was exceedingly difficult. The British govern-

From 1807 to 1853, the District of Columbia's original "Chain Bridge," hung from forty-foot stone towers, traversed the Potomac. In one of his first Senate actions Clay favored building it. Designed by James Finley, it was among the earliest suspension spans in the United States.

ment issued Orders in Council blockading the ports of France and its allies. American ships caught engaging in trade with these ports were seized and their cargoes confiscated. The British also impressed thousands of American seamen, claiming they were British subjects, taking them forcibly from the decks of American ships, and compelling them to serve in the British navy. Napoleon, to counterbalance these actions, issued decrees empowering French captains to seize American ships that traded with Britain or that obeyed the British Orders in Council.

Jefferson's answer to this treatment by both warring giants was the Embargo Act of December 22, 1807, which prohibited all commerce with foreign ports. American ships and American goods were thus kept at home. He believed that, by cutting off trade with England and France, he could force the Europeans to respect American rights on the high seas. Although later this policy proved to be ineffectual, when it was instituted the Republicans rallied to its support. Federalists, on the other hand, were critical. The main strength of the Federalist party was in commercial New England, and there the ships lay rotting at the wharves. Furthermore, Federalists were generally sympathetic toward England, for the bulk of American trade was with the British Isles and the West Indies.

A dramatic duel

Western Republicans, like their brethren in the East, rallied to Jefferson's support, and Clay took an active part in defending the President as well as his embargo. This attitude involved Clay in a series of bitter altercations with a Kentucky Federalist, Humphrey Marshall, who from his vantage point in the Kentucky legislature violently opposed the embargo. The two men had clashed earlier over the Burr affair; and since Clay had not been selected as Speaker by the legislature that met in December 1808, the two could assail each other's views almost daily on the floor of the assembly. Clay sponsored several resolutions approving the conduct of the national government and they passed in the Kentucky legislature with overwhelming majorities. Only Marshall was opposed.

Clay then, going one step further, offered a resolution to the effect that the members of the legislature should wear only clothes of American manufacture until the Orders in Council and Napoleon's decrees were repealed. Suiting action to his word, Clay appeared in the house clad in jeans, but Marshall, who had previously worn homespun, strutted up and down the aisles arrayed in a suit of English broadcloth. As the resolution neared passage, Marshall accused Clay of being a demagogue. This was too much

for the Republican and he rushed toward Marshall, who was eager for the fray. They would have exchanged blows if the huge German-American legislator, General Christopher Riffe, who occupied the seat between them, had not separated them, exclaiming, "Come poys, no fighting here. I vips you both." This ended the encounter on the floor of the house, but the next day Clay challenged Marshall to a duel.

The two men met on January 9, 1809, in Indiana territory, just across the Ohio River from Louisville. It was pistols at ten paces. Immediately afterward Clay recorded the event in a letter to a friend: "I have this moment returned from the field of battle. We had three shots. On the first I grazed him just above the navel—he missed me. On the second my damned pistol snapped and he missed me. On the third I rec'd a flesh wound in the thigh, and owing to my receiving his fire first, &c., I missed him." After the third exchange, Clay had insisted "very ardently" on another fire, but the seconds declared that honor had been satisfied, and that the duel was over.

The year 1809 was Clay's last in the Kentucky legislature. He had exhibited qualities of leadership, devotion to the national Republican party, and due respect for the needs and aspirations of Western business. His duel with Humphrey Marshall had demonstrated the sort of raw courage that was so admired by most frontiersmen. He was obviously a man of action who was bold, optimistic as to the American future, and quick to take a stand on public questions—a fit symbol of the Western spirit.

Clay was easily reelected to the legislature in 1809 for his seventh consecutive term. But in 1810 he was again selected by the Kentucky legislature to go to the United States Senate, this time to fill out the unexpired term of Senator Buckner Thruston. Clay returned to the nation's capital assured that he was a popular figure in Kentucky, and ambitious to be a leader in guiding the nation's destiny.

"I WAS A STORE KEEPER"

One of the shrewdest and most engaging observers of the passing scene in Washington during its early decades was Margaret Bayard Smith, who settled there with her husband, an editor and journalist, in 1800—the very year it became the nation's capital. Her book *The First Forty Years of Washington Society* contains many revealing comments on the Clay family. The Smiths and the Clays first became well acquainted in 1810, when they shared the same large house in Washington with several other people. In a letter to her sister about this group, Mrs. Smith wrote that year:

"I have formed habits of sociability with Mr. and Mrs. Clay only—Mrs. Clay is a woman of strong natural sense, very kind and friendly. She often brings work of an evening into our room and in the morning I go to hers—we help each other dress and she always offers us seats in her carriage when we visit together—or go a shopping, and her woman who has been the nurse of all her children, attends to mine whenever I wish it."

In 1811, when the Smiths had moved to a house of their own, Mrs. Smith wrote her sister of Mrs. Clay: "She is what you call a good woman, but has no qualities of mind to attract, none of the heart to endear. She is a most devoted mother, and to sew for her children her chief, almost exclusive occupation. She has no taste for fashionable company or amusements, and is a thousand times better pleased sitting in the room with all her children round her . . . than in the most brilliant drawing room. She has shown more affection and kindness of disposition, since my sickness, than I believed her capable of. She is always showing me and mine some attention. . . . Ann and Julia have just return'd after passing a week with her. She trim'd their bonnets for them from her own store of ribands, and bought Susan a handsome present on her birthday. This was on Thursday last and was without exception the most agreeable celebration we ever had. . . . Mrs. Clay was as much engaged as any of the children and as much delighted and she and I were as gaily deck'd as the girls."

By 1816 the two families were so intimate that Mrs. Smith could write her sister: "I have passed the last four days and nights almost exclusively with Mrs. Clay, who has lost a lovely infant of three months old with the whooping cough. . . . On Monday night it died in my arms."

Mrs. Smith was on equally close terms with Clay. In 1819 she went to hear him speak in Congress: "Mr. Clay was not only eloquent but amusing and more than once made the whole house laugh. . . . I could repeat almost the whole of it. But in losing the voice and manner of Mr. Clay, much of the effect will be lost. . . . When Mr. Clay had finished . . . he came and sat a few minutes on the steps by me, throwing himself most gracefully into a recumbent posture. I told him I had come prepared to sit till evening and was disappointed at his speech being so short; he said he had intended to have spoken longer, but his voice had given out; he had begun too loud and soon exhausted himself." The two enjoyed an occasional teasing banter, as in 1827

Margaret Bayard Smith

when he was Secretary of State and she took him to task for a nomination he had backed: "I joked him a good deal on the learned judge he had appointed in Jersey. 'At first,' said I, 'he was a saddler, then a store keeper and then when made a justice of peace, he undertook to read Blackstone, the only law-book it is said he has ever read. What a learned judge and chancellor he will make!' 'Stop, stop,' said Mr. Clay, 'you do not know, Mrs. Smith, I was a store keeper.' 'I did not,' said I, 'but I know without your telling me that your studies were not limited to Blackstone.' He took my raillery in very good part and defended the appointment very skillfully and brought me to acknowledge [one could not] please everybody."

Early in 1829, when Jackson had won the Presidency and Clay was about to lose office, the latter's personal affairs took a grim turn. One of his sons was mentally ill, another son was in jail, and Clay himself suffered a severe sickness. When the Smiths called, "Mrs. Clay was mournfully walking the room and as we entered, held up her finger, to impose silence, and pointed to the sofa. 'He sleeps,' whispered she. I felt a shock on turning my eyes as she spoke; on the sofa was stretched at full length Mr. Clay, face and all completely cover'd with a dark cloak, which looked like a black pall. We took our chairs, without speaking, and sat silent. Our entrance however had awakened him and after a minute or two, he slowly rose and putting the cloak aside reclined in one corner with his feet stretched along the sofa. I had not seen him for three weeks and was shocked at the alteration in his looks. He was much thinner, very pale, his eyes sunk in his head and his countenance sad and melancholy—that countenance generally illumined with the fire of genius and animated by some ardent feeling. His voice was feeble and mournful."

Within a fortnight, however, Clay displayed his resilience, and she noted: "No bitterness mingles its gall in the cup of disappointment and I often hear him, when only two or three friends are present, speak of General Jackson and the present state of affairs in a good humor'd sprightly way." In March 1829, just as his term as Secretary of State ended, she wrote: "Mr. Clay has, this winter, been such an object of interest to me, for to me *intellectual power* is more fascinating and interesting than any other human endowment. And never in any individual have I met with so much, as in him. Yes, he has a *natural* power and force of mind, beyond any I have ever witnessed. In Mr. Jefferson, Madison, Crawford, and other great men I have known, much of their intellectual strength was derived from education and favoring circumstances, a combination of which carried them forward in the career of greatness and raised them to the elevation they attained. Not so Mr. Clay. Whatever he is, is all his own, inherent power, bestowed by nature and not derivative from cultivation or fortune. He has an elasticity and buoyancy of spirit, that no pressure of external circumstances can confine or keep down. . . .

"Excitement is as necessary to his moral, as stimulus is to his physical, existence. Henry Clay was made for action—not for rest."

19

Chapter 2
LEADING SPOKESMAN FOR THE WEST

ALTHOUGH Henry Clay was beginning to develop a national point of view when he went to Washington in 1810, he was still essentially a regional representative for the West and its interests. That primarily agrarian section of the country was starting to manifest considerable growth in industrial activity. And in keeping with the West's expanding industrialism, the area's spokesmen were advocating a protective tariff.

Distilleries, plants for the manufacture of iron and its side products, and textile mills were starting to dot the landscape in Ohio and Tennessee. Kentucky, more advanced industrially than the other two states, produced gunpowder, hemp and rope, salt, and virtually all the cotton bagging made in the United States. The state even boasted a small wine industry, and when Clay made the long and arduous journey across the mountains to Washington he carried a bottle of Kentucky wine with him (see page 139).

Clay was not only a Westerner but also a member of the Jeffersonian-Republican party, and that party's attitude was shifting considerably from what it had been during the days of the Alien and Sedition Acts. Republicanism was still largely representative of the farming interests, and still largely opposed to the centralization of power in Washington. But it was no longer as devoted as it had been in former years to a strict interpretation of the Constitution, or to state sovereignty. The years of responsibility in national office had shown the party that there was a need for action at the center of government. The Republicans had cast off some of their former reservations about centralization and responded to this need.

Jefferson had purchased Louisiana and had established an embargo; both actions required a broader interpretation of the powers granted to Congress and the Chief Executive by the Constitution. The Sage of Monticello and his Secretary of the Treasury, Albert Gallatin, had also proposed a far-reaching program of national internal improvements, including the construction of highways and canals, which they wished to see realized through federal action. At the same time, the younger members of the Republican party—especially ambitious leaders of it such as Clay of Kentucky; John C. Calhoun, Langdon Cheves, and William Lowndes of South Carolina; and Felix Grundy of Tennessee—were endorsing governmental principles and practices upon which some of the older generation of Republicans looked askance.

Early years in Congress

The man who would soon be widely known as "Harry of the West," Henry Clay, took his seat in the Senate on February 5, 1810. It was well understood in those days that a member of Congress should represent the interests of his particular region, and consequently should respect instructions from his state legislature as to how he should vote on bills that came before the Senate or the House. Kentucky wanted economic protection, and Clay willingly voted for a protective tariff. The West opposed the first Bank of the United States—a creation of Hamilton and the Federalists, who since 1791 had exercised considerable control over efforts at state banking—and Clay helped to defeat the Bank's recharter in the spring of 1811.

The West also was concerned with the relations of the nation toward its neighbor to the south. Spain's control of the Floridas was not favored. In addition, Western interests had become increasingly hostile to Great Britain. This reaction was caused somewhat by the feeling that the Orders in Council had produced a depression in the Mississippi Valley economy, and that British policy supported the Indians at the expense of the frontiersmen. Claiming that the United States had ac-

quired West Florida east to the Perdido River by the Louisiana Purchase, President Madison seized the area in 1810. Clay not only defended this questionable act but declared that he favored obtaining East Florida "and some of the territories to the north of us also." It was not strange, then, that he supported a growing movement for war with Great Britain. A conflict with the British, he hoped, would also end the Indian menace on the frontier.

Tecumseh and his Indian warriors, reportedly supplied by Britain through Canada, were threatening any further American advance of the western frontier. General William Henry Harrison verified this situation in his accounts of the battle fought in 1811 at the Tippecanoe River in Indiana territory. In a rousing speech expressing the sentiments of the western regions, Clay opted for war, which he said would put out "the torch that lights up savage warfare." Besides, if America were victorious in invading the British domains to the north, the Canadian fur trade

Exemplifying the thesis that wars hasten technological advances, the American navy's first steam frigate, *Fulton* *the First*, was launched in New York on October 29, 1814. It was not fitted out in time to fight in the War of 1812.

would be a welcome enrichment to western economy. Addressing the Senate, Clay thumped the war drums: "The conquest of Canada is in your power. I trust that I shall not be deemed presumptuous when I state that I verily believe that the militia of Kentucky are alone competent to place Montreal and Upper Canada at your feet."

In 1811 Kentucky sent Clay to the House of Representatives, and when he came to Washington that fall, Mrs. Clay and their six children accompanied him. Clay made this trip across the mountains many times during the course of his life, usually by the road from Lexington to Maysville, Kentucky, and then along the Ohio River or by the Cumberland Road. Lucretia Clay was not at all attracted by the social life of the nation's capital. She centered her activities around the needs of the children, often entertaining them by playing the piano at their parties. Lucretia's husband, nevertheless, was a great favorite in the capital, exuding his warmth and courtly charm upon men and women alike. A story told about Clay's first visit to the White House to call on President Madison has become a legend. The door of the Executive Mansion was opened by a pretty woman, who smiled at him, whereupon he gallantly kissed her. Just at this moment the President appeared and she passed the kiss on to him. Unabashed, Clay bowed to Dolley and said, "Had I, madam, known you were Mrs. Madison, the coin would have been larger."

Leader of the "War Hawks"

While the young Kentucky lawyer found Washington society much to his taste, he was also devoted to the Bluegrass region; when Congress adjourned, he always looked forward eagerly to his return to Lexington. There, in addition to his booming law practice, he took an active part in the affairs of Transylvania University, the first institution of higher learning established west of the Alleghenies. His estate, which because of its ash trees he named Ashland, also consumed much of his time and money. By 1816, he had acquired 513 acres of land and constructed an elegant brick house that was probably designed by the famous architect Benjamin Latrobe. Situated at that time a little over a mile from Lexington itself, Ashland was a symbol of personal success. And Clay loved it. In 1811 and 1812, however, he had to center his attention on Washington, for great events were rapidly taking shape there.

Clay's fellow congressmen promptly chose him as Speaker of the House in 1811, on the first day Congress met (see pages 139–141). Never before, nor since, in the history of the United States Congress has a Speaker been selected on the first day he took his seat in the House. Clay was easily reelected to the post six times during his congressional career. Only Sam Rayburn, who filled the speakership in 1940 and was subsequently elected ten times, has served more years.

Bold of thought and action, and ready to use his power in pushing his favorite bills through the House, Clay was at times dictatorial. But he was generally courteous, and was quick and decisive in ruling on parliamentary procedure. The members especially respected him for enforcing regulations governing decorum.

The House of Representatives at the beginning of the nineteenth century was noted for its lack of etiquette. If members disagreed with the view being presented on the floor, they diverted attention by coughing, talking loudly, or slamming their desk tops. Clay made an effort to admonish congressmen who slept during sessions or relaxed with their feet on the desks. And when John Randolph of Roanoke, a brilliant but eccentric Virginia congressman, arrived accompanied by his hunting dogs, the hounds were removed at Clay's request. Heretofore, no Speaker had dared put out Randolph's dogs.

The Kentuckian's position as Speaker was particularly important during the winter of 1811–1812, for the country was moving rapidly toward war with Great Britain. The continuing seizure of United States ships and the impressment of American seamen, along with the earlier brutal attack by the British frigate *Leopard* upon the American frigate *Chesapeake* in 1807, had convinced many Americans that only by open conflict could they protect their rights on the high seas. A war with Great Britain, if the Americans were victorious, also might cut off the British supply routes to the Indians on the frontier.

The embargo had been a failure and was repealed just before Jefferson left the White House in 1809. It had been replaced by a nonintercourse policy applying only to England and France. This attempt, too, had had no effect, and neither had other measures to which Congress turned in desperation as it vainly tried to force the British and the French to end their restrictions on American foreign trade. It now became evident to a group of young and energetic leaders in Congress that the United States must take drastic action against Great Britain, and Clay vigorously urged this endeavor.

Dubbed "War Hawks" by John Randolph—who mocked them for their "whippoorwill monotony" in cries of "Canada! Canada! Canada!"—these youthful instigators included such individuals as Calhoun, Grundy, and Peter B. Porter, who came from near Buffalo on New York's western frontier. Clay, now thirty-four years of age, was the oldest of the lot and was their leader. When the Twelfth Congress began its deliberations in November 1811, Speaker Clay placed War Hawks on the most important committees and championed legislation for increasing the army, strengthening the tiny American navy (although this measure met with little favor in the landlocked West), and raising loans as well as a number of internal taxes to finance the nation's defense. Clay struggled doggedly throughout the winter and spring of 1812, insisting that the United States redress its grievances by an appeal to arms. But Congress vacillated, trying to avoid the almost certain hostilities. In May, word was received

that Britain would not repeal the Orders in Council until Napoleon had made a parallel gesture in nullifying the French decrees. The War Hawks were livid and their anger swept through the legislature. Secretary of State James Monroe drafted a war message, which was sent to the Congress asking the members for approval. On June 18, 1812, to the delight of Henry Clay and his fellow War Hawks, America declared war on Great Britain.

Humiliation on land

The Kentuckian had believed that the war would be brief and glorious for the United States; but this vision soon faded, for the country was ill-equipped to wage battle with the Mistress of the Seas. The Treasury was empty, there was no American army or navy worthy of the name, President Madison was a most unwarlike Commander in Chief, and

Here a British boarding party impresses four alleged deserters serving on the *Chesapeake*. As noted at the top of the page, this high-handed act so enraged Americans that it encouraged the War Hawks' clamor for retaliation.

Federalist New England was so opposed to the struggle that a separatist movement of dangerous proportions developed there before the conflict came to an end.

Grim as the overall American position appeared, a few naval engagements early in the war, during the late summer and fall of 1812, must have elated the citizenry. The *Constitution* won two important naval battles that year, the first against the impressive *Guerrière* off the coast of Nova Scotia in August, and the second against the *Java* in December. The capture of the *Macedonian* by the *United States*, under the command of Captain Stephen Decatur, was another triumph.

On land, however, the war was not so successful. American efforts to invade Canada ended in humiliating failure. General William Hull surrendered at Detroit, and twice American troops marched to the Canadian border with New York, only to turn back when they arrived. Finally, in April 1813, American troops captured York (now Toronto), and in September, Captain Oliver H. Perry vanquished a British fleet on Lake Erie. But then, no longer occupied with the war against Napoleon in Europe, the British could turn their attention more fully to the hostilities in America. One British force was defeated at Lake Champlain, but another, invading the Chesapeake Bay Region, reached Washington and burned the Capitol, the White House, and other buildings. The most signal triumph of American arms occurred two weeks after the peace treaty had been concluded, when General Andrew Jackson repelled another invasion at New Orleans. It is one of the great ironies of American history that the war, which Clay had done so much to bring about, produced in Andrew Jackson a military hero who was to become the Kentuckian's most formidable rival.

The Treaty of Ghent

President Madison began putting out peace feelers early in the war, and by the end of 1813, with Napoleon's power crumbling in Europe and the defeats at home, peace began to look attractive even to the War Hawks. When Britain, after rejecting a Russian proposal of mediation, offered direct negotiations, Madison promptly accepted. Although Clay had done what he could to rally Americans behind the struggle—at one time Madi-

In 1814, British troops sacked much of Washington. Fleeing the White House just before they burned it, Dolley Madison rescued Stuart's portrait of George Washington; Madison himself reportedly spent a dismal night in a henhouse.

son had even thought of putting him in command of the American armies—it was still natural that Harry of the West, the leader of the outspoken advocates of war, should be one of the five peace commissioners sent to Europe in the spring of 1814.

As Henry Clay and Jonathan Russell, a Massachusetts Republican who was to represent the interests of commerce, set sail in February, the meeting was scheduled for Gothenburg, Sweden. After a seven-week voyage, they arrived to discover that Britain wished to transfer the negotiations to London or a city in the Low Countries. James Bayard, a senator from Delaware, and Albert Gallatin, the Secretary of the Treasury, were not opposed to the British suggestion, but Clay would not agree to London. In May the British answered that Ghent would be acceptable, and by early July the five Americans had gathered in the European city. The fifth member, John Quincy Adams, minister to Russia, had joined them late in June. The British then let them cool their heels for several weeks.

Once the peace negotiations at Ghent got under way, they went on for nearly five months. Each side at first demanded major concessions from the other. The British wanted a huge Indian buffer state comprising much of the Old Northwest, cession of part of the Maine coast, and continuation of the right to navigate the Mississippi. The American commissioners came to the council table with instructions to demand that Great Britain abandon impressment, pay damages for the destruction of American property, and cede Canada. Britain was in an advantageous position, for Napoleon, its principal adversary, had been forced to abandon the French Empire and had been shipped off to exile on the Mediterranean island of Elba. The British even acted at times as though the United States had been beaten to its knees.

Despite British high-handedness, however, a variety of factors worked in favor of a stalemated peace. Both sides were weary of fighting. The British had been engaged in a long

The Maison d'Alcantara (above) housed Clay and the other American peace negotiators during their stay in Ghent.

and exhausting duel with France, and American victories on Lake Champlain at Plattsburg, New York, and at Baltimore's Fort McHenry had discouraged them about the possibilities of winning an easy war. Even the Duke of Wellington, England's renowned military leader, was pessimistic about the outcome of the struggle with the United States. On the other hand, the Americans, too, were eager to quit the fight. The attempts at invading Canada had failed, and the continuation of the war was costly, especially to the commercial community. Besides, with the end of the Napoleonic Wars, two of the vexing causes—impressment and the right of search—had become academic. It is, then, not surprising that the treaty, which was finally signed on Christmas Eve, 1814, was based on a restoration of conditions to the situation that had existed before the fighting started. Special commissions were assigned the task of agreeing on the boundary between Canada and the United States. The indecisive war thus ended in a virtual deadlock.

Henry Clay took a prominent part in these peace negotiations. He was quick to discern when the British commissioners were bluffing, and he was equally alert about putting up a stout defense for the interests of the

West, especially when rights of navigation on the Mississippi River were discussed. Some of the American delegation would have been willing to let Britain use that great river in exchange for fishing rights in Canadian waters. Clay, however, opposed any such bargain, and it was largely due to him that it was not included in the treaty.

Typically, the "Western Star" did not confine his interests to the bargaining table at Ghent. The five-member American delegation had jointly rented a single house for the duration of the proceedings. This was a mistake, for these five diverse personalities found it difficult to live in peace and quiet under one roof. Most of the friction centered around the hostility between John Quincy Adams, the strait-laced New Englander, and Clay. The two men did not see eye to eye about the New England fisheries, or about other matters as well. Following a meal, Clay liked to spend time at the dinner table drinking wine and smoking cigars, a practice that Adams held to be as absurd a waste of time as the Kentuckian's enjoyment of card games that kept him up till dawn. Gallatin had to calm many quarrels between Clay and Adams.

The final terms of the treaty did not satisfy Clay. More than once he had asserted that, rather than sign such a document, he would prefer continuing the war. When the covenant was finally concluded he accepted it only with reluctance. After the treaty was signed, Clay, having decided to remain in Europe for a few months, set out for Paris, where he attended the salon of Madame de Staël, a leading figure in Parisian society as well as a representative of the Romantic movement in literature. Quitting Paris in March, he was asked, along with Adams and Gallatin, to negotiate a commercial treaty with Great Britain. Characteristically, Clay found going to England for this conference distasteful until he heard about America's great victory in the battle of New Orleans. He could then go to London full of national pride in United States military prowess.

VIGNETTES OF GHENT

The months spent at Ghent, negotiating the treaty with the British that ended the War of 1812, allowed some time for socializing by the Americans. The *Memoirs of John Quincy Adams* provide a valuable account of these activities, although the New Englander obviously disapproved of his colleagues' conduct. Shortly after Adams arrived in the city, he confided to his diary:

"I dine again at the table d'hôte, at one. The other gentlemen dined together at four. They sit after dinner and drink bad wine and smoke cigars, which neither suits my habits nor my health, and absorbs time which I cannot spare."

The next day Adams decided to be less standoffish: "We adjourned at four o'clock, and I dined with my colleagues, as I propose to do hereafter, Mr. Clay having expressed some regret that I had withdrawn from their table yesterday."

Within a few months, however, Adams had developed a real dislike for Clay's nocturnal card games, and the animosity between the two men was evident in the manner with which Adams addressed his diary: "Just before rising, I heard Mr. Clay's company retiring from his chamber. I had left him with Mr. Russell, Mr. Bentzon, and Mr. Todd at cards. They parted as I was about to rise."

Again, a few days later: "There was another card-party in Mr. Clay's chamber last night, and I heard Mr. Bentzon retiring from it after I had risen this morning."

Not only did Adams and Clay carry on their bickering in private about Clay's social life, but the two Americans were at loggerheads in public concerning the treaty itself. Clay defended the viewpoint of the West, which came into frequent conflict with the interests of the New Englander's constituents. It was often Albert Gallatin, the Swiss-born naturalized American, who, according to his son James Gallatin, poured "oil on troubled waters." Serving as his father's secretary, James recorded this scene:

"Clay uses strong language to Adams, and Adams returns the compliment. Father looks calmly on with a twinkle in his eye. Today [August 10, 1814] there was a severe storm, and father said, 'Gentlemen . . . we must remain united or we will fall.'"

A few years later, in 1821, James Gallatin again referred to his father's part in the negotiations and to the running quarrel between Adams and

Clay: "Some very disagreeable communications from Mr. Adams to-day. I really think he, being now Secretary of State, is paying father up for imaginary wrongs when at Ghent. When I look back upon that time I am amazed that father bore so well with him and Mr. Clay; they were quarrelling like two spoiled children all the time. Father did all he could to restore peace between them, but it was of daily occurrence and most trying."

Happily, the days at Ghent were not filled solely with the sound of disputes. There were many times when Clay and Adams took a jaunt together, like ordinary tourists, to satisfy their curiosities about the ways of their European hosts. Adams records such an occasion in his diary:

John Quincy Adams

"I went with Mr. Clay to the Hôtel de Ville . . . and we saw the ceremony of the 'marriage civil' performed by the adjoint Mayor. . . . There were about twenty couples to be married this day. We saw six or seven of them go through the ceremony. . . . It appeared to consist only in the calling over the names, age, and characters of the parties and their witnesses. . . . A short passage from the register was then read by the clerk . . . and the Mayor delivered a paper to the bridegroom—I suppose the certificate of the marriage. There was a brass box on the table, into which each of the parties put a small piece of money. . . . The brides were all ugly, and almost all apparently older than the bridegrooms."

On other occasions the Americans were entertained by the citizens of Ghent themselves. The townspeople were most hospitable and cordial to the Americans and hoped to make their visitors welcome by inviting them to join local societies. Unfortunately, the European social formalities were sometimes obscure, leading to misunderstandings by the Americans. In one instance, Clay was obviously embarrassed and then piqued by the events culminating from a misdirected invitation. Adams explains the situation in his diary:

"Mr. Gallatin, Mr. Bayard, and myself had been made honorary members of this Society [the Society of Fine Arts and of Letters]. Mr. Clay, Mr. Russell, and Mr. Hughes had received the same compliment from the Society of Agriculture and Botany. The two Societies had drawn our names by lots, three and three. But this, as St. Luke's day, was the celebration only of the first Society, and the invitations were only to Mr. Gallatin, Mr. Bayard, and me. [The Society] by mistake, had told Mr. Gallatin that they were generally for us all. Mr. Russell would not go. Mr. Clay attended, and was mortified on discovering the mistake."

The next day Adams continued this account: "Mr. Clay entered a formal complaint about his having been misled in attending the meeting of the Society last evening. . . . Mr. Gallatin explained that Mr. Clay's awkward situation last evening was owing to [the] mistake in telling him that the invitation to the meeting and supper of the Society was for all. Clay had some reason to be mortified, particularly as a speech [was given] to explain how it came that Messrs. Clay, Russell, and Hughes had been made honorary members, not of that Society, but of the other."

A fitting epilogue to the Ghent negotiations is given by historian Emily Stone Whiteley in the January 1929 issue of *The Virginia Quarterly Review*. Christopher Hughes was the twenty-eight-year-old Secretary to the mission. "The news of the signing of the Treaty by the Commissioners was announced in Ghent on Christmas Day, and was received with great manifestations of joy by high and low. . . . The good people of Ghent had a real affection for their American guests. Ten years later, in 1825, when John Quincy Adams became President and made Henry Clay his Secretary of State and Christopher Hughes his representative in Brussels, it seemed to their Belgian friends a perfect end to a perfect story."

A nationalistic program

While Clay gained experience as a statesman in Europe, he also profited financially from the mission. He received $16,500 in salary and expenses, and was able to invest about $4,500 in United States government bonds bearing interest at 6 percent. On his return to America, his constituents hailed him as one who had upheld the interests of his country, and he in turn defended the war and the peace settlement. If Britain again impressed American seamen, he declared, America should again take up arms. Now, however, the country was at peace, and should devote itself to building up its economic and military strength.

Clay returned to his post in the House of Representatives, eager to play a leading part in formulating legislation. The country, fresh from a war that had demonstrated the dangers of sectionalism and of unpreparedness, and exultant over Jackson's victory at New Orleans, was ready for measures that would promote defense and prestige. Clay, Calhoun, and other young Republican leaders had plans to take advantage of this growing nationalistic fervor with a new national program. In their zeal for progress, these men cared little for the old scruples about rigid interpretation of the Constitution or about minimizing the centralization of government in Washington. Basic Hamiltonian theories, then, had been adopted by Jefferson's Republican party since 1800. The nation was expanding in both population and in wealth, and the young Republicans were determined to aid its development in every possible way.

In January 1816, the Kentuckian, who had been reelected Speaker of the House, outlined his aims. They included military and naval preparedness, construction of highways and canals plus other internal improvements at federal expense, a protective tariff to encourage domestic business interests, aid to Latin America in its struggle to free itself from the yoke of Spain, and incorporation of a national bank. Many Americans favored these pro-

The corner of F Street (foreground) and 15th Street in Washington is the subject of this 1817 watercolor by the Baroness

Hyde de Neuville, wife of the French minister. The Treasury Department is on the left, a bank on the right.

posals, and it is not surprising that during the next five years Clay played a prominent part in congressional activities.

A strengthened navy was one of the first objectives of the new Republicans in the Fourteenth Congress, and a bill for an increase in funds was sponsored by Clay, Calhoun, and Lowndes. A protective tariff, too, was passed in 1816. But, of all the Republicans' immediate concerns, the foremost was the reestablishment of a United States bank. Since the demise of the first national bank in 1811, the nation's currency had gradually weakened. Clay, reversing his earlier opposition to the institution, selected Calhoun, a staunch bank advocate, as chairman of the committee set up for its organization. Subsequently, Calhoun introduced a bill setting up a second Bank of the United States. It was passed after much discussion. Chartered in 1816 for twenty years, the institution had real powers to regulate currency. The other two programs that Clay supported—internal improvements and foreign policy—met, however, with the disapproval of the Administration of President James Monroe, who, in 1817, succeeded Madison in the White House.

There is much evidence that, during this period of his career as well as later on, Clay expected and felt that he deserved the highest political honors. His constituents sent him back to Congress again and again, though he was nearly defeated in 1816 when some of his followers deserted him because of his support of a bill to raise congressional salaries. One of several political disappointments occurred, though, early in the Monroe Administration. Clay wanted to be head of the State Department, for at that time the Secretary of State was regarded as a vital step toward the Presidency. President Monroe gave this coveted position instead to John Quincy Adams. Monroe then offered Clay the War Department, and later the mission to England. He refused both, apparently in an impetuous and imperious manner, saying that he believed he could serve better at his post in the House.

Conflict with the President

Clay's criticism of Monroe centered on the President's attitude toward foreign policy and internal improvements. The Latin American colonies of Spain, recognizing the weakness

Making political grist of Jackson's arbitrary execution of two British civilians in Florida (see next page), this cartoon used in the bitter campaign of 1828 bore the caption: "Jackson is to be President and you will be hanged."

of the mother country after the Napoleonic Wars, were striving for their independence. Clay fervently believed that the blessings of American liberty should be shared by other countries. More pragmatically, he was convinced that a free Latin America would not only have economic advantages for the United States, but would also lessen the possibility of any other powerful European nation gaining a foothold in the southern half of the Western Hemisphere. He knew that popular sympathy for the South Americans was widespread in the United States, and he made himself the outstanding champion in Congress of the Latin American cause. He pressed for recognition of the independence of the new states south of the Rio Grande, and was openly critical when the sympathetic but lethargic Administration proved slow to act.

Differences with Monroe over internal improvements at national expense made Clay still more discontented with the Administration. He wanted a program of road and canal building, because the West demanded it and also because he felt certain that increased ease of communication would bind the country together as a national unit. And no narrow interpretation of the Constitution was going to stand in his way. Monroe, however, felt that the federal government had no authority for undertaking such a program without a constitutional amendment. The President threw the weight of his influence against an internal improvements bill and, much to Clay's disgust, the New England and Virginia factions opposed the bill, preventing its passage. Thwarted in attaining this objective, the Kentuckian turned once more to urging speedy recognition of the Latin American states, only to find Monroe and Adams still hesitant.

There was good reason for the Administration's reluctance to act. Available evidence indicated that the rebellious countries were not ready for self-government. Furthermore, Secretary of State Adams was engaged in negotiating with Spain for the purchase of Florida, and hasty recognition of the rebels might terminate the good relations with the Spanish court. Clay, however, paid no heed to these considerations and repeatedly attacked the executive branch of the government for its delay in facing up to the South American situation. When the treaty ceding the Floridas to the United States was signed in 1819, Clay was still in a bitter mood. He complained because it did not include the cession of Texas to the United States, and once more pressed for immediate diplomatic recognition of those Latin American republics that had gained their freedom.

The United States, he said, should at once become the leader of a hemispheric desire for independence "which would constitute the rallying point of human wisdom against all the despotism of the Old World." Today Clay's pronouncements might be regarded as romantic, but on one point he was more perceptive than he himself realized. Documentary evidence, which was secret then, has revealed since that Spain, had it been put under pressure, would have ceded Texas along with the Floridas. But none of the American statesmen, least of all the "Kentucky Hotspur," as he was sometimes called, was then aware of this fact. As for recognition of the Latin American states, which finally came in 1822, Clay did not get the prompt action he wanted. He could, however, take comfort in knowing that by his stubborn insistence he had earned the deep and lasting gratitude of the Latin Americans.

During the course of the negotiations to acquire Florida, an event occurred that was to have considerable bearing on Clay's later career. The northern part of Florida had become a refuge for outlaws who plundered at will in American territory. In 1818, Andrew Jackson was ordered to pursue such hostile bands across the border. "Old Hickory," as he was dubbed during this campaign by his soldiers who admired his toughness, interpreted his instructions from the government liberally. He not only pursued the marauders into Florida, but also occupied Spanish towns and executed certain Indian chiefs, as well as two British subjects, Arbuthnot and Ambrister, who were suspected of supplying and spurring on the Indian attacks. Secretary of State Adams upheld the General's actions, but Clay joined Calhoun in denouncing Jackson's conduct (see pages 146–147). Thereafter Old Hickory had only hostility for the man who was later to be his rival for President.

The Missouri Compromise

While Clay was leading the debate over Monroe's handling of both internal and external affairs, there arose an ominous contention between North and South regarding slavery. The Missouri Territory, in the midst of the land acquired through the Louisiana Purchase, applied for admission to the Union as a state, and in February 1819, a petition to that effect presented by Clay was taken up in the House of Representatives. Congressman James Tallmadge of New York immediately moved to amend Missouri's state constitution so that slavery would be prohibited when the state was admitted to the Union. The battle lines of debate were drawn. Opposition to slavery expansion had been growing steadily in the North, where the practice had proved to be unprofitable and where the population, as it moved toward the West, realized it could not compete with some economic aspects of slave labor.

CLAY AND INDIAN AFFAIRS

While Henry Clay was sympathetic to the conditions that the Negro suffered under slavery, he was less concerned about another American minority group—the Indian. An entry (December 22, 1825) from the diary of President John Quincy Adams illustrates Clay's attitude toward the Indians as well as the Kentuckian's theories about their future in the United States.

"From one o'clock to near five was the Cabinet meeting upon the affairs with the Creek Indians and Georgia. The letter from the Creek delegation, finally refusing the cession of all their lands within the State of Georgia, was read. Much desultory conversation was had upon the course to be pursued. . . . Governor Barbour recurred to his plan for incorporating the Indians within the States of the Union—ceasing to make treaties with them at all, but considering them as altogether subject to our laws. . . .

"Mr. Clay said he thought it would be impracticable; that it was impossible to civilize Indians; that there never was a full-blooded Indian who took to civilization. It was not in their nature. He believed they were destined to extinction, and, although he would never use or countenance inhumanity towards them, he did not think them, as a race, worth preserving. He considered them essentially inferior to the Anglo-Saxon race, which were now taking their place on this continent. They were not an improvable breed, and their disappearance from the human family will be no great loss to the world. In point of fact they were rapidly disappearing, and he did not believe that in fifty years from this time there would be any of them left."

When Clay criticized Jackson's treatment of the Indians in Florida (on this page) or in the 1830's, the moral indignation he evinced was scarcely in accord with the sentiments Adams recorded.

The South, on the other hand, where the cotton gin had made slavery more profitable than ever before and where the number of slaves was rapidly growing, had become defensive about its "peculiar institution." Southerners wanted to retain slavery; they also wished to transport their slaves with them into the newly opening territories to the West. Sectional rivalry in the Congress was beginning to be more and more vocal. Being now in a minority in the House, the South was zealous in its desire to preserve at least a balance with the North in the United States Senate. Hence the Southern statesmen were determined that slavery should be recognized as legitimate in Missouri.

Clay personally felt that slavery was undesirable, and he continued to favor gradual emancipation as the best way of dealing with this form of human bondage. He came from a slaveholding state, however, and was himself a slaveholder. Also, as a Westerner, he disliked imposing upon a new state restrictions that did not apply to those farther east. He felt, and said, that if slavery were practiced more widely, the situation of the slaves would be improved. This point of view, called "mitigation by diffusion," was held by a number of Southerners. Weighing all of these considerations, Clay was inclined to agree with the South in this quarrel between the sections. Yet, though his loyalties lay with the South, he was genuinely alarmed by the threats of disunion coming from both North and South.

There seemed to be no escape from the dilemma of Missouri's admission when Congress adjourned in the spring of 1819. But then, following Clay's suggestion, a bill was introduced in December to admit Maine as a free state balancing Missouri's slave-state status. This settlement, though, did not solve the problem of whether the rest of the Louisiana Purchase lands were to be slave or free. It took the moderate senator from Illinois, Jesse B. Thomas, to suggest a solution, the renowned Missouri Compromise. Maine was to be admitted as a free state, Missouri as a slave state, and the rest of the Louisiana Purchase north of the 36° 30' latitude would be free. Harry of the West supported this amendment and when Randolph, the Virginian, tried to block its passage by asking for a reconsideration of the vote, Clay blocked the attempt with a bit of adept parliamentary procedure. He placed the routine business of the House first, and while the House carried on this time-consuming process, he signed the bill and dispatched it to the Senate. For the moment it looked as though a struggle that had filled the country with anxiety was over. But the crisis was not ended yet.

The constitution submitted by the Missourians excluded free Negroes and mulattoes from the state. This aroused the antislavery members of Congress, and it began to look as though Missouri might not be admitted. At this point, Clay took a leading role in putting through a second compromise. Exerting all his charm and persuasive powers, he initiated and helped carry a proposal that the Missouri legislature would be asked to accept. This was that no state constitution should ever be regarded as depriving the citizen of any other state of the privileges and immunities he enjoyed under the Constitution of the United States. Both houses of Congress finally approved this resolution, and the Missouri legislature made the required change, though adding that it had no power to bind the state. Missouri was then admitted, along with Maine, and the crisis was terminated.

The struggle over the admission of Missouri in 1821 was ominous for the future; Jefferson declared that it was "a firebell in the night" that awakened and filled him with terror. Nevertheless, Clay, placing the preservation of the Union above all other considerations, had performed with distinction, and his Kentucky admirers were enthusiastic about his conduct. When he retired from Congress that spring, on a plea of financial necessity, his friends gave him a public dinner in Lexington, and bestowed a new appellation on him—"The Great Pacificator."

Chapter 3
AN ELECTION LOST, A CABINET POST WON

ACH YEAR, during the months that Congress was not in session, Henry Clay returned to Ashland. There he entertained distinguished visitors such as the Marquis de Lafayette, James Monroe (his occasional political opponent), Daniel Webster, Harriet Martineau (the English traveler and literary figure), Aaron Burr, and William Henry Harrison. His hospitable reception of the great, however, was not less than the warmth and graciousness with which he received the plain folk who sometimes came considerable distances to see Harry of the West. The house was a marvel for the period and region. It was furnished with fine china, sofas, and rich satin drapes that Clay had brought with him when he returned from France; marabou feathers that could be washed were on display in the drawing room.

At Ashland, and on the neighboring three-hundred-acre estate of Mansfield that he was to purchase in 1831, Clay raised large quantities of hemp and considerable amounts of wheat and corn; tobacco had not yet become a staple crop in Kentucky. As the years went on, he devoted more and more time to stock-raising; he imported Hereford cattle from England, and both male and female donkeys from France and Spain to breed mules, which were very popular in the South for use by farmers as draft animals. Clay also specialized in breeding fine racehorses, buying stal-

lions in England for his stable; he also raised blooded sheep and pigs. Such animal husbandry activities were expensive, and Clay was often forced to mortgage his property. There were even times when his debts, and his generosity in endorsing the notes of his friends, brought him close to bankruptcy.

Clay's legal practice had fallen into eclipse during his absence abroad, and he practiced law only intermittently after his return from Ghent. Then financial difficulties multiplied and he began once more to appear frequently in the courts. His principal client was the Bank of the United States. With the reversal of his attitude toward a national bank in 1816, Clay had become one of the major figures in the struggle to acquire the charter of the second Bank of the United States. He then helped to get branches of the Bank established in Lexington and Louisville, bought a few shares of stock, and by 1818 had been offered a position as a director of the institution, which he refused. In 1819 he was retained as one of the Bank's lawyers and the following year took charge of its legal affairs in Kentucky and Ohio—a post that he held for about four years. The Bank paid him an annual retainer of $6,000 for his services.

As the Bank's lawyer, Clay urged leniency toward its creditors during the economic depression that gripped the country from 1819 to 1822. But at the same time, the Bank obtained through foreclosure a considerable amount of land in Cincinnati and some fifty thousand acres of farmlands in Ohio and Kentucky. Needless to say, the Bank was not popular with the former owners of these lands, nor with others who lost their jobs because of falling prices and blamed the Bank for the economic failure. Kentucky's legislature soon passed laws to alleviate the situation for debtors. But the courts proceeded to suppress some of these measures. Clay, however, suffered no immediate political damage, either from the Bank's action or from his opposition to relief measures for debtors in his own state. Only in later years did his connection with the Bank come back to haunt him, when men whom he had prosecuted and who subsequently rose to political power became his unrelenting opponents.

Craving for acclaim

It was not in the temperament of the Kentucky Hotspur to remain contented for long with the life of a lawyer and country squire. He craved both the excitement and the acclaim that go with political leadership. In 1823 the voters of Lexington returned him to Congress, where he was once more elected Speaker of the House by a large majority. There, in his speeches and by his acts, he again identified himself as a friend of human liberty, and as an advocate of action by the national government on behalf of industry and commerce. With a population that was reaching into the millions and a subsequent increase in its representation in Congress, the West's interests were rapidly broadening in scope, and Henry Clay, as one of the West's legislative leaders, was more than ever at the focus of political attention.

Still the devoted friend of Latin America, he approved the part of President Monroe's message to Congress in December 1823 that later became famous as the Monroe Doctrine —a warning to the reactionary European powers against any attempt to interfere in the affairs of the American continents.

He also spoke warmly of his sympathy for the Greeks, who were trying to establish their independence from Turkey. On the domestic scene, he urged the national government to help build roads and canals, and supported the protective tariff of 1824. A bill allocating $30,000 for surveys of national roads and canals passed the House, 115 to 86. But the vote was along sectional rather than party lines: New England and New York opposed it, the South was split, while the West supported it wholeheartedly. The tariff bill of 1824, though, gave the industrial East and the West, which would use the higher duties to construct roads and improve river transportation, a chance to form a coalition. Clay argued skillfully for this "American System," which would protect a fledgling American industry, provide money for a program of internal improvements, and, coupled with a strong national bank, give the country a sound currency policy. The tariff squeaked by in the House, 107 to 102, and passed the Senate by 4 votes. Clay had scored a victory and won the admiration of the nation's protectionists.

There is no reason to question Clay's sincerity in championing internal improvements, protection for American industry, and freedom from foreign interference for the emerging nations of the Western Hemisphere. But more than high ideals lay back of his program. He knew very well that these policies had wide popular appeal in the northern states as well as in the West, and he felt that he was ready to assume a position of national leadership in the United States. He was anxious to become President—and 1824 was a presidential election year (see pages 154–157).

A vigorous contest for the White House was inevitable in 1824. President Monroe had never been a strong Chief Executive and, especially after his reelection in 1820, there was plenty of opportunity for rival leaders to intrigue for the succession. Sectional cleavage over the tariff, internal improvements, and land policy was becoming apparent—all of which encouraged ambitious politicians to

Umbrella Manuf

No. 122½ *Market St. near the co*

(Entrance through S. Messenger's

The subscriber informs the public, tha his umbrella manufacturing establishm supply any demand for articles in that lowest prices. Merchants and others, v cles, will do well to call before they pur

Ladies and gentlemen can obtain the vance on the wholesale prices; and all retail at this establishment, *will be kep months gratis,* if they become out of r fault in the materials or workmanship.

The following articles are constantl establishment, and will always be bough barter, or good endorsed notes.

Blue & green Senshaws, Sarsnets, Levantines, Sewing silk Mantuas, Ivory,

☞ Every article for umbrella make Merchants can have their silks made up

ERASM

KEATTING'S

WHOLESALE AND RETAIL

Boot & Shoe Manufactory,

No. 254, *Market Street,*

(THIRD DOOR ABOVE THE WHITE BEAR TAVERN.)

THE Subscriber respectfully informs his numerous customers, and the public in general, that he keeps a constant supply of GENTLEMEN'S BOOTS and SHOES, first quality; and in addition, LADIES' Kid and Morocco SHOES, with a general assortment in the above line, where all orders will be thankfully received, and punctually attended to

L. KEATTING

WILLIAM WALLACE,

AT HIS

Leghorn and Split-straw Hat and Bonnet Manufactory, and Fancy Dry Goods and Millinery Store,

No. 22, South Third Street,

HAS FOR SALE A CONSTANT SUPPLY OF

Men's and Boy's improved Water-proof Leghorn Hats. 50 doz. Bermuda Chip do. 15,000 yds. do. do. Platt for making hats. Ladies' fine Yellow and Black Leghorn Hats and Bonnets, of the newest fashion. 200 Ladies' and Gentlemens' superfine White and Black Manilla Hats and Bonnets, an article equal, if not superior, to Leghorn, and comes at half the price. A large and fresh assortment of the most fashionable Split-straw Bonnets, by the case or dozen. Ladies' Black and White Chip do. Ladies' Fashionable, Plain, and Cut-silk Velvet, Satin and Silk do. A large assortment of Ribands, Plumes, Artificials, Silk Cords, Chenille, Thulle Lace, &c. &c. With a general assortment of Fancy Dry Goods, such as Laventines, Florences, Luestrings, Lace Shawls and Veils, Merino and Silk Shawls, &c. &c.

N. B. Country merchants can be supplied on the lowest terms with Straw Hats and Bonnets for cash, or acceptances in the city at four months.

Typical of the fledgling American manufacturing endeavors Clay hoped to aid with high protective tariffs were businesses such as those represented in the above advertisements by Philadelphia merchants early in the 1800's. While leghorn hats made of a smooth plaited straw were popular, Mr. Wallace (above) also sold "Manillas."

curry favor with North, or West, or South, as the case might be, in their pursuit of office. The depression of 1819–1822 also had bred discontent and a desire for change in the order of things. This reshaping of the political attitude had manifested itself in a host of local political parties with a wide variety of programs. Yet, in one way or another, all of these parties sought relief from existing conditions.

Moreover, the old party division between the Federalists and the Jeffersonian Republicans had vanished. The Federalist party had suffered a deathblow when it opposed the War of 1812, and in 1820 it offered no opposition to Monroe's reelection. The Republican party meanwhile was in the process of separating into two wings. One contained men like Clay, who believed in a strong and active national government; the other was led by individuals such as the rising New York State politician, Martin Van Buren, who felt that there should be a return to the limited national government ideal that had characterized the Republican party during the Jefferson and Gallatin era. Monroe's second term had been under way only a year when it became apparent that, among these men with their divergent views, there was bound to be a furious contest for occupancy of the Executive Mansion.

Presidential jockeying

By 1822 there were five candidates in the field, all representing various sections of the country. John Quincy Adams, cold and dour but able, carried the hopes of New England. The South claimed two representatives: Wil-

A GRASP OF REALITY

Accused of being a gambler, a ladies' man, and a drinker, even though the charges were rarely substantiated by evidence, Henry Clay frequently was the subject of criticism. Yet he was never reproached for dishonesty in his commercial dealings or during his years as the lawyer for the Bank of the United States, except from a political standpoint. Gerald Johnson makes this observation in his book *America's Silver Age,* and then states:

"By no rational interpretation of the record can it be made to appear that Henry Clay was a model of correct living, except as regards finances. On that point, he is definitely clear of suspicion. No one has ever presented any evidence that a single dollar of public money ever stuck to Clay's fingers. He remained a relatively poor man when he was holding positions that might easily have been turned to such account as to bring him a fortune. His enemies, unscrupulous as many were, did not charge him with any sort of financial dishonesty, for they knew such a charge would have been ridiculed.

"But he was charged with almost every form of duplicity that did not involve money, and in a formidable array of instances the charge was proved to the hilt. Clay was a politician, which means, as Abraham Lincoln has assured us, that he was at least one long step removed from an honest man. Throughout his public service he was the center of a succession of political intrigues. He played the game according to the rules as he found them, and the fact that it was frequently a sordid game did not deter him. He desired the Presidency so avidly that he stooped to some practices worse than doubtful to get it; but he stooped in vain. He believed in compromise and this, although it is frequently presented as proof of his insincerity, was perhaps the most honest thing about him. He really believed in it.

"Now this, plainly, is no suitable hero of copybook maxims. It would be silly, as well as useless, to try to argue that Clay has been misjudged by history, and that the sniffish reception given him by writers for nearly a hundred years is based on a total misconception of his character. The last two generations may, indeed, have felt a strong emotional need to cry Clay down in order to justify their fathers who turned their backs upon Clay and toward war; but it does not follow that they were ignorant of what manner of man he was. From the standpoint of the prude, or of the Victorian moralist, he was bad. From the standpoint of the prudent man who eschews gambling, he was bad. From the standpoint of the candid man, he was bad. From the standpoint of the strictly truthful man, he was bad. From the standpoint of the authoritarian, who thinks every man in public life should have a complete set of principles to which he adheres rigidly, he was almost fabulously bad. . . .

"To orderly souls, who like to have their historical characters all neatly labeled and filed under the appropriate index number, Clay is a dreadful annoyance. He doesn't fit into any of the more convenient categories. His career doesn't work out according to the ancient maxims. He was a trifler and an idler; at Ghent, for example, with the fate of nations in his hands, he maddened poor John Quincy Adams with his all-night card parties and other frivolities; yet he evolved a philosophy and a polity which has been adopted by the party in power in this country for the better part of a century. He was called an ignorant man, yet he had a grasp of reality that was not possessed by Calhoun, alumnus of Yale, nor by John Quincy Adams, alumnus of Harvard. He drank, he gambled, he flirted with every pretty woman who came by, he made outrageous jests upon the most awful subjects, yet he prospered, his financial affairs were always in order and conducted with a prudence not excelled by that of John Quincy Adams himself."

liam Harris Crawford, the Secretary of the Treasury, a burly Georgian who had killed his man in a duel, and the brilliant, ambitious John C. Calhoun of South Carolina. The West also had two candidates: Henry Clay, the Millboy of the Slashes, eager, impetuous and full of confidence, and Andrew Jackson, a popular hero since the battle of New Orleans, whose Tennessee friends put him forward.

All of these men were active in the government; three were in Monroe's Cabinet. Both Crawford and Calhoun—the latter being Secretary of War—spent much of their time plotting and planning their strategy for the White House. Adams regarded such intrigues with scorn, but as Secretary of State he offered missions abroad to all his rivals, hoping, though vainly, to get them out of the country.

Gradually the list narrowed. Calhoun's hopes were dashed early in Pennsylvania. In 1822 the legislature of that key state declared for Jackson, and Calhoun withdrew from the race, becoming the successful candidate for Vice-President, as it turned out. Crawford suffered a paralytic stroke in 1823; he par-tially recovered, and a group of New York politicians under Van Buren's leadership remained faithful to him. But Crawford's chances for the prize were considerably weakened when he won nomination for the Presidency from a limited caucus of Republican congressmen in February 1824. Only 66 of the 216 Republicans in Congress attended. Often conducted behind closed doors and subject to the political whims of a few party chiefs, the caucus was incurring criticism as an undemocratic method of choosing presidential candidates. However, the ailing Crawford stubbornly remained a contender in the race.

John Quincy Adams, New England's favorite, had considerable strength in New York and in the Old Northwest as well; he was a formidable candidate. So, too, was Andrew Jackson. Old Hickory had no deep-seated convictions on the tariff or on any other question of the day, and his personal actions in Tennessee indicated that he sided more often with the "haves" than with the "have-nots" in American society. Nevertheless, Jackson's friends in the state put him forward as one who had only the interests of the masses at heart. At the same time, his supporters pointed to his military record as an Indian fighter and as the man who had whipped the British at New Orleans. The state's legislature nominated him in July 1822. Thereafter his adherents steadily increased, especially in the West, the South, and in Pennsylvania.

Clay, always optimistic, did not believe that a man who was obviously a mere military hero like Jackson could be a serious political rival. The Kentucky and Missouri legislatures nominated the master of Ashland, and this reassured him that he was the candidate of the West. He was also certain that his stand on the tariff and his record of public service would win him all the strength he needed in the northern and eastern parts of the nation to carry off the prize. To ensure their candidate's victory, Clay's friends initiated a busy correspondence throughout the country. At the same time, they endeavored to form combinations with the supporters of other rival candidates who might be willing to run as Vice-President on the same ticket with Clay. The efforts of the Clayites to establish winning alliances with other candidates were in vain, however. This, together with a few instances of bad luck and the maneuvering of clever politicians, proved fatal to the Kentucky Hotspur. For example, four Clay partisans in Louisiana failed to reach the state capital in time to vote (see page 102). Added to the defection of three others, this unfortunate happenstance cost him the state's electoral vote. In New York, the Adams and Clay factions agreed on a split ticket that would have given Clay seven electors, but at the last moment the Adams manager, Thurlow Weed, failed to deliver Clay the votes that would have produced a tie with Crawford for third place in the Electoral College vote.

Ending the deadlock

When all the votes were in, the final tally in the Electoral College of the nation was Jackson 99, Adams 84, Crawford 41, and Clay 37. Only Kentucky, Missouri, and Ohio had remained steadfast in their advocacy of Clay's candidacy. No one of the four presidential aspirants had a clear majority and therefore, in accordance with the Twelfth Amendment to the Constitution, the election went to the House of Representatives, which is restricted in its choice to the three candidates on the list who receive the most electoral votes. This eliminated Clay from the contest. The President, however, still had to be selected.

Though his defeat was an obvious disappointment, Clay took it without complaint. He only wished, he said, that he could be spared "the painful duty" of having to decide between Adams, Jackson, and Crawford. It was a difficult decision to make, and it was eventually to result in a great deal of disappointment and sorrow for Harry of the West.

Early in December 1824, Clay went to Washington. Again, he was elected Speaker of the House. In that capacity, on December

10, he had the agreeable task of welcoming Lafayette officially to the lower chamber, the House of Representatives. The Marquis had been invited by the Congress to make a tour of the country, and his visit in the capital was a pleasant interlude in the principal struggle of the session—the selection in that same chamber of the next President.

Before leaving Kentucky for Washington, and soon after his arrival in the capital, Clay had told a number of friends that he had decided to vote for Adams. From his point of view this was a logical decision. Crawford was not physically fit to assume the duties of the Presidency. Jackson had emerged as Clay's political rival in the West; there was little in his public career, save his military exploits, to commend him; and, as he told one of his friends, the Kentuckian did not believe that killing 2,500 "Englishmen" at New Orleans could qualify anyone to be President of the United States. Adams, like Clay, favored a protective tariff and internal improvements at federal expense. The two men were also in general agreement about foreign affairs. Besides these points of favorable comparison, Adams had no great personal popularity, and Clay might well hope to succeed him in 1828 or, at the latest, in 1832.

Logic certainly pointed to Adams as the reasonable choice for Clay to make. There were, however, two obstacles to complete acceptance. First, General Jackson undoubtedly had amassed more electoral votes than any other single candidate, and so it might be argued that he was the people's choice. Second, the Kentucky legislature sent instructions to the state's delegation in Congress to vote for Old Hickory.

Clay was not naïve enough to make a public declaration of his decision to vote for Adams. The friends of all three candidates tried hard

Entitled "A Foot-race," this 1824 cartoon predicts a close finish between Crawford (middle) and a bald Adams, with Jackson pulling up a step behind. At right, Clay has dropped out of the contest and is being consoled.

to win him by flattery, and he doubtless enjoyed this attention. Meanwhile, his own cohorts began sounding out Adams as to whether, if he were elected, Clay would be included in the Cabinet. To this Adams replied that, if chosen by Western votes, he would naturally acknowledge Western support. After talking with one of Clay's friends, Adams wrote in his diary, "Incedo super ignes" ("I walk over fires"). Both men, however, wished to avoid the appearance of any bargain between them. It was a vain hope.

The lay of the land

Early in January, Clay called on Adams, and for three hours they exchanged views on public affairs. As Clay had anticipated, they thought alike in most matters and the Kentuckian informed the New Englander that he could count on his support. Although it is apparent that no mention of a Cabinet post was made during this conversation, Clay obviously had no doubt as to what his chances were in that regard. Shortly thereafter he wrote to his brother-in-law: "I can tell you nothing of the formation of the new Cabinet. I believe that, if I choose to go into it, I can enter in *any* situation that I may please. This opinion is formed from circumstances, not from assurances to which I should not listen, but which I should instantly check if attempted to be made."

In the days that followed Clay's meeting with Adams, the Kentucky delegation, though shaken by the instructions from their state legislature, decided to follow the dictates of Clay, their chief. Ohio also declared for Adams. Jackson's followers, furious, began to claim that a bargain had been struck. An anonymous statement that subsequently appeared in the *Columbian Observer*, a Philadelphia newspaper, charged that Clay had guaranteed certain votes to Adams in exchange for the post of Secretary of State. In a rage, Clay denied the charge and had a card that was in reality an invitation to a duel published in the *National Intelligencer*, a Wash-

---

FOR ADAMS OVER JACKSON

There can be no doubt that Henry Clay possessed exceptional political acumen. Though he never attained the nation's highest office himself, he was often instrumental in aiding or hindering those who were to become President. For example, Clay was able to cast aside his differences with John Quincy Adams when it came to opposing a greater foe, Andrew Jackson. Writing in his diary (January 9, 1825) Adams described the occasion of a visit from Clay, the purpose of which was to discuss the deadlock in the Electoral College:

"Mr. Clay came at six, and spent the evening with me in a long conversation explanatory of the past and prospective of the future. He said that the time was drawing near when the choice must be made in the House of Representatives of a President from the three candidates presented by the electoral colleges; that he had been much urged and solicited with regard to the part in that transaction that he should take, and had not been five minutes landed at his lodgings before he had been applied to by a friend of Mr. Crawford's, in a manner so gross that it had disgusted him; that some of my friends also, disclaiming, indeed, to have any authority from me, had repeatedly applied to him, directly or indirectly, urging considerations personal to himself as motives to his cause. He had thought it best to reserve for some time his determination to himself: first, to give a decent time for his own funeral solemnities as a candidate; and, secondly, to prepare and predispose all his friends to a state of neutrality between the three candidates who would be before the House, so that they might be free ultimately to take that course which might be most conducive to the public interest. The time had now come at which he might be explicit in his communication with me, and he had for that purpose asked this confidential interview. He wished me, as far as I might think proper, to satisfy him with regard to some principles of great public importance, but without any personal considerations for himself. In the question to come before the House between General Jackson, Mr. Crawford, and myself, he had no hesitation in saying that his preference would be for me."

---

ington journal. Clay's card was answered by another card that established the eccentric George Kremer, a member of Congress from Pennsylvania, as the accuser. By then, Clay's anger had cooled somewhat, and realizing that it was ridiculous to challenge such a man, he decided to ignore the duel and instead demanded that the House investigate the matter. But his accuser, obviously unable to produce any substantial evidence, refused to testify. Unfortunately, though he had escaped a farcical duel, Clay was still labeled as headstrong.

It snowed on February 9, the day of the presidential election by the House of Representatives, but the weather had no effect on the outcome. Adams was certain of twelve states; one more would give him the election. All of New England plus Maryland, Louisiana, Missouri, Illinois, Kentucky, and Ohio were in the Adams camp. The New York delegation stood 17 for Adams, 16 opposed, 1 undecided—the waverer being sixty-nine-year-old General Stephen Van Rensselaer, a Crawford supporter. Clay and Daniel Webster cornered the elderly man on the morning of the election and explained to him that, unless New York went for Adams, there would probably be no election and hence no President of the United States. Van Rensselaer entered the chamber apparently agitated by the importance of the decision he had to make. Just before his turn came to vote he bowed his head, leaned it against the edge of his desk, and prayed for divine guidance. When he opened his eyes, he saw on the floor below him a ticket with Adams' name on it. Taking this as an answer to prayer, he picked it up, dropped it in the ballot box, and Adams became President-elect.

Three days after this election, Adams offered Clay the State Department. On February 20, after several days of weighing the counsel of his friends and supporters, the Kentuckian accepted the office. Toward the end of his career, he realized his mistake and acknowledged it publicly as a blunder. The Senate confirmed his appointment on March 7 by a vote of 27 to 14. Some of those who voted "nay" were influential men, and Adams saw this dissension for what it was: the beginning of opposition to his Administration. Needless to say, one of the men who voted against confirmation was Andrew Jackson of Tennessee. Jackson believed, and continued to believe for the rest of his life, that Clay's appointment was proof of an infamous deal; that Harry of the West had sold his support for the promise of the State Department. "So you see," Old Hickory wrote to one of his friends, "the *Judas* of the West has closed the contract and will receive the thirty pieces of silver." The disappointed General sought revenge for what he considered a cynical repudiation of the will of the people, and a party of opposition to Adams and Clay and their policies began to take form, with Jackson as its leader and principal rallying point.

"OUR 'CLAY PRESIDENT' "

The bitterness stirred up at the time by the manner in which the House of Representatives decided the deadlocked presidential election is conveyed in a passage dated February 1825 in Margaret Bayard Smith's book *The First Forty Years of Washington Society.*

"When I returned to the parlor, the gentlemen were giving the family an account of the election. . . . About dusk several other members [of the House] and senators came in. . . . Two of the gentlemen proposed going to the [White House] drawing room to see how things appeared there and promised to come back and bring us some account of it. . . . Between ten and eleven the gentlemen returned, and gave us an account of the drawing room. . . . 'When we got there,' said [Mississippi Senator Thomas H.] Williams, 'Mr. Adams was not more attended to than usual, scarcely as much so as General Jackson.' 'I am pleased to hear that,' said I, 'it is honorable to human nature.' 'But it was not very honorable to human nature to see *Clay* walking about with exultation and a smiling face, with a fashionable belle hanging on each arm—the villain! He looked as proud and happy as if he had done a noble action by selling himself to Adams and securing his election. More than one, pointing to Adams, said, there is our *"Clay President,"* and he will be moulded at that man's will and pleasure as easily as clay in a potter's hands.' 'When Prometheus made a man out of clay,' said Mr. Williams, 'he stole fire from heaven to animate him. I wonder where our Speaker will get the fire with which he means to animate his Clay President.' 'Not from Heaven, I warrant,' said one of the gentlemen."

The opposition was clearly evident in Clay's own state, where a conflict continued to rage over state relief for debtors. A pro-relief faction had captured the state legislature and immediately asked for a reorganization of the Court of Appeals. Clay had stayed aloof from this struggle and Kentucky remained solidly behind him while he was in the presidential race. But with Clay out of the race, the relief party was more sympathetic to Jackson. It was this party that had instructed the Kentucky representatives in Congress to vote for Jackson. Its leaders now aligned themselves against Clay and behind the Hero of New Orleans. Even Francis P. Blair, one of Clay's closest friends, held out until March and then finally joined the opposition.

A great mistake

Clay had taken his stand with Adams for reasons that were both personal and patriotic. By throwing his political weight on the side of the New Englander, he hoped to accomplish two things at once. First, Clay was convinced that the Administration would favor the protective tariff and the internal improvements that he had declared to be fundamental parts of his American System. In addition, the arrangement also seemed calculated to advance his own interests by forging an alliance between the states of the North and West. Superficially, it looked like a good, sensible move, but unhappily it lent itself to portrayal by the opposition as corruption, and it had definitely increased Andrew Jackson's hostility to Henry Clay. Likewise, the combined Clay and Adams forces failed to realize the extent of the popular movement that was grouping behind Jackson's leadership.

The new Secretary of State had been somewhat uneasy about his personal relations with President Adams, for he remembered their bickerings at Ghent a few years earlier. Nevertheless, while there were some differences of opinion, the two men worked together with a remarkable degree of harmony. It was not his relations with his chief that

Clay found wearing, but the many petty tasks that a Secretary of State then had to perform —for example, the countless letters on unimportant subjects that he often answered when his staff was overburdened with its own tasks. Before he had been a month in office he found himself working twelve to fourteen hours a day at times.

Clay's labors were by no means confined to trivial subjects. In an effort to foster foreign trade and bolster the rights of neutrals, he negotiated more treaties than had any previous Secretary of State. He carried on a lengthy correspondence with France and Great Britain, and took a deep interest in American relations with the newly emancipated Latin American countries. Reams of paper, quarts of ink, and much mental effort went into these treaty negotiations. Yet, since most of them were concerned with matters of claims and commerce, at the end of four years the positive results were not very impressive, except for the widening of America's foreign trade.

The principal source of discussion with France was the series of American claims for damages that had originated in the wars arising out of the French Revolution. Even though the damages that the American government had presented were legitimate claims, the French were reluctant to pay. Clay wanted to make forcible collections by seizing French property, but Adams was reluctant to go that far. The consequence was that during Clay's term as Secretary the negotiations remained just where they were when they had begun in 1816.

Relations with Great Britain were about as frustrating as those with France. There were a number of vexing trade and boundary questions, as well as a dispute over damage claims. Britain did agree to pay something over $1,000,000 for property carried away during the War of 1812, but aside from this, little was accomplished. Clay tried and failed to obtain free navigation on the St. Lawrence River; his efforts to determine the boundary line between Maine and Canada, which had remained undecided since Revolutionary days, were fruitless; and Adams' unwillingness to make concessions in the way of trading privileges resulted in the closing of British West Indian ports to American ships. In retaliation, American ports were closed to British ships arriving from other ports in the Western Hemisphere. American trade with the British West Indies did not suffer much, for it continued by way of Canada and the West Indian ports of other nations. The British rebuff, however, was seized upon by the political opponents of Clay and Adams in the United States.

South of the border

As for relations with the emerging nations to the south, the Adams Administration pledged itself to encourage trade and to hamper the British in this commercial sphere.

Latin American independence movements led by such men as José de San Martín (left) and Simón Bolívar, shown here meeting at Guayaquil, aroused Clay's enthusiasm and prompted him to urge early recognition of the new nations.

Efforts were also made, albeit not very successful ones, to stimulate the growth of democracy there. Sometimes, overzealous diplomats hindered rather than helped the spread of democratic ideals by overwhelming the Latin Americans with propaganda about the North American system. Clay was aware of the dangers of what he termed "improper interference in their public councils," but his warnings apparently fell on relatively deaf ears. Samuel Larned, a diplomat in Santiago, even aided the Chileans in writing a constitution, but it was never adopted.

The Latin Americans generally felt that Great Britain was a better shield than the United States against foreign interference, and at times they actually were irritated by the attitude of their big neighbor to the north. This was especially true in Mexico, where Joel Poinsett, the American minister (and the man who introduced the poinsettia plant into United States horticulture), aroused so much resentment by his interference in internal politics and by his efforts to buy a large part of Texas for the United States that the Mexicans demanded his recall. Yet Poinsett did exemplify Adams' nonpolitical zeal for merit; Adams sent him to Mexico just after Poinsett had publicly voted for Jackson in the House election.

The most ambitious plan of Clay and Adams for extending American influence southward originated just after the Administration took office. The South American liberator, Simón Bolívar, proposed a congress of newly freed states for the purpose of forming a loose confederation. An invitation was also proffered to Great Britain, already disturbing the solidarity of the Western Hemisphere by making inroads that Monroe had envisaged —a unity the Adams Administration was trying to maintain. British Foreign Secretary George Canning, determined to act quickly in drawing an independent Latin America into the British sphere, wrote in January 1825: "Spanish America is free, and if we do not mismanage our affairs sadly, she is English."

Bolívar, afraid of the influence and power of North America but not of the British, advised against United States participation. Mexico and Colombia, however, disagreed with Bolívar and in the spring of 1825 made overtures to the North American republic about attending a meeting to be held in Panama. Clay was enthusiastic over the possibility of joining in the conference but Adams was more cautious, fearing that a confederation of American states might jeopardize the nation's sovereignty. By the time formal invitations were sent from the Latin Americans in November, Adams' anxieties had been calmed and he accepted immediately.

The President appointed two delegates to Panama, Richard C. Anderson and John Sergeant, and their names were sent to the Senate for confirmation. At once the fat was in the fire. Opposing senators raised all kinds of objections. Isolationists declared that America must beware of foreign entanglements; advocates of states' rights raised the alarming specter of an increase in the power of the government at Washington; and Southerners were frightened that slavery would be an issue at Panama, and that the Latin Americans would press for recognition of the Negro Republic of Haiti.

After long debate, the Senate finally confirmed the delegates. Unfortunately, Anderson died before reaching Panama, and Sergeant returned to the United States after waiting in vain for the Congress to reconvene in Mexico because an adjournment had been called for in Panama. Clay had spent a great deal of time and thought in drawing up their instructions, including proposals for constructing a canal "by common means" across the Isthmus of Panama. He was bitterly disappointed at this negative outcome.

Clay and Adams could not help being downcast at their meager achievements in the field of diplomacy, nor could they view with anything save chagrin the internal political developments of the four years from 1825 to 1829. During that period new political group-ings came into existence. One of these was actually the embryonic beginning of today's Democratic party. Known at first simply as the Opposition, it was originally a coalition of the followers of Jackson, Calhoun, and Crawford, united in the common aim of casting discredit upon the Administration. The supporters of Adams and Clay constituted a second party—the National Republicans. Both parties were loose combinations of various factions. Within their ranks, each contained many opposing views on tariffs, internal improvements, and states' rights. The feuding that went on between these two political agglomerations became more and more bitter as Adams' term of office neared its close.

"Bargain and sale"

Clay had entered the State Department with high hopes of a successful Administration, one that would be victoriously reelected, but as the years elapsed his hopes withered. Adams was politically inept. The South was devoted to states' rights and was alienated by the President's strong stand for internal improvements at federal expense. Both Adams and Clay believed in a protective tariff, but this was unpopular in the South and in parts of the North as well. Still another of Adams' difficulties was his devotion to the merit system in making appointments, which kept him from building up a party machine through the use of patronage. Clay tried to remedy this by appointing loyal followers, but the post offices and customs houses eventually became hotbeds of dissatisfaction with the Administration anyway.

Clay was eager to have the National Republican party accept an increased tariff as one of the main planks in its platform for the campaign of 1828, and he urged Daniel Webster and other leaders in New England and the Middle Atlantic states to help him in achieving this objective. When a group of high protectionists met at Harrisburg, Pennsylvania, in 1827 to air their views, Clay was delighted, and he stoutly defended the tariff of 1828,

43

Fearing competition from imported products, Northern manufacturers such as Samuel Slater (who ran the Rhode Island textile mill shown above) generally supported Clay's attempts to establish protective—not just revenue—tariffs.

which was very protectionist. But a Jackson majority had taken over the Congress in the mid-term elections, and the Tariff of Abominations, as the South termed it, was compiled by a Committee on Manufactures loaded with Opposition members. It was hoped by the Jacksonites that an alliance of Northerners and Southerners who opposed the bill would defeat it, since it was low in duties imposed on woolen goods but high in raw materials needed by the New Englanders. Jackson supporters, however, would back the bill and thus get credit for being protectionists; the Administration would be blamed for its defeat. Clay realized what was happening and in a letter to a friend he declared: "A viler cheat was never attempted on an intelligent people than the bill reported by the Committee." The Jackson strategy did not completely succeed; both houses passed the measure, with enough New England senators swinging over after the duty on woolens was raised slightly. Yet the Jacksonites could claim that their representatives from the Middle Atlantic and Western states voted for it, and the National

Republicans could not use the protection issue as they intended in the presidential campaign.

It was hard for Clay to watch the South turn against his leadership and even harder to see Kentucky move into the Jackson camp. One of the most vociferous voices raised against Adams and Clay in Kentucky was the Frankfort *Argus*, edited by Amos Kendall, a New Englander who had been employed in Clay's household from 1814 to 1816 as a tutor for his older children. After Clay became a Cabinet member, Kendall approached him about a position with the government. He hoped for a post that would pay about $1,500 annually, and indignantly rejected the $1,000 salary that was offered. At first, Kendall directed his diatribes solely against Adams, but when Clay removed the government printing jobs from the *Argus*, Kendall turned his attacks against Clay as well.

The most cutting abuse of all for Clay, though, was to hear the continual cry of "bargain and sale" that the Opposition raised about his appointment as Secretary of State. In 1825 he published an address to his constituents explaining and justifying his vote for Adams (see pages 158–161). He thought this would put a stop to the accusations hurled against him, but on March 27, 1826, an Opposition newspaper in Washington, the *United States Telegraph*, again sounded the charge in a full-page editorial.

Three days later, John Randolph of Roanoke rose in the Senate to charge Adams and Clay with corruption. "Let Judas have his thirty pieces of silver!" Randolph shouted and then, after a vicious attack on Adams, came an insult with a literary twist, an allusion to two of the characters in Fielding's novel *Tom Jones:* "I was defeated, horse, foot and dragoons—cut up and clean broke down—by the coalition of Blifil and Black George—by the combination, unheard of till then, of the Puritan with the blackleg." Being called a "blackleg" (a swindler, especially a dishonest gambler) was too much, and Clay challenged Randolph to a duel. They met in the late afternoon of April 8, on the Virginia side of the Potomac, Clay in his usual dress, Randolph's lean figure enveloped in a white dressing gown. The weapons chosen were pistols at a distance of ten paces. Each man's first shot missed. At the second fire, Clay's bullet passed through Randolph's gown. But Randolph raised his pistol, fired in the air, and shouted: "I do not fire at you, Mr. Clay." Then he walked toward his adversary with hand extended. Clay met him halfway and they shook hands. Obviously moved, Clay declared: "I trust in God, my dear sir, you are untouched: after what has occurred I would not have harmed you for a thousand worlds." Randolph said, "You owe me a coat, Mr. Clay." And Clay replied, "I am glad the debt is no greater." The encounter was over. But the charges of corruption were not ended; they continued throughout the campaign of 1828.

Clay watched with mounting anxiety as the Opposition put Jackson forward as its candidate for the Presidency. It was clear that Adams would be renominated by the National Republicans, and the ground swell of popu-

THE DUEL WITH RANDOLPH

Senator Thomas Hart Benton, long a congressional colleague of Clay, was a cousin of the latter's wife—whose maiden name was Lucretia Hart. Benton's massive memoirs, as long-winded as he himself often was in the Senate, describe Clay's 1826 duel with Randolph:

"Mr. Randolph came to my room at Brown's Hotel, and (without explaining the reason of the question) asked me if I was a blood-relation of Mrs. Clay? I answered that I was, and he immediately replied that that put an end to a request which he had wished to make of me [to be his second]. He told me he would make my bosom the depository of a secret which he should commit to no other person: it was, that he did not intend to fire at Mr. Clay. He told it to me because he wanted a witness of his intention, and did not mean to tell it to his second or anybody else."

Though it is often now stated that dueling suffered a sharp decline in the United States after Burr killed Hamilton in 1804, duels continued to be fought for a generation after that by very prominent Americans indeed. Clay was Secretary of State when he fought Randolph. Benton himself had killed a United States district attorney in a duel in 1817.

When he learned that the duel would be fought the next day, Benton paid an evening visit to the Clay home, and wrote: "There had been some alienation between us since the time of the presidential election in the House of Representatives [a year earlier], and I wished to give evidence that there was nothing personal in it. The family were in the parlor—company present—and . . . when all were gone, and [Mrs. Clay] also had left the parlor, I did what I came for, and said to Mr. Clay that, notwithstanding our late political differences, my personal feelings towards him were the same as formerly, and that, in whatever concerned his life or honor my best wishes were with him. He expressed his gratification at the visit and the declaration, and said it was what he would have expected of me. We parted at midnight."

When the duel ended without serious injury to either principal, Benton (who was present at it) recorded: "The joy of all was extreme at this happy termination of a most critical affair; and we immediately left. . . . I stopped to sup with Mr. Randolph and his friends—none of us wanted dinner that day. . . . It was about the last high-toned duel that I have witnessed, and among the highest-toned that I have ever witnessed. . . . Certainly duelling is bad . . . but not quite so bad as its substitute—revolvers, bowie-knives, blackguarding, and street-assassinations under the pretext of self-defence."

larity for the Hero of New Orleans became apparent as one state legislature after another endorsed his candidacy. When the contest was at its height, both sides resorted to vicious misrepresentation. Naturally, Clay received a considerable share of this political abuse. His opponents accused him of treasonable plotting with Aaron Burr, of embezzling $20,000, and even of having cheated a couple of carpenters out of their wages. Always the cry rang out of "bargain and sale." At a Jackson meeting in South Carolina those present drank a toast to "Adams, Clay and Company. Would to God they were like Jonah in the whale's belly; the whale to the devil; the devil in hell; and the door locked, key lost, and not a son of Vulcan within a million of miles to make another."

Despite the great hullabaloo of the campaign, the ordinary voters did not become greatly excited, nor did they stream to the polls in huge numbers. This was probably owing largely to the fact that in most states the outcome was never in doubt and the voters felt it was futile to exercise the ballot. When the smoke of battle cleared away, Jackson had won by a decisive majority in the Electoral College. The West, the South except Delaware and Maryland, and Pennsylvania and New York had transported the General into the Executive Mansion. The Democrats also controlled both houses of Congress. Clay's hopes of moving from the State Department into the White House had vanished. That winter, at a farewell dinner given in his honor, he warned the country of the dangers of military tyranny. Then, shortly after Jackson's inauguration on March 4, 1829, the Western Star returned to his home and family in Kentucky, a sadly disappointed man.

President-elect Andrew Jackson made frequent speaking stops during his stagecoach trip via the Cumberland Road to Washington in 1829. This and other national pikes were an essential part of Clay's American System.

Chapter 4
THE BATTLE WITH JACKSONIAN DEMOCRACY

CLAY quickly found some solace for his frustration at Jackson's triumph in the enthusiasm of the crowds that gathered in every village and town to do him honor as he journeyed homeward in the spring of 1829. A sizable throng was also on hand to greet him in Lexington when he arrived. Pleasant as this personal triumphal tour may have been, it could not have completely gladdened the heart of a man who had been buffeted by political defeat and personal tragedy as well. Commencing with the deaths of two daughters, Eliza and Susan Duralde, in 1825, the Clay family was struck with misfortune during these trying years. At the end of 1829 Clay's mother, stepfather, and brother John were interred within a two-week period. A favorite sister-in-law, Nancy Brown, died a year later after a long illness. One son, Thomas, was unable to control his excessive drinking and even was jailed in Philadelphia. Another son, Theodore, was afflicted with a mental illness and deemed insane.

Upon his return to Ashland, Clay busied himself first in caring for and enlarging his landholdings, which by 1831, according to the county tax lists, had an assessed valuation of $72,500—exclusive, as the old record has it, of "Studs, Jack Asses and Billiard Tables." Yet the life of a country squire was tame for a man who loved to be at the center of a wider stage, and it soon became apparent that the Kentucky Hotspur was still politically minded. In May 1829, he leveled his first major attack at the Administration in power by denouncing Jackson as a spoilsman.

The Jacksonian promise during the 1828 campaign had been "retrenchment and reform." For a while after Old Hickory was installed in the White House, there was a general lowering of governmental expenditures. But the downward trend lasted only a few years, and by 1833, the navy was spending as much as it had during the last years of the Adams Administration, the Treasury expenditures had leaped about $7,000,000 more than in 1828, and deficits in the Post Office were higher than ever. Reformation in government by the Jackson Administration was also an ill-kept promise. The new President believed in rotation in office so that as many as possible might have a chance to share in the business of government. In addition, he saw nothing wrong in rewarding his loyal supporters by patronage. The result was that although corruption was muzzled in certain cases, there was still as much inefficiency and dishonesty as had existed previously.

Clay, confident that the people would soon have their fill of Jackson, charged that the National Republican officeholders were being turned out in droves. This was not entirely true, though it must be said that Old Hickory's use of the appointing power did lower the standards of public service. Spoilsmanship was not the only charge that Clay brought against Jackson. He denounced the Administration for truckling to Great Britain when, by admitting that Adams and Clay had adopted an erroneous policy, it prevailed on the British government in 1830 to reopen the West Indian trade to American ships. He criticized the President as well for the arbitrary way in which he forced the Cherokee and other Indian tribes to give up their lands in the Deep South and move to reservations beyond the Mississippi.

Clay was also irate about Jackson's changing position on a number of internal improvements bills, for Jackson vacillated on the issue, approving some and vetoing others. The Kentuckian was particularly incensed by the veto of a bill for improving the Maysville Road, which connected Lexington with the town of Maysville on the Ohio River. The road was wholly within the state of Kentucky. This veto centered public attention on the issue, not only because of the outraged cries of Clay and his supporters but also because it demonstrated a principle of Jacksonian democracy —that roads and canals should be built and improved by the states, rather than by the national government.

There was really only one aspect of government policy on which both Clay and Jackson agreed—nullification. South Carolina, aroused by the tariff of 1828, threatened to declare that bill null and void, and to leave the Union. Clay, like Jackson, denounced this attitude, and applauded Webster's famous two-day reply to Senator Robert Young Hayne of South Carolina in which Webster declaimed: "Liberty *and* Union, now and forever, one and inseparable."

A third political party

Despite attacks upon Jackson's policies by Clay and other National Republicans, the Democratic Administration retained its popularity with the voters in the election of 1830. This was a cross that Harry of the West found hard to bear, especially since the National Republicans made no gains in Kentucky or Ohio. More important, the rise of a third political party, which was diverting some of the opposition to Jackson, provided still another source of worry and discontent. In the fall of 1826, William Morgan, a stonemason of Batavia, New York, had been seized in a nearby town and taken to the Niagara frontier, where all trace of him disappeared. He was a member of the Masonic Order, but not in good standing, for he had written a book entitled *Illustrations of Masonry*, which disclosed the secrets of the first three degrees of the society. When it became apparent that investigations into his disappearance were being obstructed by influential Masons, a wave of popular indignation rose in western New York and swept from there into the other Middle Atlantic states, New England, and Ohio. Out of this furor came the Anti-Masonic party, pledged to war against the secret and exclusive Order of Masonry, and for morality and the rights of the common man. In New York, where the party soon gained strength, the Anti-Masons in 1828 won four seats in the state's Senate, and seventeen in the Assembly. It also counted among its ranks such leaders in the state as Thurlow Weed and William Henry Seward.

Clay was a Mason, but an inactive one. Had he been willing to come out against the Order, he might have received the Anti-Masonic nomination. This he refused to do, for he did not believe that Masonry should be a political issue. The leaders of the new party became convinced that Harry of the West was no friend of theirs, and they selected William Wirt of Maryland as their candidate for President during a nominating convention held in Baltimore in the fall of 1831. (This convention also set a national precedent by being the first to choose its two candidates for the presidential ticket in an open meeting, a practice that was quickly adopted by the other political parties.) A breach soon developed between Clay and the rising Anti-Masonic politicians—a breach that deepened after the fall elections of 1831 when the New Yorkers suspected Clay's followers in that state of knifing the Anti-Masonic state ticket by voting instead for Jacksonites. A rivalry between Clay on the one hand and Weed and Seward on the other had begun. It was to do Clay political injury in the years that lay ahead.

Apparently believing that the Anti-Masons more actively championed rural democracy, many National Republicans switched over to the new party, but Clay was nevertheless de-

A sinister-appearing magazine illustration portrays the suspected abduction of William Morgan by irate Masons who considered him a traitor to their Order. Gagged, he was supposedly taken to the Canadian border in a yellow carriage.

The four 1832 presidential candidates join in "A Political Game of Brag." Clay, left, shows his cards; the Anti-Mason, Wirt, passes; Jackson curses, seeing Clay's hand; Calhoun (foreground) hides Nullification and Anti-Tariff cards.

termined to run for President on his party's ticket. The Kentucky legislature elected him to the United States Senate in 1831, and, shortly after he arrived in Washington that December, the National Republicans held a national nominating convention. It made him their candidate and selected John Sergeant for Vice-President. Jackson was the over-whelming choice of the Democrats for re-election, and the two rival chieftains and their partisans began marshaling their ranks for the coming campaign.

The 1832 campaign

The National Republican platform had three main planks. Clay and his party stood for a protective tariff, for renewal of the char-ter of the Bank of the United States, and for maintaining the price of public lands and dis-tributing the proceeds from the sales to the individual states. Employing these three mea-sures, which were the core of his American System, Clay hoped to promote increased na-tional prosperity. The Bank, by reason of its ability to discount the notes of state banks, would help to maintain a sound and stable national currency; the tariff would furnish revenue for the expenses of the national gov-ernment; the public-lands policy would aid the states that wished to make their own in-ternal improvements and, by keeping up the price of land, would please Eastern manufac-turers who feared that cheap or free land would deplete their available labor force by tempting workers to migrate westward.

Clay's program was viewed with much favor in the Eastern states, particularly by businessmen, but it had its weaknesses from a political point of view in other sections. The South was not enamored of the Bank of the United States, hated the high tariff, and had little or no interest in internal improvements.

The West, while it liked the protective tariff well enough, disliked the Bank and wanted cheap or, if possible, free land. These regional differences presented weighty problems for a unified political stand, but Clay brushed them aside. He was especially committed to a protective tariff, which he regarded as vital to his system. To preserve the tariff, he declared, he "would defy the South, the President and the Devil."

During 1831 and early 1832, Jackson's Administration showed signs of moving cautiously toward a lower tariff, cheaper public-lands policy, but the major conflict with Clay and the National Republicans developed over the recharter of the Bank of the United States. President Jackson disapproved of the Bank, partly because he was suspicious of banks in general, partly because he was convinced that in several states the Bank had favored Adams in the 1828 election. The charter of "the Monster," as he called it, was to expire in 1836, and by 1832 it was clear that he would oppose its renewal.

Clay and Webster (one of the Bank's most prominent lawyers) hoped to make the institution's recharter an issue in the 1832 election. They argued that a bill for recharter was certain to pass Congress and that Jackson would be obliged to sign it in a presidential year, while he could veto it later without political damage to himself. If the President refused to sign, they said, he would certainly lose the key state of Pennsylvania, where the Bank was popular, as well as those voters in the West who were sympathetic to the institution. Nicholas Biddle, president of the Bank, was reluctant at first to follow their advice, for he preferred to keep the Bank out of the political arena. Finally this able administrator yielded upon the suggestion of his Washington agent, Thomas Cadwalader. Biddle was probably also swayed somewhat to support recharter of the Bank in 1832 by the fact that Clay and Webster were anxious to champion the measure at this time. As Clay and Webster predicted, the Bank bill passed Con-

gress. Jackson instantly took up the battle. To Van Buren he said: "The Bank is trying to kill me, but I will kill it." On July 10, Old Hickory unexpectedly vetoed the recharter in a ringing message that declared the Bank unconstitutional, a dangerous concentration of power, and a device for advancing the interests of the few at the expense of the many. While the veto message was weak in its condemnation of the Bank's economic policies, its appeal to the masses made it a potent weapon in the presidential campaign.

The result of the campaign of 1832 was never in doubt. Jackson was enormously popular, the opposition vote was split between Clay and Wirt, and the Bank was an excellent Democratic issue. The National Republicans, blindly believing that the veto would alienate the people from Jackson, helped to bring on their own destruction by scattering thousands of copies of the veto message around the country. Wirt carried only Vermont. South Carolina wasted its vote on John Floyd. Clay carried Massachusetts, Rhode Island, Connecticut, Maryland, Delaware, and Kentucky. Jackson topped them in all the other states for a total of 219 electoral votes to Clay's 49, and a sizable popular majority of about 100,000 votes. The National Republican party had been routed, and Henry Clay's presidential aspirations had suffered a bad setback. Saddened by the 1832 defeat, Clay tried to resign his seat in the Senate, but John J. Crittenden, who was approached to take it, rejected it. Clay reluctantly stayed on in Washington and soon was enveloped in the pressing problems intrinsic to his position as a leader of the opposition.

The nullification crisis

Shortly after the election, a crisis developed over the tariff question, and in the resolving of this difficult situation Clay played an important role. The tariff of 1832, which became law in July of that year, was framed in a House of Representatives committee headed by John Quincy Adams. It reduced the duties on imported goods to about the level of the tariff of 1824. Andrew Jackson thought it was a good bill, but South Carolina was furious. The state threw away its presidential vote in protest and then, in a special convention held in November, declared the tariffs of 1828 and 1832 null and void, not to be enforced in South Carolina after February 1, 1833. This Ordinance of Nullification also forbade collection of federal duties in the state, prohibited appeal of nullification to the Supreme Court of the United States, and declared that any attempt to coerce the state would mean the end of South Carolina's allegiance to the Union.

Jackson's response to the South Carolinians was to use a carrot-and-stick policy. He supported the Verplanck bill, a new tariff measure introduced in the House of Representatives, which would have made some reductions immediately and lowered the tariff generally 50 percent by 1834. At the same time, he issued a strong Proclamation to the People of South Carolina insisting that nullification of a federal law by a state was "incompatible with the existence of the Union, contradicted expressly by the letter of the Constitution, unauthorized by its spirit, inconsistent with every principle on which it was founded, and destructive of the great object for which it was formed." As for secession, Jackson told the people of his native state that "disunion by armed force is *treason*. Are you really ready to incur its guilt?" South Carolina, however, refused to listen to the President, and the state began to prepare itself militarily. Calhoun gave up his post as Vice-President and took the vacant Senate seat of Robert Y. Hayne, who had just won the state's governorship. Meanwhile, Jackson asked Congress for a "Force Bill" that would give him additional powers needed to collect import duties under any circumstances. Nationalists, even members of the opposition like Webster, rallied to Jackson; states' rights advocates, on the other hand, abandoned him.

Clay was tempted to keep clear of this collision between the President and South Caro-

"A SAGACIOUS MAN OF AMBITION"

Miss Harriet Martineau, a leading English literary figure in the first half of the nineteenth century, traveled extensively in America and saw much of Clay, both in Washington and Kentucky. Her *Retrospect of Western Travel*, published in London in 1838, has many vivid passages about him:

"Mr. Clay, sitting upright on the sofa, with his snuff-box ever in his hand, would discourse for many an hour, in his even, soft, deliberate tone, on any one of the great subjects of American policy . . . always amazing us with the moderation of estimate and speech which so impetuous a nature has been able to attain. . . . There can scarcely be a stronger contrast than between the eloquence of Webster and that of Clay. Mr. Clay is now my personal friend, but I have a distinct recollection of his speaking, while he was yet merely an acquaintance. His appearance is plain in the extreme, being that of a mere west-country farmer. He is tall and thin, with a weather-beaten complexion, small grey eyes which convey an idea of something more than his well-known sagacity—even of slyness. It is only after much intercourse that Mr. Clay's personal appearance can be discovered to do him any justice at all. All attempts to take his likeness have been in vain, though upwards of thirty portraits of him by different artists, were in existence when I was in America. No one has succeeded in catching the subtle expression of placid kindness, mingled with astuteness, which becomes visible to the eyes of those who are in daily intercourse with him. His mode of talking, deliberate and somewhat formal, including sometimes a grave humor, and sometimes a gentle sentiment, very touching from the lips of a sagacious man of ambition, has but one fault—its obvious adaptation to the supposed state of mind of the person to whom it is addressed.

"Mr. Clay is a man of an irritable and impetuous nature, over which he has obtained a truly noble mastery. His moderation is now his most striking characteristic; obtained, no doubt, at the cost of prodigious self-denial . . . of some of the ease, naturalness, and self-forgetfulness of his manner and discourse. But his conversation is rich in information, and full charged with the spirit of justice and kindliness, rising, on occasion, to a moving magnanimity. By chances, of some of which he was totally unaware, I became acquainted with several acts of his life, political and private, which prove that his moderation is not the mere diffusion of oil upon the waves, but the true stilling of the storm of passion and selfishness. . . .

"Mr. Clay is sometimes spoken of as a 'disappointed statesman,' and he would probably not object to call himself so; for it makes no part of his idea of dignity to pretend to be satisfied when he is sorry, or delighted with what he would fain have prevented. . . . He once held the balance of the Union in his hand [at the time of the Missouri Compromise] and now belongs to the losing party; he more than once expected to be President. . . . Thus far he is a disappointed statesman; but . . . he is in possession of . . . the imperishable reality of great deeds done. . . .

Harriet Martineau

"The one act of Mr. Clay's public life, for which he must be held to require pardon from posterity, is that by which he secured the continuance of slavery in Missouri; and, in consequence, its establishment in Arkansas and Florida. When he held the destinies of American slavery in his hand, he had unhappily more regard for precedent in human arrangements than for the spirit of the divine laws in the light of which such arrangements should be ever regarded. He acted to avert the conflict which cannot be averted. It has still to take place—it is now taking place—under less favorable circumstances; and his measure of expediency is already meeting with the retribution which ever follows the shift from] a higher principle to a lower. . . .

"His recollections of Europe are very vivid and pleasurable. We spent many an hour of my visit to him in Kentucky in talking over our mutual English friends, till we forgot the time and space we had both traversed since we parted from them, and looked up surprised to find ourselves, not at a London dinner-table, but in the wild woods of the west. . . .

"The finest speech I heard from Mr. Clay in the Senate was on the sad subject of the injuries of the Indians. He exposed the facts of the treatment of the Cherokees by Georgia. . . . Some of the foreign ambassadors might be seen leaning against the pillars behind the chair; and many members of the other House appeared behind, and in the passages, and one sat on the steps of the platform, his hands clasped, and his eyes fixed on Mr. Clay, as if life hung upon his words. As many as could crowd into the gallery leaned over the balustrade; and the lower circle was thronged with ladies and gentlemen, in the center of whom stood a group of Cherokee chiefs, listening immoveably. I never saw so deep a moral impression produced by a speech. The best testimony to this was the general disgust excited by the empty and abusive reply of the senator from Georgia. . . . This gentleman's speech, however, showed us one good thing—that Mr. Clay is as excellent in reply as in proposition, prompt, earnest, temperate, and graceful. The chief characteristic of his eloquence is its earnestness. Every tone of his voice, every fibre of his frame bears testimony to this. His attitudes are, from the beginning to the close, very graceful. His first sentences are homely, and given with a little hesitation and repetition, and with an agitation shown by a frequent putting on and taking off of the spectacles, and a trembling of the hands among the documents on the desk. Then as the speaker becomes possessed with his subject, the agitation changes its character, but does not subside. His utterance is still deliberate, but his voice becomes deliciously winning. Its higher tones disappointed me at first; but the lower ones, trembling with emotion, swelling and falling with the earnestness of the speaker, are very moving, and his whole manner becomes irresistibly persuasive. I saw tears, of which I am sure he was wholly unconscious, falling on his papers, as he vividly described the woes and injuries of the aborigines. I saw Webster draw his hand across his eyes; I saw every one deeply moved except two persons."

President Jackson's reshuffling of his Cabinet provoked this hostile cartoon, "The Rats Leaving a Falling House." Secretary of State Van Buren, who tactfully resigned with the others, is restrained by a heavy Jackson foot.

lina but, for a variety of reasons, finally decided to intervene. He did not favor the Verplanck bill's drastic lowering of duties; he feared the possibility of other states joining South Carolina; he distrusted Jackson; and he wanted acclaim in the South for lowering the tariff. All of these factors prompted him to bring forward the Compromise Tariff of 1833. It provided for a gradual reduction of duties annually until 1840 and then two sharp reductions, so that by 1842, there would be a top duty rate of only 20 percent. The Compromise Tariff passed (see pages 188–191) and Jackson signed it as well as the Force Bill on March 2, 1833. South Carolina nullified the Force Bill (a move on its part that did not have any practical effect) but accepted the tariff (which did), and the danger of secession had passed.

Clay, for his part, had won new laurels as a Great Pacificator. The part he played also gained him the political friendship of Calhoun, who had been a prime mover in nullification. It appeared that there would be a new union between South and West (though the alliance between the two was short-lived). The breach with Webster arising from his support of Jackson was healed before the end of the year and John Randolph patched up his differences with Clay a few months before the Virginian's death. Clay returned to Ashland that spring, feeling relatively relaxed.

The tranquility of the Bluegrass country, though, was broken by the devastations of a cholera epidemic that had swept through most of the nation the year before, reserving its most potent onslaught for the Lexington area. More than fifty people died within three days in the town, and by early July over five hundred had succumbed to the disease. Ashland and the Clay family were untouched by the epidemic, although a planned visit to Kentucky by Webster was postponed.

In the fall, Clay and his wife took a trip that included Philadelphia, New York, Boston, Albany, and then continued via New Jersey on to Washington. Lucretia found the trip exhausting but Clay was exhilarated by the receptions he received, which were certainly cordial except in Boston—where Webster's backers were somewhat standoffish. Reassured that New England still supported him, Clay returned for the winter session of Congress.

The rise of the Whigs

During the year and a half that followed the struggle over nullification and the tariff, two political parties died and a new one was born. The National Republican party, never a very strong organization, had been demoralized by its defeat in 1832, and now it disintegrated. The Anti-Masonic party, primarily a revolt against a secret society, had too narrow a base for permanence on a national basis. Its leaders recognized this, and maneuvered it into a new political organization that was formed in 1834. With a title adopted from British politics, the Whig party was an uneasy coalition of National Republicans, Anti-Masons, and those dissident Democrats who had come to dislike Old Hickory either because of his attack on the Bank or because of his treatment of South Carolina.

Henry Clay and Daniel Webster were the principal Whig leaders, with Calhoun as a temporary ally. Their party attracted the socially conservative—men who distrusted the impulses of the masses. There was a saying among the Whigs that they knew one another "by the instinct of gentlemen." It also appealed to men of economic foresight, who saw great possibilities in Clay's American System, and were impatient with Jacksonian democracy because it put more emphasis on maintaining equality of opportunity for everyone than it did on measures that would promote the economic growth of the nation.

It was the new party's economic vision that enticed men like Horace Greeley and Abraham Lincoln to join the Whig ranks. There were, however, many differing viewpoints among the Whigs as to what was best for the country, and in its early years the party held together mainly because its members were united in their dislike of Jackson and in their fear of his policies. They referred to the President as "King Andrew" and declared that his vetoes alone demonstrated his tendencies to be those of a tyrant and a despot. He and his followers, the Whigs said, were Tories; the Whigs, they maintained, were the true lovers of liberty.

Clay stated, and doubtlessly felt, that in leading the fight against Jackson he was struggling for the benefit of the country, as well as preserving its liberty, property interests, and virtue. He viewed everything Jackson did with deep suspicion, and in 1834 plunged into another struggle with him.

Since the Bank's charter would not expire until 1836, the institution had plenty of time to strike back at the Administration by causing financial stress before it went out of business. At least so thought the President. He had to dismiss two Secretaries of the Treasury before he found in Roger B. Taney a man who felt as he did, and who began removing the government deposits from "the Monster" and putting them in what were soon known as "pet banks." This procedure was bound to

The Capitol and White House can easily be identified in this view of a pastoral Washington as it appeared in 1833.

weaken the Bank, for it not only lessened the overall amount of money in its vaults, but also forced it to curtail its lending operations. Biddle's loan curtailment, however, went beyond what was necessary to safeguard the Bank's legitimate interests. He, and Clay also, hoped that this policy would create pressure from the business community for the restoration of the deposits, and might even force Jackson to allow a recharter.

Humiliations for Clay

Upon his return from New England, Clay threw himself into the fray. And later in the spring of 1834, with a dramatic move in the Senate, he capped his pro-Bank campaign. On March 28, he persuaded that body to pass a resolution of censure on Jackson for trying to gain a control over the Treasury not conferred by the Constitution. He was convinced that the President's dismissal of Cabinet members such as the Treasury Secretaries was dangerous to popular liberty. Jackson was changing the republican form of the government into a tyranny, according to Clay, by uniting in his person the power of the purse and the sword. Clay hoped that this censure resolution, and the long debate that would surely accompany it, would destroy the country's faith in the President, and so prepare the way for the Bank's recharter. The debate lasted for three months, longer than any previous debate since the establishment of the Congress. At the same time, the lack of Bank credit was being felt throughout the nation, and meetings of protest were a common occurrence. One Whig in Cincinnati addressed his complaint directly to Jackson: "Damn your old soul, remove them deposites back again, and recharter the bank, or you will certainly be shot in less than two weeks and that by myself!!!" Clay was eloquent on the Senate

In a nightmarish cartoon, "Political Quixotism," Jackson battles with the "Monster," the Bank of the United States.

Weary of the conflict, the public hauls on the President's suspenders, trying to get him back into bed.

floor, pleading the "heart-rending wretched-ness" of the jobless, of "unclad and unfed orphans," and "the tears of helpless widows."

But Old Hickory would not be moved. He protested the censure resolution, declaring that he would "not bow down to the golden calf"—the Bank. Those who wanted the deposits restored had better not come to him. Let them "go to Nicholas Biddle," he cried. The President's party rallied behind him and the deposits remained in the "pet banks." Finally, in 1837, the episode was literally written off the record when a Democratic majority in the Senate voted to expunge the censure resolution from the Senate Journal. The Whig Senators, not wishing to witness what they considered unconstitutional conduct, left the room. Then, the secretary of the Senate drew black lines through the offending words and wrote over them: "Expunged by order of the Senate," followed by the date. Clay's effort to use the Bank as a weapon in his assault upon Jackson had ended three years later in a Democratic triumph led by Thomas Hart Benton, Clay's onetime political ally.

The outcome of the Bank struggle was only one of the humiliations that Clay suffered during Jackson's second term in office. Foremost among these other defeats was that of his public-lands policy. There were millions of acres of these lands, and Clay was determined to keep the price at $1.25 per acre and distribute the proceeds to the states, with special consideration for those states in which the land lay. Repeatedly he introduced bills to this effect, but the Democrats blocked them all.

Still another issue of the time involved land speculation and the means of checking it. The country was prosperous during the early and middle 1830's, and there were enormous sales of public lands and of private real estate as well. Land speculation was widespread, prices rose, and there was a wave of inflation. Bank credits piled up on paper, because speculators bought land with bank notes, which in turn went to deposit banks where funds were re-lent to speculators. A surplus of paper

On the day the Senate passed the expunging resolution over Clay's opposition, boos and hisses expressed the discontent of spectators. But Jackson, gratified, invited the expungers and their wives to a "grand dinner."

without any specie support was developing. After a badly conceived attempt to distribute the surplus among the states resulted in further inflation, Jackson finally realized that this boom might be followed by a crash, and sought to protect the country from such a catastrophe by issuing the Specie Circular of July 11, 1836. This stipulated that purchasers of government lands must pay for them with gold and silver, rather than with the paper money of state banks.

The Specie Circular was meant to be a curb on land speculation, but there were some consequences that the President had not foreseen. It drained specie from the East into the West, thus making money on the Atlantic seaboard very "tight." Distrust of the country's banks also spread, fostering a spirit of pessimism about the economic future. Thus the Circular helped to precipitate the panic that broke out in 1837. The Whigs promptly denounced the Specie Circular, and Clay introduced a bill providing that the notes of sound banks would be receivable in payment for public lands, which would have lessened the shock of the Circular. The bill passed both the Senate and the House, but Jackson, finding it too inconsistent with existing laws, pocket-vetoed it. Old Hickory seldom changed his mind once he had made it up on any issue.

Victories for moderation

On more than one occasion Clay said that Jackson's violent emotions and prejudices were a danger to the country. The Kentuckian honestly believed this, and in one particular instance sought through moderation to diminish the danger of a foreign war being provoked by the President. During the latter's first term, a treaty had been signed by which France agreed to pay 25,000,000 francs for the damage done to American commerce during the Napoleonic Wars. Payment in six annual installments was to begin in 1833, but the French legislature did not make the necessary appropriations even though King Louis Philippe pressed for acceptance. Jackson waited some two years and then, in his message to Congress, threatened to seize French property unless payments began in the very near future. This warlike proposal angered the French, and there was great excitement in both countries. The French minister in Washington was recalled to Paris. Clay, as chairman of the Senate Committee on Foreign Relations, brought in a resolution that counseled delay and that soothed the French spirit. His action obviously helped to smooth over what might have been a very unpleasant crisis. Subsequently, the French approved the payments if the Americans would present their government with some explanation for

Jackson's harsh language. Again the tempers flared. Old Hickory refused and the American legation in Paris was shut. But another message was written by Jackson during the winter of 1835, and its language was softened by Congress; it offered no menace to France. Britain also made an effort to calm the two ruffled nations, and the French, though not fully appeased, began to pay for the damages in the spring of 1836. Thirty years later the United States minister to France, John Bigelow, found that the incident still rankled in the minds of leading Frenchmen.

Clay also took a moderate and pacific stand on another question of policy that arose during Jackson's second term—the possible acquisition of Texas. That great territory belonged to Mexico. Its cotton lands had attracted immigrants from the United States, and by 1836 there were some thirty thousand American settlers living in the area. They were mainly Southerners and slaveholders, who had evaded Mexican laws forbidding slavery by bringing in their Negroes as indentured servants. Mexico, belatedly alarmed by this influx of American pioneers, tried to abolish slavery in Texas and to establish more effective control of the province from Mexico City. General Santa Anna, then president of Mexico, crossed the Rio Grande to establish order. The Texans rebelled, declared their independence, and even wrote a constitution. When Santa Anna arrived at San Antonio, he was met by a small band of 190 determined Texans garrisoned in a mission named the Alamo. Victories at San Antonio and later at Goliad by the Mexicans only served to enrage the Texans further, and at the San Jacinto River, an army commanded by Sam Houston defeated the Mexicans and captured Santa Anna. Texans proclaimed their freedom, and wanted to be Americans.

Jackson was much interested in Texas. Sam Houston was an old friend. Twice the President had tried to buy the Mexican territory, and was willing to pay $5,000,000 for it, but both times he had been rebuffed by the

DEATH OF THE LAST DAUGHTER

On Christmas Day in 1835, the Clays' longtime Washington friend, Margaret Bayard Smith, wrote her sister: "Poor Mr. Clay was laughing and talking and joking with some friends when his papers and letters were brought to him; he naturally first opened the letter from home. A friend who was with him says he started up and then fell, as if shot, and his first words were 'Every tie to life is broken!' He continued that day in almost a state of distraction, but has, I am told, become more composed, though in the deepest affliction. Anne was his pride as well as his joy, and of all his children his greatest comfort. She was my favorite, so frank, gay, and warmhearted. . . . Of five daughters, she was the last, and now she is gone and poor Mrs. Clay in her declining age is left alone and bereaved of the support and comfort which daughters and only daughters can afford."

Mexican government. Now he moved cautiously toward recognition of Texan independence and its eventual annexation, but the powerful Senate Committee on Foreign Relations was even more cautious than the President. Under Clay's leadership, the Committee recommended delay in recognizing the independence of Texas until there was proof that it had a stable government capable of functioning as an "independent power." In the speech that accompanied this resolution, and in the months that followed, Clay favored a waiting policy. Already there were signs of a crisis over the expansion of slavery, similar to the one that had accompanied the admission of Missouri to the Union. Antislavery sentiment was growing in the North; abolitionist literature was increasing in volume, and a considerable amount of this propaganda was finding its way into the South, irritating an already excitable situation.

Northern hostility, together with a Negro uprising in Virginia in 1831—Nat Turner's Rebellion—had made Southerners defensive about their "peculiar institution" and anxious to protect it. One way of solidifying their position would be to extend slavery into a large block of unsettled territory out of which

Southerners blamed abolitionists for inciting slave rebellions such as the bloody one led by Nat Turner (standing, left) in 1831.

new states might be carved. Rumors of a Southern conspiracy to acquire Texas added to the gravity of a situation that caused Clay growing concern. Jackson saw the situation much as Clay did, and it was only on the day before he left the White House, March 3, 1837, that the government formally recognized the independence of the Lone Star State.

Van Buren as President

An additional reason for the reluctance of both Whigs and Democrats to act swiftly about Texas was a feeling on both sides that the issue of annexation would be a dangerous one in the presidential campaign of 1836. In that contest, Martin Van Buren was the Democratic choice. The Whigs, split by their various attitudes on national problems, could not agree on a single candidate. They experimented with the idea of running several candidates in different sections of the country, such as Daniel Webster in New England and William Henry Harrison in the West, hoping in this way to throw the election into the

House of Representatives. Van Buren won an easy victory, for the country was still true to King Andrew, and the Red Fox of Kinderhook (as Van Buren was known) was his choice for succession. Much to his disappointment, Clay had been passed over by the Whigs, but with his usual optimism he began laying plans to win the Whig nomination in 1840.

Van Buren had no sooner taken office than it became woefully apparent that the United States was in for a period of difficult times. The Panic of 1837 hit the country hard. Land values tumbled, unemployment rose, breadlines formed in the cities, bankruptcies were frequent, and currency was unsound. The inflation and speculation of the early 1830's was followed by a period of depression that lasted for almost six years.

Clay asserted that this economic situation was the fault of Jackson and his policies, and that it was up to the Democrats and not the Whigs to devise means of relief. But the Democrats refused to assume this responsibility. Van Buren's principal answer to the depression, if answer it could be called, was the Independent Treasury Bill. This measure separated the government from all direct relationship to banks and banking, its "hard money" advocates believing that—in ways they found difficult to explain—it might help the suffering country. At least it would keep the revenue safe, and the government from falling into the clutches of the money changers. Clay and the Whigs fought hard against this measure. The Kentuckian's remedy for the depression was the reestablishment of a national bank as a means of procuring a stable and sound paper currency. But he could not prevent the ultimate passage of the Independent Treasury Act; after two years of submission and resubmission, debate, passage by the Senate, and refusal by the House, it finally became law in 1840.

Thwarted in his attempts to revise financial policy, the Kentuckian was also harassed and perplexed by the rising tumult over slavery. William Lloyd Garrison and other antislavery zealots denounced the South in unsparing terms. Newspapers, such as the *Liberator*, became more insistent about emancipating the Negroes. Abolitionist societies grew in number; there were 369 antislavery groups in New York alone by 1838. Abolitionist petitions flooded into Congress, where the Southerners tried to stifle them with gag resolutions prohibiting their printing, debate, and even reception by the House. Postmaster General Amos Kendall collaborated with the South in an attempt to prevent the circulation of antislavery literature through the mails. All of these things produced national controversy and Clay, like the other political leaders of his time, was forced to define his position.

"A grievous wrong"

Clay still disliked slavery. It was, he said in 1836, "a curse to the master; a wrong, a grievous wrong to the slave." On the other hand, he was a slaveholder in a state where majority sentiment supported the institution. Another more important element was his con-

tinued ambition to be President, which made him anxious to avoid alienating large masses of public opinion in either North or South. It was almost inevitable that he should take a middle course in the growing excitement over human bondage.

When Calhoun in 1836 tried to push through Congress a measure prohibiting the circulation of antislavery propaganda through the mails, Clay joined Northerners in opposing the move. In so doing, he upheld the rights of free speech and petition. However, he censured the abolitionists for stirring up a controversy that threatened the destruction of the Union, and declared that Congress had no power over slavery within the states or over interstate slave trade.

Jackson's Spoils System, often attacked by cartoonists, was expanded substantially by his successor, Van Buren.

To the thorny slavery problem, his answer was colonization of freed Negroes in Africa. Foreseeing an increase in immigration into the United States, he reasoned that cheaper white labor would eventually make slavery too expensive for the slave owners. As the Negroes' conditions became worse, there would be more crime and rebellion; the shipment of emancipated slaves to areas in Africa would then become desirable. It was not a completely practical solution, being both very costly and also unpopular among Negroes, but Clay continued to support it in dogged fashion. It gave a sop to his humanitarian instincts, and provided the middle-of-the-road position that he felt was necessary from a political point of view (see pages 200–204).

Clay was eager to be the Whig candidate for President in 1840. He had powerful support among Northern business interests, Southern Whigs favored him, and victory prospects were bright, for the Democratic

---

CLAY VERSUS CALHOUN

During their early years together in Congress, Clay and John C. Calhoun had been good friends and associates. Subsequently, they were often vehement opponents. A notable instance of this animosity occurred in 1838, when Calhoun stopped cooperating with Webster and Clay in their opposition to the Van Buren Administration. For all practical purposes, Calhoun became a Democrat—and Democratic Senator Thomas Hart Benton was delighted. "The opposition," Benton recorded, "took deeply to heart this withdrawal of one of their leaders, and his appearance on the other side. It created a feeling of personal resentment against Mr. Calhoun. . . . Some sharp passages took place between himself and Mr. Webster, but . . . Mr. Webster was but slightly inclined towards that kind of speaking which mingles personality with argument. . . . Mr. Clay had a turn that way; and, certainly, a great ability for it. Invective, mingled with sarcasm, was one of the phases of his oratory. He was supreme . . . where the political attack on a public man's measure was to be enforced and heightened by a personal attack on his conduct. He owed much of his fascinating power over his hearers to the exercise of this talent . . . and to him it naturally fell to become the organ of the feelings of his party towards Mr. Calhoun."

After giving some fiery examples of Clay's attack on Calhoun, Benton continued with Calhoun's harsh counterattack: "Instead of leaving not a hair in the head of my arguments, as the senator [Clay] threatened (to use his not very dignified expression), he has not even attempted to answer a large, and not the least weighty, portion; and of that which he has, there is not one fairly stated, or fairly answered. . . . But the senator did not restrict himself to a reply to my arguments. He introduced personal remarks, which neither self-respect, nor a regard to the cause I support, will permit me to pass without notice, as adverse as I am to all personal controversies. Not only my education and disposition, but, above all, my conception of the duties belonging to the station I occupy, indisposes me to such controversies. We are sent here, not to wrangle, or indulge in personal abuse, but to deliberate and decide on the common interests of the States of this Union."

In his own autobiography, President Van Buren says of this same clash: "When Mr. Calhoun came to the support of my administration . . . there arose a bitter feud between him and Mr. Clay. . . . Mr. Calhoun insisted that Mr. Clay was then in his power—that he was 'his master'! 'He my master'! replied Mr. Clay, with indignation, and in his best and loftiest manner —'I would not accept him for my slave.' "

The upshot was that for a long time after this quarrel, Calhoun and Clay never spoke to each other on a personal level. Then, in 1842, Clay resigned from the Senate and made a moving speech of adieu. Even his old adversary Benton paid somewhat grumpy tribute to Clay's unprecedented farewell, noting: "The resignation which had just taken place was an epoch in the annals of the country. . . . But the valedictory, though well performed, did not escape the criticism of senators, as being out of keeping with the usages of the body. It was the first occasion of the kind; and, thus far, has been the last; and it might not be recommendable for any one, except another Henry Clay—if another should ever appear—to attempt its imitation." The iron-willed Calhoun was even more deeply stirred by the event. Nathan Sargent, long a journalist and public official in Washington, dramatically reported the reconciliation that took place just after Clay finished his adieu: "Members of the Senate, all save one, then gathered around the retiring Senator, and took leave individually of him. . . . As Mr. Clay became somewhat free from the crowd of friends, he noticed Mr. Calhoun standing at a little distance; they met and embraced in silence. The two distinguished statesmen had held no social intercourse with each other for nearly five years; yet as they were about to be separated the past rushed to their memory, and the real admiration they entertained for each other overrode every less noble feeling."

Administration was unpopular because of the continued depression. Yet there were obstacles in his path. The former Anti-Masons had no liking for him, Western advocates of cheap lands opposed his candidacy, and the growing antislavery group was not enthralled with the idea of supporting a slaveholder for the Presidency. He was, moreover, a Bank man, and shrewd politicians felt that the Bank had been proven to be far more of a political liability than an asset.

New York was important in determining the Whig nomination and, unfortunately for Clay, Thurlow Weed and Governor William Henry Seward controlled the state's Whig party organization. They believed that the Bank issue, Anti-Masonic antipathy, and antislavery opposition would kill Clay in the estimation of New Yorkers, and that as a result the Whigs would lose control of the state if Clay received the nomination. Clay sensed their hostility, and in the fall of 1839 made a trip to their state in an effort to win support. It was a futile effort, and the New York delegation opposed Clay at the Whig national convention, held at Harrisburg, Pennsylvania, in December 1839. The New Yorkers' first choice was Winfield Scott, a hero of the War of 1812, but they finally settled for William Henry Harrison, who had received more popular votes than any of the other Whig candidates in the 1836 campaign. He was another war hero, famous for his battles against the Indians and British in the Northwest Territory, and had acquired a nickname, "Old Tippecanoe," from the site of a fight in the Indiana Territory. Clay and his backers were bitterly disappointed and, to salve their feelings somewhat, the convention nominated John Tyler of Virginia as Vice-President. A Clay supporter, Tyler wept, it was rumored, when Clay was not nominated as President.

The campaign of 1840 was a slam-bang affair, for the Whigs borrowed the tactics the Democrats had used against John Quincy Adams, with a few additions of their own. Log cabins, hard cider, and coonskins (all supposedly symbols of the common man) were employed to depict Harrison, while Van Buren was denounced as a spendthrift who used cologne, wore corsets, and ate from silver plates. All these devices were utilized by the Whigs in a major attempt to convince the people that they, rather than the Van Burenites, were the true champions of the democratic way of life. These tactics, plus the persistence of the continuing depression, brought a decisive Whig victory that swept Harrison into the White House. He carried nineteen of the twenty-six states in the Union at the time. Clay did not endorse this kind of political campaign, but he worked hard for Harrison and was overjoyed to see the Whigs win. He still felt that, from his post in the Senate, he would be able to control the President and to establish the policies of the incoming Administration.

A country gentleman with simple tastes, Harrison fitted the presidential image advanced by the Whigs in 1840.

Chapter 5
CONTINUED EFFORT
AMID DISAPPOINTMENTS

HARRY OF THE WEST had lost the Whig nomination at a time when he would probably have won an easy victory. This was a bitter pill to swallow, but he was still determined to remain the leader of his party, even though the White House was occupied by another man. Harrison, who was sixty-eight and not in the best of physical condition, journeyed to Kentucky after the election. Supposedly this trip was for the purpose of conferring about a land company with Charles Wickliffe, an old enemy of Clay, but actually it was engineered so that Harrison could take counsel with the political leadership at Frankfort.

Fearful of sharing power, the President-elect at first planned to see Clay, but then thought their contact should be through a mutual friend. Clay, however, invited him to Lexington in such a way that to refuse would have signalized an open breach between the two men. Harrison came over from Frankfort to "the Athens of the West," and spent most of the week with Clay and his son, Henry Junior. Reportedly the two men reached agreement on some matters of public policy, although Harrison was reluctant to reveal his selections for the Cabinet. The President-elect had already made it clear that Clay could have the State Department, but the latter had made it equally evident that he would not accept the post. He suggested Webster, and Black

Dan—so-called because of his swarthy visage —received the top post in Harrison's Cabinet.

With or without the counsel of Clay, his supporters were fairly represented in the Cabinet. John J. Crittenden of Kentucky was chosen Attorney General, and Thomas Ewing of Ohio became head of the Treasury Department. Despite Clay's best efforts, however, he could not secure a Cabinet berth for another friend, John M. Clayton of Delaware, and the very lucrative post of Collector of the Port of New York fell to Edward Curtis, a protégé of Webster's who, along with Weed and Seward, had worked for Clay's defeat in the Whig nomination. This last appointment made Clay furious, and when Democrat William Learned Marcy twitted him privately about his New York friends he spoke out, as Marcy told one of his correspondents, "and said what I am not at liberty to repeat. He has just views of their character and motives of their conduct." When sufficiently aroused, Clay indulged in bursts of profanity, and this was undoubtedly one of those occasions.

During the winter and spring of 1841, an uneasy truce existed between Harrison and Clay. The former agreed to an extra session of Congress urged by the Kentuckian, but the President had more than his share of vanity and was increasingly irked by Clay's domineering manner. Old Tip would not be dictated to on appointments, and on one occasion exclaimed, "Mr. Clay, you forget that I am President." Relations between the two men became so tense that finally Harrison refused a request for an interview, and Clay complained to a friend: "And it has come to this! I am civilly but virtually requested not to visit the White House—not to see the President personally, but hereafter only communicate with him in writing! . . . Here is my table loaded with letters from my friends in every part of the Union, applying to me to obtain offices for them, when I have not one to give, nor influence enough to procure the appointment of a friend to the most humble position!"

An unforeseen succession

How this growing hostility between the President and the Senator from Kentucky might have ended no one can say, for Harrison was only in office a month. The insistent claims of wrangling politicians, the clamor of office seekers, and the complaints of those ejected from office, sapped his strength. He caught cold one spring day when, as was his wont, he went out bareheaded and without an overcoat to shop for White House food supplies. Pneumonia speedily developed, and on April 4 he died. Suddenly, Virginia's John Tyler, a friend of Clay, was the tenth President of the United States.

A states' rights Democrat who had joined the Whigs because of his dislike for Andrew Jackson, Tyler prided himself on being consistent in his views and attitudes toward public policy. And he was anxious to be regarded as the leader of his country, a position that fate now seemed to have thrust upon him. Since no occupant of the White House had ever died in office until Harrison did, there was some question as to whether Tyler was really President or merely the Vice-President acting as the Chief Executive. Tyler insisted

Desiring party unity, eminent Whigs induced Harrison to let Clay read the inaugural address before its delivery (above).

The oft-sought goal of Clay's ambitions, the White House, appears in an 1841 engraving done during Tyler's occupancy.

that he was actually President, and so established a precedent that has lasted down to the present. Never a leader on the national scene, Tyler had no hope of becoming the party's chief. Whigs still suffered when reminded of Jackson's domination of party and legislature while he was President, and as a result preferred that a member of the legislature be their guide in the party. There was no doubt that Clay felt this leadership was his and his alone. Besides, despite his personal friendship for Harry of the West, Tyler had a long record of opposition to a national bank, to internal improvements at national expense, and to a high tariff—Clay's pet projects. Under these circumstances, a clash between the two men was inescapable.

When Congress met that spring in extra session, Clay was in a position of great power. He headed the Committee on Finance in the Senate, and a close supporter was chairman of the Committee on Public Lands. Another ally, John White of Kentucky, became Speaker of the House, and Clay's friends chaired most of the important committees in the lower chamber. Confident of his control over Con-

gress, Harry of the West lost no time in outlining a program for the Whigs. He declared that the Independent Treasury Act must be repealed, a national bank reestablished, the tariff adjusted upward, and provision made for distribution of the proceeds from the public land sales. These were some of the foremost elements of the American System, and it appeared that Clay finally was going to enact his program. States' rights Whigs, Tyler among them, took alarm.

The inevitable dispute between the President and the imperious Senator came over the reestablishment of a national bank. Secretary of the Treasury Ewing worked out a plan for such an institution, one that had the approval of Tyler and all the Cabinet, including Secretary of State Webster. But from Clay's point of view this proposal was fatally defective. It provided that the bank, which would be chartered in the District of Columbia under congressional jurisdiction, could establish branches elsewhere only with the consent of the states involved. This satisfied Tyler's states' rights scruples, but disgusted Clay. "What a bank would that be!" he exclaimed, and insisted upon an institution with un-limited branching power, like the old Bank of the United States. He wanted a bank bill stamped with his own signature; he also wanted to make it clear that he, rather than the President, was the leader of the Whigs. As chairman of the Committee on Finance, Clay was in a position to wield power, and the Committee wrote his sort of bill.

The states' rights members of the party, however, were unwilling to follow Clay's dictatorial leadership and refused to accept his bill. After an abortive attempt by William C. Rives of Virginia to attach an amendment that was close to the Ewing proposal, Clay finally had to accept a compromise amendment proposed by Peter B. Porter of New York. The Porter amendment gave a state the right to prevent establishment of a branch within its borders, if its legislature passed an act to that effect at its first session after the bank bill became law. Even so, Clay's bill provided that Congress could establish a branch in such a state, if it were found necessary in order to carry out powers granted in the Constitution.

Clay's bill squeezed through Congress by three votes and went to the White House early in August. Tyler vetoed it, primarily because it gave the Bank the power to establish branches. The Cabinet, Tyler, and various members of Congress—not including Clay—then went about the task of framing a new bill. The Kentuckian announced that he would take no part in these proceedings.

The break with Tyler

While this second bank bill was in preparation, Congress repealed the Independent Treasury Act, and passed a land bill that in-

---

LIKE A SOARING EAGLE

Pleading his various causes either in opposition to the prevailing Administration or in concert with it, Clay had to make use of both his personality and his oratorical powers. The journalist Oliver Dyer, in Washington at the time, made this compelling capsule portrait of the man in his 1889 study *Great Senators of the United States Forty Years Ago.*

"Henry Clay was the tallest of the great Senators of his era, his height being six feet and one inch, in his stockings. He was also the most brilliant, the most chivalric, and by far the most popular. . . .

"The leading characteristic of Henry Clay's mind was penetration. His perceptive and knowing faculties were so enormously developed that nothing could escape his alert observation. . . . In controversy he was logical, witty, humorous, forcible, sarcastic, eloquent. His style was vehement and impassioned. His voice was full, rich, clear, sweet, musical, and as inspiring as a trumpet; it was also so penetrating that in the ordinary tones of conversation it would be heard further than the thick vocal bray of some of his rivals. When he became excited in debate, his manner was peculiarly . . . ambitious and sometimes arrogant. As he set forth proposition after proposition with increasing energy and fire, his tall form would seem to grow taller and taller with every new statement, until it reached a supernatural height; his eyes flashed and his hair waved wildly about his head; his long arms swept through the air; every lineament of his countenance spoke and glowed, until the beholder might imagine that he saw a great soul on fire and expressing itself through an organism which spontaneously responded to its every emotion.

"The effect of Clay's oratory was much enhanced by the peculiar conformation of his forehead and that portion of his head which lay above it. His perceptive organs projected far out, the crown of his head was unusually high, and a grand curvilinear line swept from the frontal sinus between his eyes to the apex of his head. This peculiar conformation gave him a commanding, eagle-like, soaring expression which, in combination with his glowing features, his blazing eyes and his fiery eloquence, sometimes excited the beholder's imagination until he seemed to be rising in the air with the orator. . . .

"Henry Clay's speeches derived their irresistible power from his irresistible personality. It was *that*—his personality which took people captive. He spoke to an audience very much as an ardent lover speaks to his sweetheart when pleading for her hand. Everybody knows that the more successful a lover's speech is on such an occasion, the less readable it is when it gets into cold print. . . . It was the same with Henry Clay. He spoke to win his cause right there and then and gain a favorable verdict on the spot; and no lover was ever more ardent, more vehement, more impassioned, or more successful in his appeal than Clay; and he was content with his immediate success."

cluded Clay's plan for distributing the proceeds of the land sales to the states. Clay was not entirely content with the latter, for it contained a provision suspending distribution if the tariff went above the 20 percent ad valorem level; but he submitted rather than risk another veto.

By August 1841, the new bank bill was ready to be submitted to Congress. Entitled "Fiscal Corporation of the United States," the institution was enabled to set up "agencies" throughout the nation to handle public monies as well as foreign and interstate bills of exchange. Tyler's suggestion, however, that there be some stipulation allowing the states to prevent installation of an agency if it was contrary to their laws, had been omitted. In addition, the bill had not been submitted to him for a final inspection and he was sus-

picious of it. Obviously, any presidential support for the bill was lost, and Webster, foreseeing that the Cabinet would be forced to resign if the President vetoed a bill that it had been instrumental in framing, tried to influence a vote postponement in Congress. Clay, on the other hand, was adamant, and he pressed for passage and the ultimate showdown. The bill passed Congress and on September 9 was vetoed by Tyler. Two days later, the Cabinet, except for Webster, resigned. The New Englander was furious with Clay, who he argued had deliberately split the Whigs in his own self-interest. Webster was in the President's office when Ewing's resignation was presented. And when he offered to stick by the President, Tyler exclaimed: "Give me your hand on that, and now I will say to you that Henry Clay is a doomed man from this hour."

The breach between the President and his party had become irreparable. Whig wits throughout the country began referring to Tyler as "His Accidency," in mockery of the manner in which he attained the Presidency. Everywhere, save for a coterie of Tyler's fellow-Virginians, the Whigs turned to Clay as their real leader.

During the fall lull, while Congress was adjourned, Tyler regrouped his forces, loading the Cabinet with Jacksonites. A few months later, the President proposed a bill to establish a "Board of Exchequer," which in some respects resembled a bank, though it had no authority to discount the notes of state institutions and was distinctly limited in its branching power. Webster thought it a practicable and valuable plan, but Clay was savagely against it and it was promptly defeated.

Weary and dispirited, with most of his program deadlocked by the intransigency of the President and the lack of enough support to override the veto, Clay resigned from the Senate on March 31, 1842. In a winning speech filled with emotion, he asked forgiveness for the ardor he had displayed in debate, denied any wish to play the dictator, and pleaded his

Webster suffered cruel lampooning for yielding part of Maine to the British Lion while in Tyler's Cabinet.

anxiety for the good of the nation. It was a dramatic and effective display of his eloquence and warmth, and at its close the Senate, unable to consider any other proceedings, adjourned for the day. (See also pages 209–210.)

Though Clay had failed to put through Congress most of the measures he had planned, in one sense he had emerged victorious from the struggle with Tyler. He was now the generally acknowledged head of his party, and his policies had been accepted, though with some reluctance, by the Whigs. Sentiment for a national bank and for internal improvements was increasing in all sections of the country, and in the summer of 1842 a tariff bill passed and was signed by the President, raising the level of duties approximately to what it had been under the tariff of 1832. By August of that year over two hundred Whig newspapers had indicated their approval of Harry of the West as their presidential candidate for 1844. He was clearly the logical Whig choice, but the path to the White House was still full of traps for unwary feet.

In retirement at Ashland, Clay protested that he had no interest in the White House. He busied himself with all the varied details of farm life, among other things greatly enlarging the production of hemp on his estate. He also had to contend in 1842 with serious financial difficulties, for his son Thomas failed for $30,000, two-thirds of which he had borrowed from his father. So deeply involved was the master of Ashland that he had to put a heavy mortgage on his own estate, go to New Orleans to collect debts owed him, and obtain orders for rope and bagging. He even offered his services as a lawyer again.

"Go slop your hogs"

Debts or no debts, the financial troubles at Ashland could not replace the primary concern of a still ambitious Henry Clay. The political fever continued to burn in his veins. During that spring of 1842, Van Buren, returning from a tour through the South, rested for a few days at Clay's home. The two men

AN "HONEST OPINION" ALTERED

Henry Clay, in addition to his home at Ashland, owned other property throughout the state of Illinois. On occasion, he made visits to these holdings, and usually he rode horseback the entire way. Nathan Sargent, a respected Whig journalist, relates in his book *Public Men And Events* a humorous incident that is said to have occurred during one of these visits.

"Coming to a farm-house on his road, near the close of the day, he courteously inquired of the owner . . . if he could be permitted to stop there overnight, and was answered in the affirmative. Alighting, and relieving his horse of his saddle-bags . . . the animal was taken to the stable and suitably cared for.

"It happened that the farmer had some fine stock, of which he was very proud. These cattle attracted the attention of Mr. Clay, who possessed the finest stock in Kentucky and was a connoisseur and amateur of blooded animals. He spoke of them, went among the herd, was greatly pleased, and criticised their various points in a manner that showed he was no 'prentice han' in that business.

"Of course the farmer was delighted with his guest. But another subject came up just before Mr. Clay returned to rest, upon which they did not agree so well,—to wit, politics. The farmer proved to be a Jackson man,—red-hot,—and in the course of conversation spoke of 'that fellow Henry Clay,' and of his bargain and corruption. Mr. Clay said it was possible he might be mistaken; that there might not have been any such corrupt bargaining as he had spoken of, and that possibly Mr. Clay was not exactly the man he seemed to think him. The farmer, however, was positive,—could not be mistaken; Mr. Clay was a very dangerous man; whereupon Mr. Clay dropped the subject and retired to bed.

"By some means or other, before morning the farmer learned, to his astonishment, that his guest was the veritable Henry Clay himself! What could he say to him? What apology could he make? Mr. Clay rose early . . . and went out to look at the fine cattle again. There he found the farmer, who, in a confused, embarrassed manner, addressing Mr. Clay by name, began an excuse for his rudeness, which Mr. Clay at once cut off, assuring him that he had committed no offense, and therefore no apology was needed. 'You spoke,' said Mr. Clay, 'your honest opinion, which I hope you will find reason to change; but so long as it shall be your honest conviction I cannot object to your expressing it.'

"It is hardly necessary to add that from that day the farmer was one of the most devoted friends Mr. Clay had in the State of Illinois."

Clay deplored mistreatment of slaves but never outrightly condemned sales of Negroes, such as this one.

The assemblage jeered the abolitionist, but Clay quieted them. Then he launched into a defense of colonization and an attack upon immediate emancipation which, he said, would inevitably produce a struggle between blacks and whites for political supremacy. All of his own slaves, said Clay, were well cared for, some of them would not accept freedom if it were offered to them, and others were incapable of fending for themselves. What would happen to these last if he turned them loose? Growing emphatic at the close of his remarks, he told Mendenhall: "Go home and mind your own business, and leave other people to take care of theirs. Limit your benevolent exertions to your own neighborhood . . . and you will be a better and wiser man than you have this day shown yourself." One witness of this interchange reported that Clay began his retaliation to Mendenhall with a curt, "Go home and slop your hogs."

This Indiana incident made the rounds of the press, and it deepened the feelings of anti-slaveryites against Clay. Northern Whig politicians, busily weighing the political significance of the crusade against human bondage, thought that Harry of the West had made a bad mistake. Benjamin Wade, a rising Ohio politician, said that Clay had "committed the unpardonable sin against the North," and William Henry Seward, now Governor of New York, remarked that the Mendenhalls of the country would reply to Clay through the ballot box.

Despite the misgivings of such Northern Whigs, Clay remained the party's leading candidate, and by early 1844, Whig conventions and legislatures in seventeen states had declared for him. Early in the spring, he made a triumphal tour through Alabama, Georgia, and the Carolinas, arriving in Raleigh, North Carolina, on April 12. There the Whigs gave him a prodigious welcome worthy of a hero. But the North Carolina city acquired a prominent place in the Clay annals for another reason: It was there, on April 17, that he wrote his celebrated "Raleigh letter."

had a real liking for one another, and all indications were that the Red Fox of Kinderhook would be the Democratic candidate who would run against Clay in 1844. They undoubtedly talked about politics, and it has always been believed that, in this series of conversations, they made an agreement not to allow Texas to become an issue in the next presidential campaign. Later in the spring, Clay made a speech at Lexington defending his past record and proposing economy in government, distribution of land sales, a sound currency, and "reasonable" protection through tariffs.

In the fall, Clay made a political tour through Ohio and Indiana, with large crowds gathering to hear him speak. At Richmond, Indiana, a Quaker abolitionist named Mendenhall presented him with a petition urging the emancipation of the Kentuckian's slaves.

The Texas controversy

The annexation of Texas had finally, after seven years of procrastination, become a critical national issue. Webster, as Tyler's Secretary of State, was cool to the idea of taking the Lone Star State into the Union. Having settled the question of the Maine boundary, he decided to resign in May 1843. Webster was back in the Whig fold. His successor, Abel P. Upshur of Virginia, was an avid expansionist and, with Tyler's hearty consent, prepared to bring the former Mexican province under the Stars and Stripes. On February 28, 1844, this strategy was interrupted when Upshur lost his life in a gun explosion on board the battleship *Princeton*. Tyler promptly filled the State Department post by appointing John C. Calhoun, an even more ardent annexationist than Upshur, and on April 22, 1844, a treaty of annexation was placed before the Senate. It was not a startling event. The news that such a treaty was in the making had been in the press for weeks.

Obviously, Texas had become a political question of the first magnitude. It even entered into the international realm. Calhoun stated the Administration's position in a note to Sir Richard Pakenham, British envoy at Washington, in retaliation for a move by Lord Aberdeen, the British Foreign Secretary, who supposedly had offered a loan to Texas if slavery were abolished. In his statement to the British minister, Calhoun defended slavery as a beneficent institution, and declared that the annexation of Texas, with slavery, was necessary to the peace and security of the United States. This note, which Calhoun also forwarded to Congress (and which also promptly found its way into the press), made it appear that Texas was being annexed primarily to protect slavery in the South.

Five days after the treaty of annexation reached the Senate, Clay's Raleigh letter was published in Washington's *National Intelligencer*. In it, Clay opposed annexation because (1) it did not have the support of public opinion, (2) the Texas debt of $13,000,000

When the *Princeton's* new naval gun burst while being tested in 1844, it killed two Cabinet members and others.

would have to be assumed by the United States, (3) it menaced the integrity of the Union, and (4) it could lead to a war with Mexico (see pages 210–211). A similar stand was taken in a letter appearing the same day in the Washington *Globe* under Van Buren's signature. The two men hoped they had eliminated Texas as a campaign issue.

This hope appeared to be well founded when the Whig convention met at Baltimore. In the midst of great enthusiasm, with flags, bunting, live raccoons and little foxes in cages cluttering up the streets, the Whigs unanimously nominated Clay for President. Pious Theodore Frelinghuysen of New Jersey was put on the ticket as his running mate. Accompanying these nominations was a series of resolutions that avoided any reference whatsoever to an expansion of territory.

But the Democratic convention, held at Baltimore on May 27 (a full month after the appearance of Van Buren's letter on annexation), was another story. Annexationists had had time to assemble their forces. Van Buren had never been popular in the South, and his stand on Texas definitely dampened his chances in that section of the country. Old Hickory, once his supporter, now turned against him; one Southern state after another made clear its decided opposition to his candidacy. Nevertheless, as the convention opened, the Red Fox had a majority of the delegates, but his opponents invoked, ironically enough, the rule making a two-thirds majority necessary for nomination—a rule that had been used in his favor in 1832 and 1836.

The convention was deadlocked until the ninth ballot, when it finally stampeded for a dark horse, James K. Polk of Tennessee, a friend of Andrew Jackson as well as a dedicated expansionist. The convention also adopted a platform that included a demand for the "reannexation" of Texas at the "earliest practicable period." The "reoccupation" of Oregon, where a hassle with Great Britain over possession of the Far Northwest had been developing, was also among the Democratic platform guarantees.

"Manifest destiny"

The Whigs professed jubilation over the Democratic choice of a presidential candidate. "Who is James K. Polk?" they scornfully asked. The fact was, however, that the Democratic convention had made a very shrewd move. Expansionist fever was sweeping the country. Northerners as well as Southerners were saying that it was America's "manifest destiny" to acquire more territory, either to protect its borders against possible foes, or to carry the blessings of American freedom across the continent, or because a nation had to grow or it would die.

Sentiment for the acquisition of all the Oregon Territory up to the latitude of 54° 40' had powerful support in the northern tier of Western states—Illinois, Indiana, and Ohio—while California and the Southwest were objects of great interest for expansionists, especially in the South. The Democratic convention took advantage of this state of the American mind; its presidential candidate symbolized the nation's expansionist mood.

Clay believed at first that he could win the election simply by formulating solutions to problems of internal policy. He wanted to concentrate on the tariff, distribution of the revenues of land sales, a national bank, and restriction of the powers of the President; but these were at best only side issues in the contest. There was one chief issue—Texas. And there was a subsidiary question—Mr. Clay's moral character.

The Democrats declared over and over again that Clay was a man devoid of principle. They raked up once more the old charge of "bargain and sale." They accused him of being a duelist, a gambler, and a Sabbath-breaker. Clay's standard, said a Democratic congressman, should be "a pistol, a pack of cards, and a brandy bottle." The abolitionists of the North alleged that he was proslavery, and the Democrats of the South insisted that he was a friend of the abolitionists. This flood of accusation quite overshadowed Whig charges that Polk favored free trade and disunion and was under the influence of the British.

Democratic vilification of Clay, and Democratic pretensions in industrial Pennsylvania that Polk was a better protectionist than his adversary, certainly played a part in deciding the election, but the crucial campaign issue was Texas. The attitude of both parties made it clear that the Democrats were the annexationists, and as the Democratic campaign harped on this argument, Clay's strength in the South began to slip away. By July, Clay recognized the danger to his ambitions for winning the Presidency, and the old campaigner wrote two letters to an Alabama newspaper editor to explain and defend his position. He certainly wished them to be read by a national audience. Clay stated that although he opposed annexation "at the present time," this did not mean that Texas should never be admitted to the Union. He had no personal objection to the annexation of Texas, he said. His only desire was to preserve the Union, and he would be glad to see Texas become part of the nation when this could come about with the common consent of the American people and without war. He did not think that slavery should affect the question one way or the other. Later, in September, he wrote still another letter to the *National Intelligencer*, declaring that his position on Texas had been consistent throughout, and that he opposed immediate annexation. It was an attempt to adopt a middle-of-the-road policy, but it was not explicit enough to win the needed votes.

Undoubtedly, these letters, especially the ones to Alabama, helped Clay in North Carolina, Kentucky, and Tennessee, but they backfired in the North. Pennsylvania had already succumbed to the misleading representation of Polk as an advocate of "incidental protection." New York was the pivotal state, and there the abolitionists redoubled their efforts. An antislavery party, known as the Liberty party, had put a third ticket in the field in 1844, with James G. Birney, a former slave owner, as its candidate for the Presidency. Birney polled 15,812 votes in New York. Had he not run, most of those ballots would have gone for Clay, who ran only 5,106 votes behind Polk in the state. If New York's 36 electoral votes had gone to Clay, Polk's apparently substantial victory of 170 to 105 over Clay would have had a different result—141 votes for Clay to Polk's 134.

War with Mexico

Clay was bitterly disappointed by the result. An eyewitness claimed that when he lost the 1840 Whig nomination he had also lost his temper, stamping up and down the room, cursing, and swearing that his friends were not worth the powder and shot that it would

An Eastern cartoon, "Volunteers for Texas," poked fun at Southerners and Westerners eager to fight in Mexico.

take to blow them up. In 1844, perhaps because he had some forewarning of defeat, he took it much more calmly.

Clay and his wife were at a wedding in Lexington when the news reached them. According to his friend Mrs. Robert S. Todd, as Clay read the paper containing the tabulation of the New York vote: "I saw a distinct blue shade begin at the roots of his hair, pass slowly over his face like a cloud and then disappear. He laid down the paper, and, turning to a table, filled a glass with wine, and raising it to his lips said: 'I drink to the health and happiness of all assembled here.' Setting down his glass, he resumed his conversation as if nothing had occurred and was, as usual, the life and light of the company." Despite such a display of equanimity, defeat filled his spirit with gloom, and he repeatedly announced that he would retire from politics. In time it would be shown that no such resolve could be kept by Harry of the West.

Like most defeated politicians of any generation, Clay viewed with dismay the state of the country after the election of 1844. The annexation of Texas, which followed hard on Polk's victory, filled the Kentuckian with alarm, and when the Democrats lowered the tariff barriers by enacting the Walker tariff of 1846, he publicly protested what he called this subversion of the policy of protection.

Personal worries and griefs gave Clay no opportunity to enjoy his well-earned retirement. Near bankruptcy, he was forced to sell thousands of acres in Missouri and Kentucky. Ashland was mortgaged, and debts, including one of $15,000 to John Jacob Astor, increased the burden. Luckily, Clay had won a loyal and generous retinue of friends, acquaintances, and supporters who now came to his financial assistance. The Northern Bank of Kentucky, which held most of Clay's mortgages, received substantial (chiefly anonymous) contributions deposited to the Clay accounts. By April 1845, a total of about $26,000 had saved the homestead. Although Clay was reluctant to accept these gifts, he was extremely appreciative of his friends' generosity. By relieving him of his financial indebtedness, they had freed his mind from an anxiety that would have made his last years hard indeed. Tragedy also struck within the family circle. The youngest son, twenty-four-year-old John Morrison Clay, began to demonstrate the same symptoms of mental instability that had resulted in his brother Theodore's commitment to an asylum. Fortunately, John was kept only a few weeks in the Lexington institution. But the greatest calamity of all was yet to come.

Mexican resentment over the annexation of Texas by the United States, boundary disputes between the two countries, bickerings over American claims against Mexico, and finally Polk's determination to acquire California proved to be the necessary catalysts to initiate the war with Mexico in the spring of 1846. Clay had long dreaded this seemingly inevitable conflict and continued to be critical of the policy that had ignited the conflagration. Henry Junior had joined the 2nd Regiment of Kentucky Volunteer Infantry and was quickly made a lieutenant colonel. His father's fears were doubly justified when this son, serving in Zachary Taylor's army, was killed in combat at the battle of Buena Vista (see page 111). An indication of the extent of his personal loss and his contempt for this conflict was given in a letter he wrote to John Middleton Clayton: "If I could derive any consolation from the fall of my beloved son on the bloody field of Buena Vista, it would be from that fact that, if he were to die, I know he preferred to meet death on the field of battle, in the service of his Country. That consolation would be greater, if I did not believe that this Mexican War was unnecessary and of an aggressive character." A year later, Henry Clay bowed before this accumulation of personal sorrow and sought the consolation of religion. On June 22, 1847, he was baptized at Ashland.

Always in contact with the nation's political leadership and ever ambitious even though he was approaching seventy, Clay again began to court Whig politicians in the hope that he might receive the nomination for the presidential election of 1848. All the signs indicated that there would be another colossal domestic struggle between the North and the South over any territory that would be acquired in a forthcoming treaty with Mexico, and Clay felt he could direct the forces involved. The Wilmot Proviso, an amendment attached to a bill for appropriations to buy territory that Mexico might cede in a peace treaty, prohibited the introduction of slavery into any such territory. This amendment heralded the conflict that was to arise. Already it had been passed twice in the House, to be defeated both times in the Senate.

Aware of the situation, Clay made a significant speech in November 1847 at Lexington, dealing with the Mexican War and with the probable increase of territory that would result from that struggle. The war, he said, had been brought on by deceit and was both "lamentable" and "unnatural." Congress had the right and the duty to define the objectives of the war. The United States should be magnanimous toward Mexico, which under no circumstances should be annexed, and the nation should emphatically disavow any intention of obtaining foreign territory for the purpose of fostering or expanding slavery. This speech placed Clay among the supporters of the Wilmot Proviso and was definitely a bid for the 1848 Whig nomination. The Kentuckian's statement of principles was well received by the Whigs throughout the country.

Whig politicians were chary of nominating a candidate who had been three times defeated and who, if elected, would be only a few weeks short of seventy-two before he entered the White House. While there were many who rallied to his banner, and a number of Clay delegates were chosen for the 1848 Whig national convention, another candidate dazzled the more practical Whig leaders.

"Old Rough and Ready"

Out of the Mexican conflict emerged a war hero, General Zachary Taylor, who, with forces much inferior in numbers, had been victorious in one battle after another against the Mexicans. Ever since the Jacksonian era it had been evident that military prowess was a great asset in a presidential aspirant. Men like Thurlow Weed in New York and John J. Crittenden in Clay's own state of Kentucky therefore saw Taylor as a distinctly available candidate, even though the General had but a poor command of the English language, no experience in politics or civil administration, and for some time even had difficulty in deciding whether or not he was a Whig.

Nevertheless, the Taylor bandwagon had begun to roll. Alexander H. Stephens had engineered Taylor's nomination by the Whigs in Georgia. A young congressman from Illinois named Abraham Lincoln and other Whig leaders in Congress formed a Taylor club, the "Young Indians," to whip up enthusiasm for "Old Rough and Ready." Even in Kentucky there was strong support for Taylor, and a

---

"BAPTIZED IN A PUNCH BOWL"

Henry Clay's reputation suffered, both during his life and after its end, from the contention that he was impious. Thomas Hart Clay tried to refute this in the biography he wrote of his grandfather.

"Mr. Clay became a communicant of the Episcopal Church in 1847. He had been a pewholder in Christ Church, Lexington, from the time of his marriage, was a constant attendant there when at home, and was always deeply interested in its welfare. His father-in-law, Colonel Hart, was a member of this church, the first Episcopal church in Kentucky, and a liberal friend to it. Mr. Clay was baptized in the parlor at Ashland, June 22, 1847, and the rector of Christ Church, the Rev. Edward F. Berkley, who officiated, gave an account of the ceremony. It had been stated that Mr. Clay had been immersed in a pond on his estate, and Mr. Berkley wrote to one who had made inquiry concerning the truth of this report: 'I baptized Mr. Clay in his parlor at Ashland, at the same time administering the same ordinance to his daughter-in-law, Mrs. Thomas H. Clay, and four of her children, on the 22nd of June, 1847, a few special friends being present. The water was applied by the hand, out of a large cut-glass urn which was numbered among his many rare presents and had been given him by a manufacturer of such wares in Pittsburgh. It was said that this was the largest piece of cut glass then in existence. [The social critic Gamaliel Bradford in *As God Made Them* suggests it was a punch bowl and then makes the comment: "Baptized at seventy in a punch bowl! Could there be a more delightful epitome of Kentucky life a century ago?"] It may interest you to know that in the baptismal service of the Protestant Episcopal Church there are asked certain questions which the candidate is supposed to answer from the book. Seeing that Mr. Clay did not have a Prayer-Book in his hand, I suggested that the use of one might enable him more readily to reply to the questions. He replied, "I think I shall be able to answer them," and the readiness with which he answered, and his familiarity with the service gave evidence that he had made it a personal study and was ready to stand by his declaration.' "

Whig convention in Frankfort refused to name any candidate, thus leaving the state's delegation at the national convention open, uncommitted to Taylor or Clay. Undaunted, Henry Clay finally decided to be a candidate for the Whig nomination on April 10, 1848.

Clay blithely reads Horace Greeley's influential Whig newspaper, the New York *Tribune*, as other Whigs initiate "The Assassination of the Sage of Ashland." This lithograph's title refers to Taylor's nomination over Clay.

By the time the Whigs gathered for the national nominating convention in the great hall of Philadelphia's Chinese Museum on June 7, the Taylor boom had grown to such proportions that it could not be stopped. He received the nomination on the fourth ballot—a nomination that was, so Horace Greeley declared, "though perfectly true, nevertheless impossible." To placate the Northern delegates, Millard Fillmore, a New Yorker and an antislaveryite, was selected for Vice-President.

The Clay supporters at Philadelphia charged treachery and double-dealing, and Clay shared their bitterness and chagrin. He knew that Crittenden and Kentucky had played him false, and he severed relations with his old friend. He felt that the Whigs had nominated for the Presidency "the merest military man ever offered to the American people for that office"—a war hero who had no other qualifications. On the broader basis

of party principles, Clay feared that, since the Whigs had provided Taylor with no platform, they were bypassing the standard issues of bank, tariff, and land policy, and were thus creating a vacuum into which the issue of slavery was bound to rush. This was largely correct. The old issues were dead, and slavery and expansion had arisen to take their places.

Crestfallen and disappointed, Clay refused to accept the Senate seat left vacant by Crittenden, who resigned in 1848 to run for governor of Kentucky. Harry of the West remained in retirement at Ashland. Some of his more zealous supporters proposed to nominate him as an independent candidate, but he would not consent. Stricken at the beginning of November by a serious illness, Clay was probably glad that he could use his malady as an excuse for not going to the polls on election day. His sons cast their ballots for Taylor; after all, he was the Whig candidate.

Chapter 6
THE STRUGGLE
TO SAVE THE UNION

WHEN THE WHIGS sent Zachary Taylor to the White House, Clay was seventy-one years old. The "Old Prince," as his devoted followers now frequently referred to him, showed some signs of his advancing years; he was often absentminded, there were hollows in his cheeks, his nose was more pinched, his fair hair had receded and become white. However, he still had the quick temper that was apt to flare up at his opponents. The wit and warmth that had so long exercised a fascination upon all except the most rabid of his political opponents were as apparent as ever.

Women liked Clay, and he returned their admiration. Feminine grace and beauty had always charmed him, and the belles of the period, young and old, found his sensitive nature and courtly manners very attractive. It was an age that found it in good taste to overwhelm the feminine sex with compliments, and Clay was a master of this sort of flirtation. Evidently he enjoyed kissing beautiful girls and sought their attentions, yet there was never any scandal involving his good name. His correspondence gives ample proof of his affection for his wife.

Throughout his life, Henry Clay was a man who had a keen appreciation of luxury, as well as female beauty. One of his favorite pastimes was to visit the watering places such as White Sulphur Springs in what is now West Virginia, or Saratoga Springs in New York—resorts much frequented by fashionable and pleasure-loving society in the era before the Civil War. During the latter part of his life, he often sought the genial climate of New Orleans during the winters that he was not in the Senate. When public life kept him in Washington during the summer, he would find respite from the humid heat of the nation's capital by vacationing at Newport or Cape May. On one occasion, he took a sea voyage for his health, from New York to New Orleans with a stopover in Cuba.

A major new crisis

It was while spending the winter in New Orleans, in the early part of 1849, that Clay received the news he had been reelected to the United States Senate. Kentuckians had rebuffed his presidential aspirations in 1848, but they still held him in high regard. This time he accepted the post. That summer—as a vacation prelude to what looked as though it would be a strenuous winter, and because he was weak from sickness during a cholera epidemic that had ravaged Lexington—he and Mrs. Clay took a trip to Saratoga Springs and Newport, and Clay visited Van Buren at Lindenwald, the latter's home at Kinderhook. They then returned to Ashland. In November, Clay made the long trek to Washington, took rooms at the National Hotel, and on December 3, 1849, sat in his old place in the Senate.

Harry of the West arrived in a capital buzzing with excitement, for a major crisis was at hand. The war with Mexico had added California and a vast block of territory in the Southwest to the United States, and by so doing had roused the tumult over slavery to greater heights than ever. The question as to whether these new lands were to be slave or free was crucial enough in itself; to make matters worse, it was joined to other controversies that were splitting the North and the South: the return of fugitive slaves and continuation of slavery in the District of Columbia. Furious propaganda by the abolitionists and bitter Southern response served only to irritate the already delicate situation. Real diplomacy had to be practiced in Congress to pass any bill concerning slavery. The Oregon Territory, for example, was established in 1848 only after a rancorous congressional struggle over the exclusion of slavery. During those last months of the Polk Administration, no decisions at all were reached on the extension of the Missouri Compromise line to the Pacific or on territorial govern-

ments for California and New Mexico. Excitement reached such a peak in the Thirtieth Congress that tempers flared and fistfights broke out on the chamber floors. Things finally bogged down so completely that Polk had no chance to sign the last appropriations bill until after his term had actually expired.

The early months of Taylor's Presidency were rife with these same conflicts plus new problems. The discovery of gold in California had created a rush of adventurers to that territory. By the close of 1849, it was ready for admission as a state; a constitutional convention had prepared a document with a clause that prohibited slavery, and a governor and legislature had been elected. Another added problem for Polk was the squabble between Texas and New Mexico over their boundary line. To make affairs still more complicated, neither the Whig nor the Democratic party controlled the House of Representatives. A third party had been organized in 1848, taking as its slogan "free soil, free speech, free labor, and free men." This Free Soil party, after absorbing the Liberty party

Famed for their curative mineral waters, spas such as Saratoga Springs (depicted here) often attracted Clay for visits.

members, had held a national convention and nominated Martin Van Buren for President. He had not carried a single state, but he had obtained 10 percent of the total popular vote; fourteen Free Soilers had been elected to Congress, where they held the balance of power in the lower house.

Clay had watched these developments with deep foreboding. Southern determination to expand slavery into the Southwest and California particularly alarmed him, for he felt sure that it would result in a conflict menacing to the Union. This conviction was no whit allayed by the turmoil that now filled Congress. The House found it difficult to choose even a doorkeeper, and took sixty-three ballots to elect Howell Cobb of Georgia as Speaker. When Robert Toombs of Georgia made a speech threatening secession, Southern members cheered. Contention also marked proceedings in the Senate.

The Compromise of 1850

President Taylor, who had come to depend more and more upon the advice of the New Yorker, William H. Seward, one of the leading antislavery Whigs, sent a message to Congress asking admission of California as a free state. Such a step would upset the exact balance of free and slave state representation in the Senate, and it roused the irascible passions of the Southern members to an even higher pitch.

During December 1849 and January 1850, proslavery and antislavery members of Congress were busy introducing a bewildering variety of bills that dealt with various aspects of the complex and highly dangerous situation. There were bills to readjust the Texas boundary with compensation for lost territory, to bypass territorial status of California and New Mexico by admitting them directly to the Union, to enact a law dealing more effectively with fugitive slaves, and to prohibit slavery in the District of Columbia. Compromise was obviously the only way out of this legislative labyrinth, and Henry Clay,

---

AN AMAZING MEMORY

One of the most striking facets of a many-faceted man was Henry Clay's ability to remember everything and everyone with whom he came in contact. Various writers have commented on this facility, which is most essential to a successful politician and statesman. Oliver Dyer reports of Clay in his book on Senators he had known:

"He had a marvelous faculty for seeing everything and remembering everything—names, faces, places, events, scenes, and the topographical features of a country through which he traveled. If he met a man and spoke with him, he never forgot him or the circumstances under which they met. After spending a few hours in any place through which he passed, he could recall its features and peculiarities at any subsequent time, however remote, and remember the people he met there, and what their vocations were, to the minutest particulars. This gave him surpassing influence and popularity, inasmuch as it is pleasant to anybody to be remembered for years by a distinguished personage."

Thomas Hart Clay also tells the following anecdote that illustrates his grandfather's power of recollection: "Once, during a visit to Mississippi, Mr. Clay stopped for a few minutes at a place called Clinton. A crowd gathered around the train and an old man with one eye made his way to the front.

" 'Don't introduce me,' he said, 'for I want to see if Mr. Clay will know me.'

" 'Where did I last see you?' asked Mr. Clay, taking the old man's hand.

" 'In Kentucky,' he answered.

" 'Have you lost that eye since I saw you?'

" 'Yes.'

" 'Turn the good eye to me that I may see your profile. I have it,' said Clay. 'Did you not give me a verdict as a juror at Frankfort, Kentucky, twenty-one years ago?'

" 'I did, I did!' exclaimed the man in delight.

" 'And is not your name Hardwicke?'

" 'It is,' and turning to his friends he said triumphantly, 'Didn't I tell you that Harry Clay would know me, though he hadn't seen me for over twenty years?' "

---

now the elder statesman, assumed again the mantle of compromiser. Painfully, for his health was frail and his cough was bad, Harry of the West put together a number of proposals, the adoption of which he hoped would end the crisis and preserve the Union.

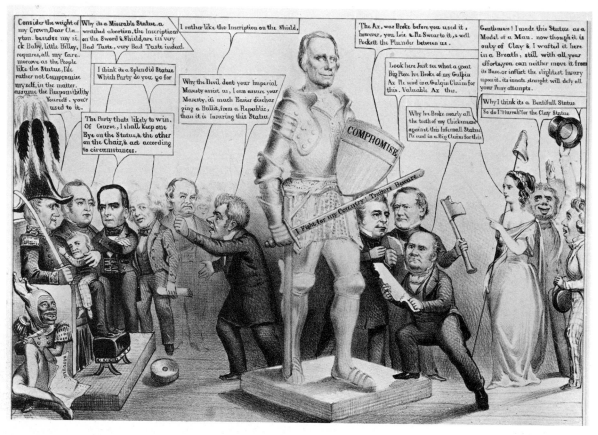

Molded by the Goddess of Liberty (right), the Clay statue personifying Compromise is attacked by the ministers of Zachary I (Taylor, on throne at left). Their effort fails, owing to the derision of the "people" (far right). Senator William H. Seward sits on Taylor's lap, while Senator Thomas Hart Benton (back of Seward) scoffs.

On January 29, 1850, Clay rose to his feet on the Senate floor to introduce these proposals in the form of a series of resolutions: (1) California would be admitted as a free state, the other lands acquired from Mexico being organized as territories without reference to slavery; (2) a boundary line would be drawn between Texas and New Mexico giving to the latter the land in dispute, but on the other hand, the United States would assume the public debt, amounting to more than $5,000,000, owed by Texas at the time it came into the Union; (3) the traffic in slaves brought into the District of Columbia for sale or transportation would be stopped, but slavery would not be abolished there without compensation and the consent of Maryland and the people of the District; (4) Congress would declare itself powerless to interfere with the interstate slave trade; and (5) Congress would pass a more effective fugitive slave law. Most of these measures, which Clay now grouped together, had been previously proposed as individual measures in the Senate.

Clay spoke only briefly that first day in support of his resolutions, but a number of Southern senators immediately challenged his proposals. Senator Jefferson Davis of Mississippi declared that the Kentuckian offered nothing that was of any value to the South; for that section, only one settlement was possible—the extension of the Missouri Compromise line of 36° 30' to the Pacific, with no restriction on slavery below that latitude. Clay replied abruptly that no power on earth would make him support planting slavery anywhere by Congressional decree. He refused to be drawn into debate, saying that he wanted his propositions to be considered as a unit, and that he hoped the Congress would give them the most careful scrutiny.

Just a week later, on February 5, 1850, so feeble that he had to be helped up the steps to the Capitol, Clay began his great two-day argument defending these resolutions. Initially, he spoke for two-and-one-half hours in a Senate chamber so tightly packed with spectators that the temperature climbed to a suffocating one hundred degrees. The following day he concluded his remarks. His theme was compromise for the sake of the Union; he took up each of his proposals in turn.

California had a right to declare itself a free state, and it would be an abuse of democracy to force the state to accept a principle it did not wish. New Mexico and Utah did not need the Wilmot Proviso to protect them against slavery, for in those regions nature itself—climatic conditions and the fact that the soil is generally more conducive to grazing than to planting—obviated the necessity for slavery. Addressing the Northerners, Clay stated: "You have got what is worth more than a thousand Wilmot Provisos. You have nature on your side." Prohibition of the slave trade in the District of Columbia would be pleasing to the North, and Southern complaints about this would be stilled by a more effective fugitive slave law, and by the acknowledgment that Congress had no power to interfere with the interstate slave trade.

His other proposals, he said, were matters of simple justice. The boundary line between Texas and New Mexico was a compromise between those who wished to see slaveholding Texas held to limited confines and those who wanted the territory enlarged. Besides, it still allowed a substantial increase in territory for the state and paid off its public debt as well. He made it clear that what he asked would give the South more than it gave the North, and he appealed to the latter section to be magnanimous. He closed with the solemn declaration that no state or collection of states had the right to secede, and asserted that the dissolution of the Union would mean civil war and after that the rise of despotism. In his concluding statement he expressed the earnest hope "that if the direful and sad event of the dissolution of the Union shall happen, I may not survive to behold the sad and heart-rending spectacle."

A long, bitter debate

Clay's Compromise was now before the Senate, and there began a lengthy period of debate. Led by the three Senate elders—Clay, Calhoun, and Webster, all of whom were approaching the ends of their careers—the debate was to last until the following September, a record-breaking nine months. Calhoun, who was in the last stages of tuberculosis and whose speech was read for him by Senator Mason of Virginia, declared that what Clay asked was merely a modification of the Wilmot Proviso. The only way to end the crisis, said the South Carolinian, was for the North

Clay's Compromise aimed at halting the traffic in slaves (such as these on a Washington street) throughout D.C.

to give the slave states equal rights in the new territories, faithfully return fugitive slaves, suppress antislavery agitation, and restore the political balance between the sections with a constitutional amendment. If these actions were not taken, the South should secede, by force if necessary.

Webster, in his famous "Seventh of March Speech," the last great one the New Englander made in the Senate, supported the Compromise. Agreeing in substance with Clay, Webster added his literary style to the Compromise debate. Northern businessmen praised him for his stand, but abolitionists were bitterly critical and the Quaker antislavery poet, John Greenleaf Whittier, pilloried him in "Ichabod," a poem more biting because its upbraiding was so gentle:

"So fallen! so lost! the light withdrawn
    Which once he wore!
The glory from his gray hairs gone
    Forevermore!"

Antislavery leaders joined Calhoun in criticizing the Compromise, though of course from a different angle. Both Salmon P. Chase of Ohio and John P. Hale of New Hampshire denounced Clay's proposals because of their concessions to the South. One of the most striking speeches came from William Henry Seward on March 11, when he argued that the conciliation of slavery which Clay advocated was little short of vicious. In this speech Seward used the phrase, "a higher law than the Constitution," an appeal to the judgment of the Almighty, which disgusted Clay. Then, March 31, the South lost its leading orator, when John Calhoun died "a little after sunrise."

President Taylor had no liking for Clay's method of settling the crisis. Old Rough and Ready's plan for dealing with the situation was that California should be admitted at once as a free state, and that no action should be taken by the national legislature on the other new lands until they asked for admission as states. This, Taylor thought, would end the turmoil, even though it left a number of questions unsolved.

CLAY AND WEBSTER

Two of America's greatest orators and parliamentarians, Henry Clay and Daniel Webster strode across the national scene at approximately the same time. Their parallel careers touched frequently throughout their public lives. Sometimes they clashed, sometimes they criticized each other and sometimes they were affable as one supported the other's viewpoint.

An indication of the two men's personalities may be derived from Oliver Dyer's description of their respective reactions when strangers were introduced to them: "Webster evidently felt such introductions to be an intolerable bore, and seldom took the trouble to conceal his annoyance. Usually, his manner, on such occasions, was freezingly indifferent. He seemed to be preoccupied and . . . sometimes he did not even look at the person introduced, but mechanically extended his hand, and permitted the stranger to shake it. . . . Clay's manner to a member of Congress who introduced a constituent to him was such as led the stranger to imagine that his Representative was one of the most intimate and cherished friends that Clay had on earth; and his reception of the stranger caused him to feel that for some reason it gave Clay a peculiar personal gratification to make his acquaintance."

Since both Clay and Webster were pillars of the Whig party, representing the West and New England, they often had to ignore their differences for the sake of party unity. Martin Van Buren, regarding this situation from the vantage point of the opposing political party, makes a rather succinct analysis of this rivalry in his own autobiography.

"Mr. Webster had a right to think that his talents were, in some respects superior, and in all at least equal, to those of Mr. Clay. The latter, however, soon acquired a popularity and influence in the ranks of their common party, which eclipsed his own, notwithstanding what he naturally regarded as his superior advantages. It was not in human nature that he could ever become perfectly reconciled to this preference, even if his dispositions had been more magnanimous and placable than they were."

Webster apparently recognized the condition of his acquaintance with Clay—that they were partners yet adversaries. Joseph M. Rogers in his biography *The True Henry Clay* has presented

Webster's description of this relationship: "Webster was once asked why he did not have more enthusiasm for Clay. He replied that neither God nor nature had given him much sentiment, but that he had always believed that if Henry Clay had been a woman, and he (Webster) had met her in early life, they would have loved, quarrelled, and married, and probably quarrelled afterwards; but he could not conceive how he might, in any case, have regretted the event."

Henry B. Stanton, New York lawyer and journalist, in his volume *Random Recollections*, recalls how Clay felt about Webster in 1841: "In the stormy days of John Tyler, while Webster was his Secretary of State and Rufus Choate was in the

Daniel Webster

Senate, and Congress was in extra session in the fall of 1841, the question of chartering a United States bank was shaking the country. . . . A conference of leading Whig Senators was held. Clay, with lofty mien, was for waging relentless war on the accidental President. . . . Choate again and again told what Webster thought ought to be done. Clay was restive and exclaimed: 'Who cares a damn about what Webster thinks?' "

By the time that these two political stalwarts reached the end of their lives, the differences that had irritated earlier conflicts between them had mellowed. In January 1850, Clay paid a visit to Webster to acquire the latter's support for the Compromise of 1850, which he was formulating.

The meeting and conversation which took place that evening were recounted "by a gentleman who was at Mr. Webster's home during the interview" to Henry Hilliard, who then described it in his work *Politics and Pen Pictures:*

" 'At seven o'clock . . . Mr. Clay came to Mr. Webster's house and held a long interview with him concerning the best mode of action to settle the difficulties growing out of slavery and the newly acquired Territories. I heard a part of the conversation. Mr. Clay retired after an interview of about an hour. Mr. Webster called me to his side, and spoke to me of Mr. Clay in words of great kindness. He said he agreed in substance with Mr. Clay; that he thought Mr. Clay's objects were great and highly patriotic; Mr. Clay seemed to be very feeble, had a very bad cough, and became quite exhausted during the interview; that he had no doubt that it was Mr. Clay's anxious desire to accomplish something for the good of the country during the little time he had left upon earth. That perhaps Providence had designed the return of Mr. Clay to the Senate to afford the means and the way of averting a great evil from our country.' "

As Clay was succumbing to his final illness, Webster paid him tribute tinged with some acid criticism in a conversation with Charles Lanman, newspaperman, author, and artist, who recorded the New Englander's words in his book *Haphazard Personalities:* " 'Mr. Clay is a great man; beyond all question, a true patriot. He has done much for his country. He ought long ago to have been elected President. I think, however, he was never a man of books, a hard student, but he has displayed remarkable genius. I never could imagine him sitting comfortably in his library and reading quietly out of the great books of the past. He has been too fond of the world to enjoy anything like that. He has been too fond of excitement; he has lived upon it. He has been too fond of company, not enough alone, and has had few resources within himself. Now a man who cannot, to some extent, depend upon himself for happiness is, to my mind, one of the unfortunates. But Clay is a great man, and if he ever had animosities against me, I forgive him and forget them.' "

The two statesmen who were so often in contact during life followed each other into death as well. Webster died on October 24, 1852, a mere four months after Clay. Ever since, both men have ranked high in the list of great Senators.

The lack of Administration support for the Compromise, and the opposition of the extremists, North and South, made progress difficult. On March 25, the first step toward putting the resolution into law was taken when Stephen A. Douglas' Committee on Territories reported two bills, one to admit California as a free state, and another to establish Utah and New Mexico as territories, with a provision for the Texas boundary. But even this positive undertaking became enmeshed in legislative harangue. So Clay, who at first had expected that each of his resolutions would be acted on separately, finally agreed to the appointment of a Committee of Thirteen to deal with the whole problem. Clay was elected chairman of this committee. It met, deliberated, and on May 8 he presented its report.

The Committee of Thirteen proposed first an "Omnibus" bill that lumped together the admission of California as a free state, the organization of Utah and New Mexico territories without reference to slavery, and adjustment of the Texas-New Mexico boundary in favor of the latter, with compensation to the former. The second measure was a more effective fugitive slave law. The third prohibited importation of slaves into the District of Columbia for subsequent transportation or sale. In making these recommendations, the committee had taken into consideration the proposal by Douglas and another conciliatory measure by Senator John Bell of Tennessee, but the report was essentially what Clay had first proposed. The major differences were that no mention was made of the interstate slave trade, and that several of the measures were tied together into one package.

"Five bleeding wounds"

Debate now began all over again, this time centering on the Omnibus; and it continued through the hot summer months. The main question was whether the Omnibus measures could be passed together as a unit. Clay led the fight, beginning with a two-hour speech on May 13. Repeatedly he spoke in favor of the Committee's report, declaring that it was distinctly preferable to Taylor's plan for admitting California and leaving things to take their course in New Mexico and Utah.

There were, Clay said, "five bleeding wounds" that threatened the very existence of the nation. The President proposed to heal only one of them. The Committee's plan, if adopted, would heal them all. On into the summer he carried the struggle, refusing to consent to adjournment even for the purpose of removing the heavy draperies and carpet that helped to stifle the air in the Senate chamber. He kept the Senate in daily session and spent his energy without stint, while the breach between himself and the White House became wider and wider, and both Northern and Southern ultras continued their attacks on the Compromise.

Taylor died unexpectedly on July 9, from acute gastroenteritis or cholera morbus, brought on by overindulgence in raw vegetables and fruit washed down by copious iced drinks on a torrid Fourth of July. A tragic event, the President's death actually proved to be an asset for the Compromise, for Millard Fillmore, the new President, favored the measure. Still, progress was agonizingly slow. In an eloquent speech on July 22, Clay summarized the situation and pleaded again for unity: "Let us go to the limpid fountain of unadulterated patriotism, and, performing a solemn lustration, return divested of all selfish, sinister, and sordid impurities, and think alone of our God, our country, our consciences, and our glorious Union; that Union without which we shall be torn into hostile fragments, and sooner or later become the victims of military despotism, or foreign domination." But the stalemate continued. Then, to gain a few Southern votes, the section concerning the Texas boundary was struck from the Omnibus bill and replaced by amendments that set up a joint Texas-United States commission to draw the boundary and that delayed the commencement of the New Mexico territorial government until the boundary had been established. On July 30, Clay was confident that the bill would pass. But the next day, the Omnibus went down to defeat, as Northern Whigs deserted it and one after another of its stipulations was stripped from the body of the bill.

Disheartened by this turn of events and exhausted by his efforts throughout this parliamentary wrangle, Clay went off to Newport in August to escape the Washington heat and to gain back some of his strength. While he was gone, the Omnibus was broken up into separate bills. These and the other measures of the Compromise, save for the District of Columbia bill, were then passed separately under the astute leadership of Senator Douglas. When Clay returned, he shepherded this last measure through the Senate, and the Compromise of 1850 became law.

In the final analysis, a large part of the credit for the Compromise of 1850 should go to Douglas, who believed from the start that it would be impossible to pass the Omnibus. By joining the Northern moderates and Southern moderates, the Senator from Illinois was able to win passage. It should be noted that in the end more Democrats than Whigs voted for the Compromise measures.

Nevertheless, Clay played a most significant part in creating the Compromise. It was he who first brought its different parts into relation with one another, showing the advantages that would be gained by each geographical region. Moreover, with his original proposal and his subsequent tireless efforts, he was able to direct the attention of the country to the Compromise. The pressure of public opinion was an important factor in effecting the passage of this great piece of legislation, and Clay, with his enormous prestige and personal appeal, had much to do with formulating that opinion. Harry of the West was still admired by thousands of dedicated followers and he still spoke for them in the tones of reason, common sense, and conciliation.

The closing years

The remaining years of Clay's life contained no grand moments such as those connected with the Compromise of 1850, but he retained his interest in public affairs, despite being plagued by increasingly bad health. In Congress, he showed flashes of his old imperious ways, but in general he took a moderate attitude toward both foreign and domestic affairs. Two opportunities to display this moderation came during the Fillmore Administration. Both of them were related to the Austrian empire. Webster, again Secretary of State, sent a bombastic note to Chevalier Hülsemann, the Austrian chargé d'affaires in Washington, defending American expressions of sympathy for rebellious Hungary and informing Austria that the United States was a country "in comparison with which the possessions of the House of Hapsburg are but a

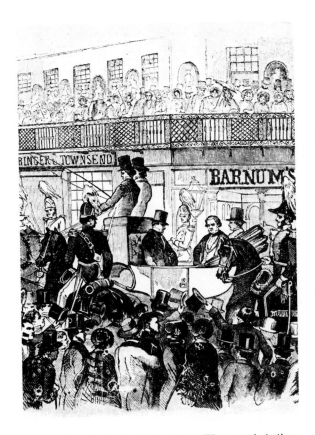

During a New York parade, President Fillmore rode hatless past the museum of P. T. Barnum, later of circus fame.

patch on the earth's surface." A motion to print ten thousand copies of this effusion was made in the Senate, but Clay protested. What was the use, he asked, of irritating the Austrians any further? The motion to print was defeated by a margin of three votes.

Some time later the exiled Hungarian patriot, Louis Kossuth, was in America, appealing for aid for his hapless fellow countrymen in their struggle against Austrian domination. He called on Clay, who was then living in the National Hotel, and in the course of their conversation remarked that he hoped for American intervention in the affairs of Europe. Clay replied that he was sympathetic with struggles for liberty everywhere, but could see no point in American intervention on the other side of the Atlantic. The greatest service the United States could give the cause of liberty, he declared, was to continue exhibiting at home the beneficent results of freedom.

In domestic as well as in foreign affairs, Clay's attitude was thoroughly conservative during the last years of his life. He sought to preserve intact the Compromise of 1850 as the best guarantee of the Union's permanence, and he had no patience with those who sought to modify or repeal the Fugitive Slave Law, the one part of the 1850 legislation that continued to be resented and attacked in the North. He also persisted in asserting his belief that no state had the right to secede from the Union, and that, whenever necessary, force must be used to put down resistance to the Union, the Constitution, and the laws of the country.

During the summer of 1851, Clay made his last will and testament. In addition to providing for his wife and children, the document contained special provisions regarding the future of his slaves (see pages 207–208). The owner of Ashland hoped in this way to further the cause of colonization—his answer to the slavery problem.

Clay went to Washington for the last time in the late fall of 1851. He was feeble before he left Lexington and the trip exhausted him. After answering the roll call on the first day, he did not appear again on the floor of the Senate. His tubercular condition had weakened him considerably and, though he went for occasional carriage rides and received friends who called upon him, he was more and more closely confined to his rooms in the National Hotel.

In that suite he died, June 29, 1852. His son Thomas, who had been summoned late in

---

"A MERE FRENCH ACTOR"

The Clay wit never faltered, and the graciousness embodied in the man was evident even during his last active years. Only occasionally trapped by his own repartee, Clay was always able to charm his way out of a bad situation. Such an incident is retold by John W. Forney, the Philadelphia (and later Washington) journalist and editor, in his book *Anecdotes of Public Men.*

"In 1850, after the triumph of the Compromise Measures, Henry Clay visited Philadelphia. . . . Ex-Mayor John Swift . . . in the 84th year of his age, dropped in at my editorial rooms the morning after Clay's arrival, in company with my esteemed friend, Edwin Forrest, the tragedian. Mr. Swift, who has been one of Mr. Clay's active and unselfish champions, gladly acceded to my request to be presented to Mr. Clay, whom I had never met. . . . Forrest expressed the wish to accompany us. . . . [Clay] looked feeble and worn—he was then over seventy-three years old—but he soon brightened. Anxious to rouse him, I quietly ventured to suggest that I had heard the speech of Pierre Soulé, Senator in Congress from Louisiana—an extremist especially distasteful to Mr. Clay—and that I thought it a very thorough and able presentation of the side adverse to the Compromise measures. I saw the old man's eye flash as I spoke, and was not surprised when, with much vehemence, he proceeded to denounce Soulé. . . . He wound up by saying: 'He is nothing but an actor, sir—a mere actor.' Then suddenly recollecting the presence of our favorite tragedian, he dropped his tone, and waved his hand, as he turned to Mr. Forrest—'*I mean, my dear sir, a mere French actor!*' We soon after took our leave, and as we descended the stairs, Forrest turned to Mr. Swift and myself, and said: 'Mr. Clay has proved, by the skill with which he can change his manner, and the grace with which he can make an apology, that he is a better actor than Soulé!' "

April, attended Clay during those last hours and was clasping his father's hand as the family patriarch slipped quietly into death. A state funeral was held in the Senate chamber, and political enemies and friends were both present. At Lexington thirty thousand people gathered in streets draped with black crepe in mournful remembrance as the body of the Millboy of the Slashes was returned to its final resting place in the town that he had adopted, known, and loved. On the marble shaft above his grave are the words, "No North—no South—no East—no West," a phrase he had used in the great debate of 1850 and one that epitomizes his lifetime of service for the entire Union.

The summing up

At a superficial glance, Clay's public life would seem to have been chiefly one beset by a series of mistakes and frustrations. He never achieved his great ambition to become President of the United States, a goal that remained a vital part of his life until he was past seventy years of age. The disappointing stalemate ending the War of 1812 had been an early blow to his pride. His years as head of the State Department had been barren of great achievement, as were his conflicts with President Jackson. His acceptance of the State Department at the hands of John Quincy Adams had been a mistake damaging to his political fortunes; the same was true of his attempt to force a recharter of the Bank of the United States in 1832, and of his failure to see the annexation of Texas as a vital issue in 1844.

Even worse in long-range perspective, perhaps, was the fate suffered during his lifetime by his cherished American System—that combination of national bank, protective tariff, and distribution of land sales—by which he hoped to unite the industrial East and the agricultural West under one banner while promoting national growth and national prosperity at the same time. The bank issue proved to be a Whig handicap; the West

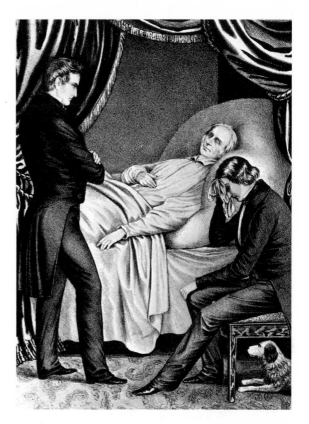

The sedate scene at Clay's death, with his son seated by him, was lithographed by the renowned Nathaniel Currier.

rejected distribution in favor of a cheap-and-easy land policy; the tariff, with the exception of the short-lived act of 1842, moved steadily downward rather than upward during the last twenty years of his life. By 1850 all three fundamental features had ceased being cardinal issues between Whigs and Democrats, and the American System, as a program, had been consigned to limbo by the very party that was supposed to embrace it.

Despite all these disappointments, defeats, and frustrations, Clay remains a giant in the history of American political life. His sympathy with the Latin American liberals, expressed in his acts and speeches, made him a hero in the countries south of the Rio Grande. This attitude on his part promoted good relations between North and South America in an era when little thought was given to the United States' Latin neighbors. His vision of

87

"BUT I CHAWS"

Henry Clay followed his chosen profession as a lawyer throughout his life. While his aptitude as a counselor may be criticized from the standpoint of the little time he had spent in formal study of the law, the length and extent of his legal education was about average for the period.

When past seventy, Clay was still displaying his talents in front of a jury. A grandson of Kentucky's early governor, Isaac Shelby, had been accused of murdering a companion after a nonsensical argument. In what was probably his last address before a jury, Clay (according to Joseph M. Rogers, in his book *The True Henry Clay*) "thrilled with emotion as he offered such defence as he could for the atrocious deed. His silver voice never sounded sweeter, and every one of the audience was in tears." One man at the hearing said Clay "reminded him of a catamount in a cave." The plea succeeded.

In an earlier case, Clay used other tactics. Rogers writes: "In those days, as now, lawyers were not above finding out all that was possible about the jury in advance, so as to work on them in turn. In an important case which he was trying, Clay found he had succeeded in winning over eleven men of the jury, but the twelfth was obdurate. Every one of his arts was tried in vain upon the twelfth man, a sturdy old farmer who had evidently made up his mind and was not to be moved. Finally he began an impassioned passage, and in the very midst of his eloquence suddenly stopped and, pointing his graceful finger at the obdurate juryman, said, 'Mr. X———, a pinch of snuff, if you please.'

"The old man was overcome with the attention paid him by the distinguished lawyer, and finally managed to blurt out, 'I don't snuff, Mr. Clay, but I chaws.' " Clay won the verdict.

Gerald Johnson, in *America's Silver Age*, tells another story of Clay's prowess in court: "A certain Mrs. Phelps had blown her sister-in-law into eternity with a shotgun. It was done in the presence of Phelps himself, and of other witnesses, so there was no question as to the facts. Everything depended upon the argument of counsel for the defense, and Clay's speech was such a masterpiece of sentimentality that the flustered jury brought in a verdict of manslaughter. It was the one verdict that was patently impossible; but it saved the life of his client, which was all Clay hoped to achieve. Incidentally, it gave criminal lawyers a new weapon, which they have employed assiduously ever since." According to Johnson, Clay "has the questionable distinction of being the first American to plead emotional insanity to a charge of murder."

the two American continents united in their common defense of freedom made him one of the originators of the Pan-American idea that has since manifested itself during the twentieth century in the Good Neighbor Policy of Franklin D. Roosevelt and the Alliance for Progress of John F. Kennedy and Lyndon B. Johnson.

In the realm of domestic policy, Clay also made a number of extremely important contributions. He believed wholeheartedly in fostering American economic growth and in promoting national prosperity by every means possible. His emphasis on measures leading to these ends entitles him, as the historian Clement Eaton has written, to rank with Alexander Hamilton as one of the great promoters of economic nationalism. His protective tariff policy was resurrected in later years to become a major element of the post-Civil War period.

Again, through his leadership of the Whig party, he helped to solidify and strengthen the two-party tradition that had been initiated in the days of Washington and Jefferson, after it had foundered in the political chaos of the 1820's. This two-party system has developed into a supporting pillar of American political life.

Finally, the Whig party was national in its outlook and aims, and greatest of all Clay's achievements as one of its chiefs was his function as a national leader who clearly saw the true value of the Union and strove energetically to preserve it. To accomplish this, he carried on the great tradition of compromise used by the Founding Fathers in framing the Constitution. At three times of crisis—in 1820–1821, in 1833, and again in 1849–1850—he acted commendably as a compromiser, an adjuster of the grievances that were dividing two sections of the nation. Henry Clay offered to the people of the United States an outstanding example of patriotic devotion that has justifiably made his name and career a noteworthy and lasting monument in the American tradition.

EARLY LIFE IN AN EARLY WEST

HENRY CLAY, a self-made man in a land of self-made men, did more than most to mold his nation. In the years of swift national growth from the Revolution until the Civil War, he personified the desire for advancement so typical of the ambitious middle-class American.

By origin neither an aristocrat like Washington nor an impoverished frontiersman like Lincoln, Clay was born on the Virginia farm seen below, in the not too fertile re-gion, "the slashes," of Hanover County north of Richmond. The farm, if no estate, was well above the average. Clay received little schooling, but he had a sharp mind and the benefit of tutoring by canny George Wythe, who had been one of Jefferson's mentors. Eventually his horizons broadened from his little corner of Virginia to encompass Latin America and the whole world. Clay's passion for agriculture and his concern for world affairs so characterized him that when John

Neagle painted the noteworthy portrait (see page 89) that hangs in the Capitol, he included a plow and a globe with Latin America facing outward.

Amiable and self-confident, the young Clay quickly acquired the social graces and the ability to express himself cogently. By the time he got his license to practice law, at the age of twenty, he was equally at ease in a ballroom, a country store, or a tavern such as the one his mother and stepfather kept in the Kentucky Bluegrass country. In a rapidly changing, westward-flowing society, Clay had the attributes necessary for

In the Virginia of Clay's boyhood, as in most of America until the early 1900's, the general store (pictured above by Thomas Wood) was a center of community life. Clay, though his preacher-father and his stepfather were prosperous by the standards of the day, worked in such a store as a lad. At fifteen he became George Wythe's secretary. Clay later moved easily in all classes of society and undoubtedly took part in the hunts that were a favorite sport of the gentry. The painting below, "Start of the Hunt," was done when Clay was a child. His lifelong love of horses was probably fostered by such episodes and the excitement they generated.

EARLY LIFE IN AN EARLY WEST

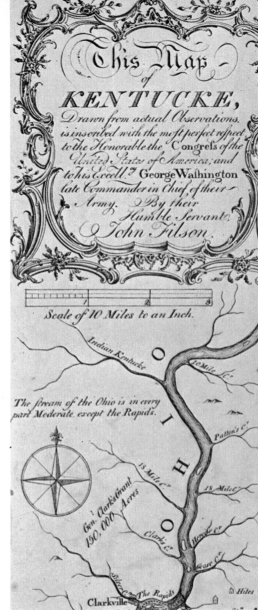

success, and Kentucky, a frontier area with the manners of Virginia, promised that success quickly. Kentucky, rich in land, produced tobacco and hemp as well as thoroughbreds. It was also full of litigations over land, bringing sizable fees to lawyers. The courthouse (above) was as much a social center as the general store. The whole region was growing fast, and Lexington (at the center of John Filson's classic 1784 map), where Clay settled soon after his admittance to the bar, dominated it intellectually, industrially, and commercially. A pleasant town in rolling country, Lexington

Rivers served as main arteries of trade, but much freight moved west in Conestoga wagons of this type.

EXPLANATION.

⚏ Stations or Forts.
☼ Salt Springs & Licks.
▢ Towns.
▢ Dwelling-houses & Mills.
△ Wigwams.
The dotted lines represent
Roads, some Cleard, others
not.

While this Work shall live,
this Inscription remain a Monument of
the Gratitude of the Author, to Col.ᵒ Dan.ˡ Boon,
Levi Todd, & Ja.ˢ Harrod, Capt.ⁿ Chriſt.ᵉ Greenbex
Inᵒ Cowan, & W.ᵐ Kennedy Eſq.ⁿ of Kentucke; for
the diſtinguiſh'd Aſſiſtance, with which they have
honord him, in its Compoſition: & a teſtimony,
that it has recieved the Aprobation of thoſe
whom he juſtly Eſteems, the beſt qualified to
Judge of its Merit.

INDIAN TERRITORY

Natural Meadow

Mingo Nation live here

Point Cr.

Old Shawane Town

Scrotha River very gentle and runs thro' excellent land

FAYETTE

Fine Cane Land

Main Licking

the Blue licks a fine salt spring

Upper Blue licks

Hincᵗ ſton Fork

Abundance of Cane

Fine Cane

Elkhorn

C O U N T Y

Greenville

Lee's-town

Col Marshal's Office

Lexington

Bryan's

Strouds

RED RIVER

Bibbe's Cr.

N. Fork

Boon's

Col. Todd's

Col. Boen's

Boonsbuᵗ

Morrison's

Morgan's Mill

War Cr.

F E R R Y R I V E R

Big Benson

Harrod's Town.

Fine Cane

Grant's Mill

L I N C O L N

Blue lick

Dick's R.

Danville

Craig's

Knob lick

Warrens

Flat licks

Warrior's Path

boasted a university, and during Clay's first decade of residence added distilleries, breweries, powder and textile mills, hat and rope factories, and a thriving trade in fine silverware. Basically, however, the fertility of the soil, symbolized in the photograph at the left, motivated the westward surge of emigration for which Pittsburgh was the gateway during most of Clay's lifetime. At Pittsburgh's "Golden Triangle," the Monongahela and Allegheny rivers join to form the Ohio (at left in painting below), an ideal avenue for travel and trade at the time. In 1811, the year that Clay became Speaker of the House of Representatives, Nicholas Roosevelt launched from Pittsburgh the first Mississippi-Ohio River steamboat service. Clay, long before, had developed an intense concern for better transport. From the very beginning of his career as an officeholder, in the Kentucky legislature of 1803, he pressed for improved roads and canals, and when he went on to the federal Senate in 1806, for the few remaining months of an unexpired term, one of his earliest votes was cast for construction of a bridge across the Potomac. Well ahead of the times, he argued that the federal government should pay the cost of new highways and waterways. As an ebullient, farsighted Westerner, he knew that his country had to grow and that this growth required new arteries.

Clay of Kentucky

Calhoun of South Carolina

Cheves of South Carolina

WAR OF 1812

BEFORE CLAY was thirty-four, he had
served twice, if briefly, as a federal senator and had gained broad recognition as a
spokesman for the West. He sprang to the
top rank of national leadership, however, in
the House of Representative in 1811. On his
first day there, the House—in an action still
without parallel in congressional history—
elected him Speaker. Clay began by trans-
forming the House, ejecting crusty John
Randolph's hunting dogs from the chamber,
and ordering dozing Congressmen to stay
awake—with feet off desks—or go home. He
transformed the Speakership too. Assuming
powers nowhere specified, he made the
Speaker, who had been little more than a
classroom proctor, one of the most potent
men in government and a shaper of national
policy. He used his newly acquired influence
to help precipitate the War of 1812—often
called "Mr. Clay's War." Although Clay was
an expansionist, his motivation was not expansionism but the conviction that no independent country could ignore such affronts
as Britain's impressment of American sail-
ors or apparent incitement of Indian attacks
on the frontier. Such young men as John
Calhoun, Langdon Cheves, Felix Grundy,
Peter B. Porter, and Richard Johnson—the
War Hawks—shared his views, and were put
in strategic House committee posts, encouraging the war spirit. Despite some American
victories, like the *Constitution* — Old Iron-
sides—over the *Guerrière* (right), the war

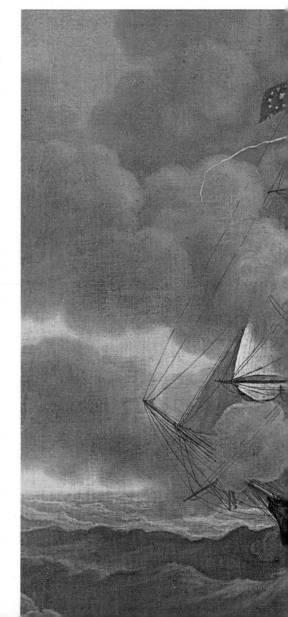

96

Grundy of Tennessee

Porter of New York

Johnson of Kentucky

WAR OF 1812

proved a bloody fiasco; and President Madison, unenthusiastic about it from the first, grasped an opportunity to negotiate peace. Clay resigned his Speakership to become one of five commissioners dispatched to Ghent to deal with the British. Emboldened by Napoleon's defeat, the British made demands that Clay and his associates considered unacceptable at best, and insolent at worst. Clay, however, played his cards frontier-style—adept at brag, a forerunner of poker, he could bluff and he could see through an opponent's bluff. The treaty that emerged from almost five

months of haggling did not satisfy him—he growled that it was "damned bad"—but it satisfied the folks back home, and his part in it raised his popularity to new heights; his eventual election to the Presidency, an honor and a responsibility that he was beginning to covet, seemed likely. But news traveled slowly; the greatest battle of the war that Clay had helped begin and helped end was fought at New Orleans after the treaty had been signed. It was to make the victor, Andrew Jackson, a hero—and President instead of Clay.

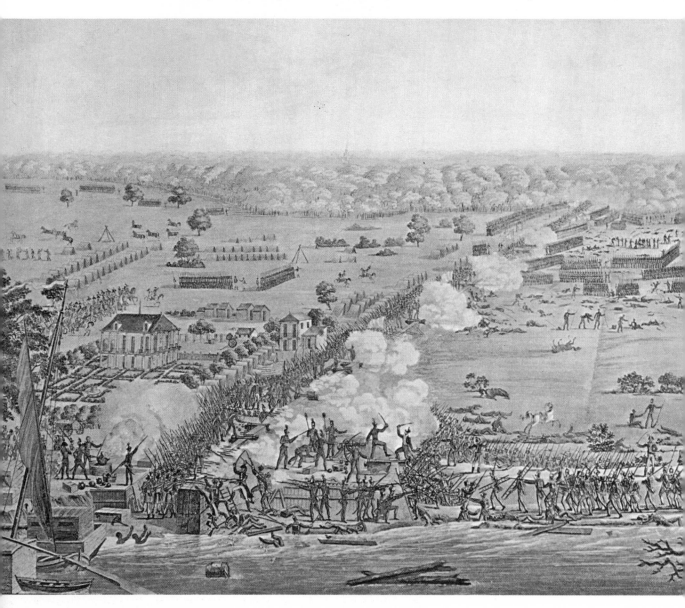

Andrew Jackson (right, in an 1819 portrait by Rembrandt Peale) led American troops into battle against the British at New Orleans (below) on January 8, 1815, unaware that John Quincy Adams (fifth from left in painting at bottom right; Clay is seated at the extreme right) had exchanged copies of the Treaty of Ghent with British chief delegate Lord Gambier on December 24, 1814. Jackson, standing near the American flag in the large painting, had placed his men in impregnable positions dug along the Rodriguez Canal, and the British, marching from right to left as though they were on parade, were slaughtered there, while the American right flank repelled another redcoat attack that was attempted along the Mississippi in the foreground.

A NEW POLITICS

UNTIL 1824, the year when Clay first ran for the office, presidential elections had been decorous affairs in which aspirants gave the appearance of letting the office seek the man. Candidates stayed home, presumably pondering great thoughts, while friends soberly propounded their merits; only in the press did the debate become raucous. But as the country's center of population moved westward, election contests became less serious. They acquired, in fact, a lusty, ribald character that George Caleb Bingham, himself a Missouri politician, depicted in such paintings as "Canvassing for a Vote" (left); "County Election" (below), in which a party worker is carrying a voter to the polls; and "The Verdict of the People" (right). American political behavior moved Bingham to write: "God help poor human nature."

THE ELUSIVE PRESIDENCY

CLAY MERITED the Presidency far more than some men—William Henry Harrison, for example—who attained the office. Until his last years he never stopped trying for it. Between 1824 and 1848 he ran for election three times, and twice unsuccessfully sought his party's nomination. The buttons above survive from his actual campaigns in (left to right) 1832, 1824, and 1844. Except for mischance and trickery he might have made it in the four-man race of 1824. Several Clay supporters in Louisiana were delayed on their way to the legislature, so that Clay lost the state's electoral vote in a close contest. In New York enough Clay votes were miscounted to put him in last place. When the election went to the House of Representatives, where Clay was popular, he had been eliminated as a contestant. In then throwing his own support to John Quincy Adams, he made an unforgiving enemy of Andrew Jackson. But Jackson was only one of many antagonists Clay inevitably acquired in his long career. Involved in politics since the century's beginning—and in national affairs since 1806—Clay had eschewed political deals, sacrificing potentially useful alliances. He had taken controversial positions out of principle on such issues as the tariff (see 1844 campaign banner at right), which was part of his "American System" represented in the poster at lower left. He had spoken out against war with Mexico, subject of the song (below, center) dedicated to him in 1848. Many—although not enough—already had sung his praises with "The Whig Chief," an 1844 song that won a $50 prize; its sheet music (below, right) was adorned with three pictures: Clay's birthplace, Ashland, and the White House. But Clay was

Clay poster shows "American System."

1848 song about Mexican War hails Clay.

1844 song is entitled "The Whig Chief."

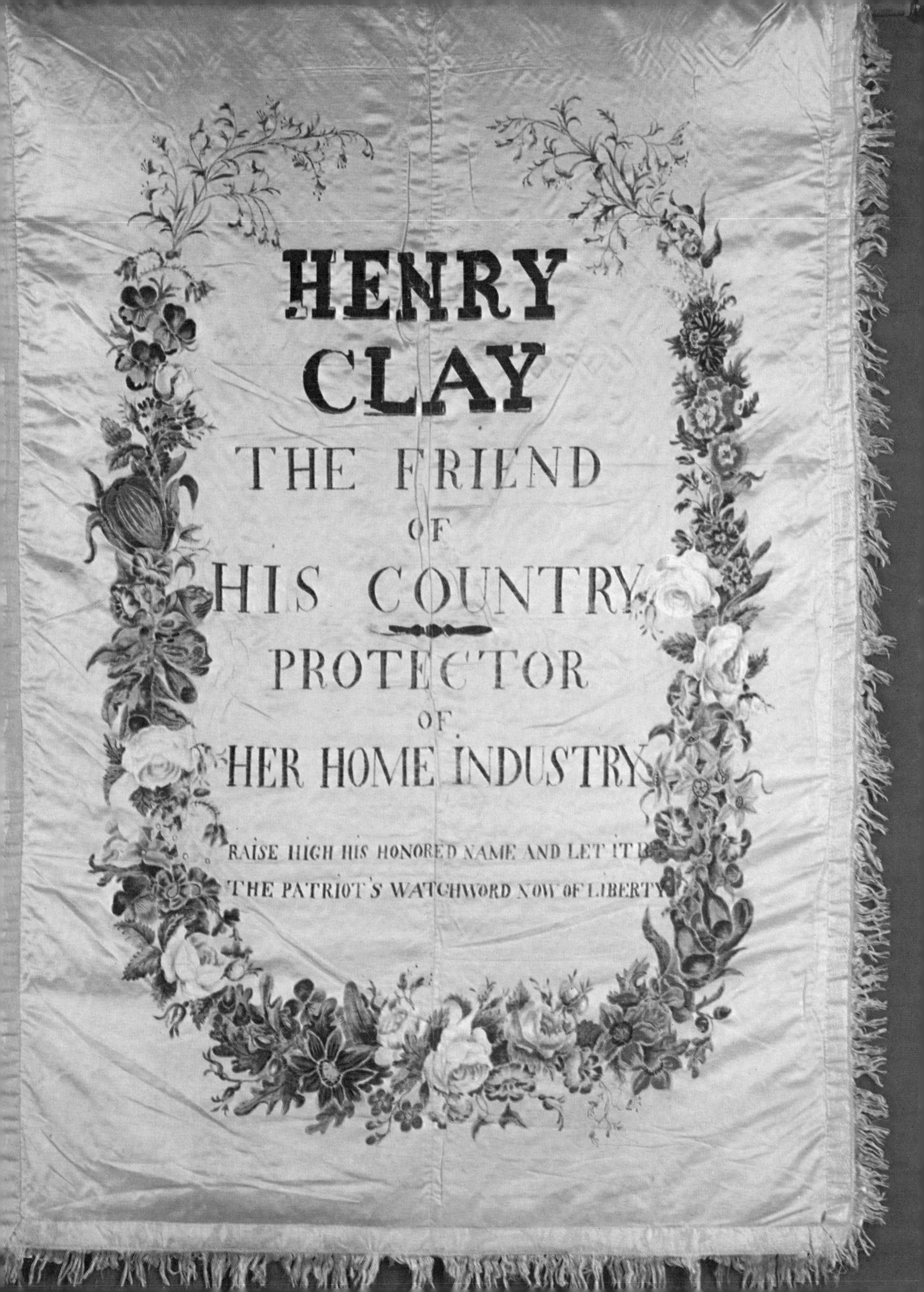

HENRY
CLAY

THE FRIEND

OF

HIS COUNTRY

PROTECTOR

OF

HER HOME INDUSTRY

RAISE HIGH HIS HONORED NAME AND LET IT BE
THE PATRIOT'S WATCHWORD NOW OF LIBERTY

THE ELUSIVE PRESIDENCY

no match for a war hero like Zachary Taylor, or for other men new to politics and accordingly less burdened by commitments. The slavery issue, however, proved to be Clay's greatest dilemma. He had held slaves since childhood—inheriting two from his father—and as a landowner recognized the institution's practicality for the South, and yet as a humane man he abhorred it. Even his genius for compromise, often displayed in the Senate (below, with Clay standing before post at far left), failed to conceive a solution that would satisfy all sides and win for him a majority in the Electoral College.

Contrasting Northern and Southern views of slavery are epitomized in paintings at top and bottom right. One shows a Negro family being separated after the sale of some of its members; the other depicts well-fed, well-dressed slaves dancing at a kitchen ball. The cartoon (middle), showing Clay defending slavery in a Senate speech, charges him with taking different positions above and below the Mason-Dixon line.

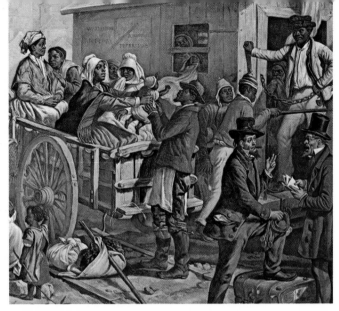

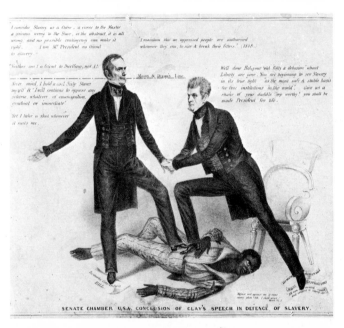

SENATE CHAMBER U.S.A. CONCLUSION OF CLAY'S SPEECH IN DEFENCE OF SLAVERY.

PRIVATE LIFE

POLITICALLY, Clay suffered from legends about his private life. To self-righteous folk, of whom there were many, Clay was a profane, godless, hard-drinking, card-playing womanizer, the prototype of the Mississippi riverboat gambler. But this image, based on Clay's lusty youth in a frontier society, was badly distorted; in his maturity Clay lived a life astonishingly blameless for its times. He admired—and charmed—pretty women, loved to dance with them, and kissed and flattered them freely. But he was devoted to his wife, Lucretia, who bore him eleven children, and apparently remained faithful to her throughout their fifty-three years of marriage. He *could* swear expertly, but generally displayed his skill only under extreme provocation. In his frequent travels, he often drank ale and played cards in places like Delaware's Red Lion Inn common room, a re-creation of which (right) is at Winterthur Museum near Wilmington. But he gave up brag (the fiercest gambling game of the period, at which he used to win or lose as much as $8,000 in a single night) for whist (a genteel ancestor of contract bridge), and he told one bigoted critic that he had never

The couples above are dancing "Jullien's Original Mazurka," a contemporary step Clay probably knew.

in his life played cards on the Sabbath. If he skipped a Sunday morning service on a Mississippi steamboat, he explained, it was because he did not care to listen to a sermon by a "ranting, canting" parson.

He had become a Southern gentleman despite his somewhat humble origins, his limited fortune, and his lack of education. His manners and morals were doubtless better than those of most of his contemporaries.

Until his old age, he dressed carefully, scorning the Jacksonian era's custom of donning ragged clothes when campaigning, and he enjoyed luxurious dinner parties, music, and books. He shared his neighbors' passion for horse racing and often witnessed scenes like that depicted below. On a shelf (lower right) in his home, Ashland, racing calendars that he owned, covering the years 1830 to 1835, still hold an honored place between volumes of his biography and a contemporary edition of his collected speeches.

A horse breeder himself, Clay helped to make the limestone region around Lexington the home of the thoroughbred that it is today. As early as 1808, he put up $1,000 for a one-fifth share in a famous English horse, Buzzard, that went into stud service on his farm. Subsequently, he paid Virginia's Governor James Barbour $1,500 for an imported brood mare, and he bought a half-interest in a magnificent Arabian stallion that had belonged to Sultan Mahmud II of Turkey.

Clay's interest in stockbreeding extended beyond race horses. To produce mules, which were in great demand as draft animals, he imported jacks and jennets from France, Spain, and Malta and sold their get as far away as Alabama and eastern North Carolina. He bought Merino and Saxon sheep from Pennsylvania and New York, respectively, for improvement of his stock. In addition, he raised large numbers of Berkshire, China, and Portuguese pigs, which he often fed himself. In his dining room, the story goes, he kept shelled corn handy for taking out of doors to bring his chickens running.

Clay's interests and the social contacts that they compelled inevitably influenced the ideas he expressed in Washington's salons. By instinct, he was a democrat and a friend of the common man. But he had raised himself to the level of the rural aristocracy, and his social experiences and associations resulted in a modification of his political stance that made him a much less obvious leader of the underprivileged than, say, his longtime rival, Andrew Jackson.

In rooms adorned by paintings and costly draperies, like the one at left depicted by Henry Sargent in "The Dinner Party," Clay not only felt at home but also accomplished much business. When the talk turned to horses, Clay was equally at ease; the shorter books below are some of the racing calendars that, as an enthusiastic follower of the horses, he needed to have on hand. He built a track at Ashland to exercise the horses that he himself bred and trained. The racing scene at lower left, which Clay would have found familiar, now hangs in New York's Jockey Club.

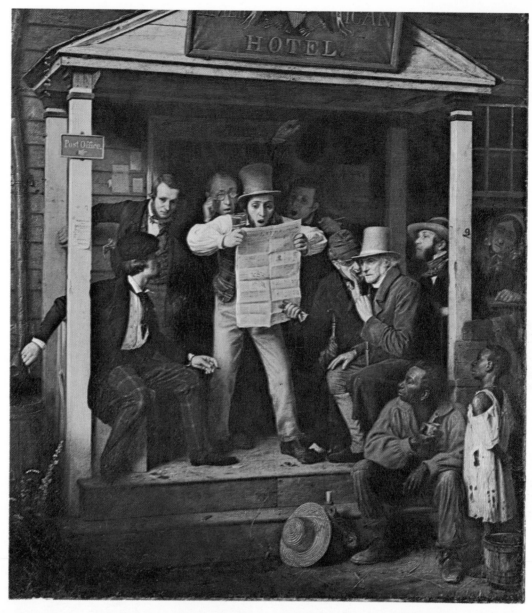

WAR ON MEXICO

HAD CLAY been elected President in 1844, the Mexican War almost surely would not have occurred, for he disapproved of war as a means of advancing the sort of American expansionism in which he so strongly believed. But his counsels of caution on the annexation of Texas went almost unheard in the din of Polk's jingoism, and when Clay qualified his stand, he alienated many of his supporters.

Once war came, however, Clay followed its progress as avidly as did his compatriots, who got the news quickly (left) by Morse's new invention, the telegraph. Clay had a more personal interest than most, for his favorite son was at the front when the Mexican General Antonio López de Santa Anna attacked General Zachary Taylor's invading forces at Buena Vista, a few miles south of Monterrey, on February 23, 1847 (at lower left). Both sides fought gallantly, but Mexican cavalry charges could not overcome American artillery, and Taylor's 5,000 men beat off Santa Anna's 20,000. Among the Americans killed in action that day was Henry Clay, Jr. The father, just short of seventy, never quite recovered from the blow. Yet his mind may have been distracted from the tragedy somewhat by the upcoming elections of 1848. He was still hopeful of attaining the Presidency.

Dying at Buena Vista, Henry Clay, Jr. (below), a West Point graduate who was a lieutenant colonel in the 2nd Regiment of Kentucky Volunteers, is reported to have said: "Leave me and take care of yourselves. Give these pistols to my father, and tell him I have done all I can with them, and return them to him."

CLAY'S SYSTEM

THOUGH CLAY never satisfied his ambition
to occupy the White House, he contributed more to the shape of American life than
did many Presidents. Soon after his return
from the peace conference at Ghent, when
he was just entering his middle years, he
proposed an ingeniously worked out program
that became known as the "American System." It embraced the building of more national roads like the National Turnpike, or
Cumberland Road (above), begun by Jefferson and the main route out of Baltimore for
families migrating to Ohio, Indiana, and
Illinois. (The Cumberland Road is now U.S.
40.) Clay's program also embraced the dig-
ging of more canals like the Erie (right),
which cut freight charges between Buffalo
and Albany in New York State from $100 a
ton to $8. Four horses on a turnpike could
haul 3,000 pounds eighteen miles in a day,
but four horses pulling a barge could move
200,000 pounds of goods twenty-three miles
in the same period. Of equal or perhaps even
greater importance was Clay's insistence, as
part of the "American System," on the impo-

This portrait of Clay, painted in his sixties, now hangs at Ashland. The Cumberland Road scene on the left is at the Fairview Inn near Baltimore, a starting point for settlers' westward-bound Conestoga wagons.

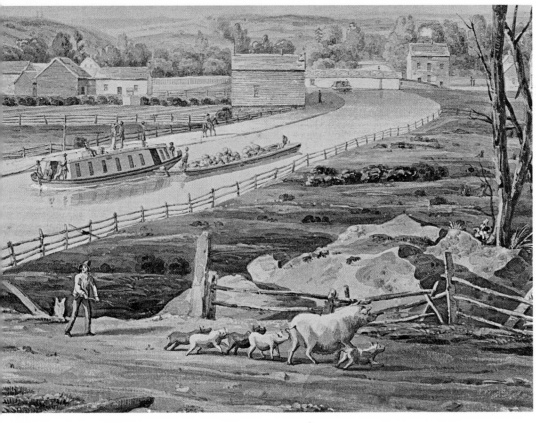

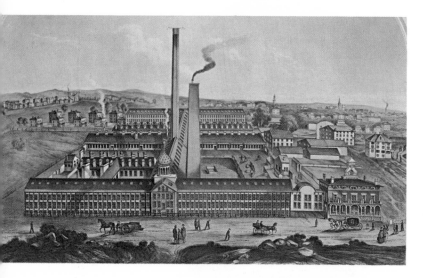

Mister Bull you ca
of the exhibition "to m
your "Crystal Palace" i
across the pond, and y
to the Pacific & China -
longer, we will show y

sition of protective tariffs against imports pouring into the country (below) from all over the world. Tariffs, Clay argued, would encourage American industry (such as the Colt Patent Fire Arms Manufactory in Hartford, Connecticut, above) and make the nation self-sufficient in wartime; they would provide domestic markets for domestic agricultural products, like cotton; and they would help to finance the roads and canals. Later, Clay's ideas won more approval than they did when he was vigorously advocating them. Yet when the Great Exhibition of 1851 took place in London's Crystal Palace, the advanced state of the American economy so surprised the British that an American cartoonist (right), reflecting characteristic bumptiousness, bragged unduly.

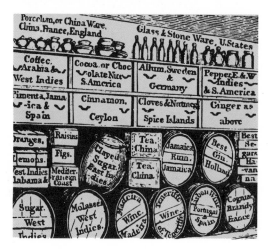

KENTUCKY HOME

Ashland's dining-room table is set with Mrs. Clay's ice cream dishes.

CLAY ONCE said of his wife, Lucretia (right): "Again and again she has saved our home from bankruptcy." Lucretia was indeed the kind of wife Clay needed. Her practicality countered Clay's easygoing approach to financial matters, and she managed skillfully the household at Ashland (above), which burned in the early 1900's but has been faithfully rebuilt. Wellborn, she provided Clay with useful connections; she disdained social life, but proved a kind and amiable hostess to Clay's friends who came to discuss politics in Ashland's library (far right) and stayed for dinner and the ice cream she made herself. Clay took pride in his gardens, lawns, and cattle; in 1845 a visitor said Clay "seemed more like the quiet happy farmer than anything else."

Lucretia Hart Clay

The library at Ashland was familiar to such visitors as Monroe, Daniel Webster, and Lafayette.

The finding of gold, some of it in nuggets as large as the chunk shown in the top picture, drew great hordes of immigrants to California. Not all the newcomers, however, went prospecting; many stayed in San Francisco, where a great parade celebrated California's admittance to statehood on October 29, 1850 (right). Others went into commerce in small towns like Sierra City, whose 1870–1880 business directory appears immediately above.

118

CLAY'S FINAL SERVICE to his nation is also one of his greatest. Conceived of contradictions and born amid frustrations, the Compromise of 1850 survived only briefly, but it saved the Union for ten years and its facets reflected the whole man and his destiny. As a result of the Mexican War (which Clay had opposed), the United States now sprawled to the Pacific (as Clay had foreseen). Discovery of gold and the ensuing tides of immigration made quick statehood for California inevitable. But a new state would upset the numerical balance between slave and free states. The North pressed for the Wilmot Proviso, which would have excluded slavery from all the land acquired from Mexico. The South was vehemently opposed, although some Southerners de-

THE LAST GREAT COMPROMISE

manded a western extension of the Missouri Compromise line to the Pacific, which would have divided California just south of San Francisco. Despite being a Southerner and slaveholder, Clay objected to imposing slavery where it did not exist. He worried equally about the increase in talk of secession. Once again, he displayed his genius at compromise; he bundled together an "Omnibus" of eight proposals, barring slavery from California but offering the South so many advantages that it could not reject the package. The fate of Clay's Omnibus Bill curiously resembled his own; it did not prevail, but

its ideas did. When it was broken up into its components, seven were finally enacted. Without Clay, the Compromise of 1850 might never have been effected, and secession, coming earlier, might have had a different outcome.

The man who "would rather be right than President," Clay never received the reward he so desired. But he was as beloved in the South (especially in New Orleans, where his statue, below, dominates an 1872 parade) as in the North. And a century after his death, the United States Senate voted Henry Clay one of the five greatest senators of all time.

HIS OWN WORDS

A PLUNGE INTO PUBLIC AFFAIRS

The earliest existing document written by Henry Clay was penned soon after he reached Kentucky in 1797. He plunged wholeheartedly into the political battles then raging in the newly admitted state. Dissatisfied with a constitution that permitted indirect election of the governor and state senators by means of electors, many people in Kentucky were clamoring for a constitutional convention to revise the state's principal document. Others saw this as an opportunity to end slavery within the state. A young aspiring lawyer— already a political animal in spirit—Clay added the force of his pen to the rising tide of indignation. He later changed some of the opinions he expressed here, notably those concerning the abolition of slavery. But this address to the electors of Fayette County, dated April 1798, only four days after his twenty-first birthday, shows his mastery of the political situation, his analytical clarity and rhetorical skill, and his potential as one of the outstanding public servants in American history.

■ That there exist defects in the constitution is not denied by the most violent opposers of a convention. But it is said, that, if we attempt an alteration of it now, we shall expose it to the attacks of the wicked and designing, and that, by endeavouring to expunge the defective parts, we hazard a loss of the perfect. . . .

How do we endanger the good parts of the constitution, by a convention? Those who urge this objection seem to suppose that, instead of an assemblage of the most wise and enlightened citizens of the state, canvassing the constitution and availing themselves of the lessons of experience, and the dictates of reason, we are to expect a convention of the most wicked and ignorant, shaking government and attacking property. They pay but a poor compliment to the discernment and integrity of the people. . . .

It is not however true that the people of Kentucky are contented and happy under the present government. The vote of so large a number, in favor of a convention, at the last election, and the present stir in the country, prove the contrary. Can any humane man be happy and contented when he sees near thirty thousand of his fellow beings around him, deprived of all the rights which make life desirable, transferred like cattle from the possession of one to another; when he sees the trembling slave, under the hammer, surrounded by a number of eager purchasers, and feeling all the emotions which arise when one is uncertain into whose tyrannic hands he must next fall; when he beholds the anguish and hears the piercing cries of husbands separated from wives and children from parents; when in a word, all the tender and endearing ties of nature are broken asunder and disregarded; and when he reflects that no gradual mode of emancipation is adopted either for these slaves or their posterity, doubling their number every twenty-five years.

Permit me to hint at some of the alterations which appear to me to be necessary to our constitution. In addition to other misrepresentation, to which the enemies to a convention, despairing of success by a fair mode of reasoning, have had recourse, they had addressed themselves insidiously to the fears of the slaveholders, and held out as the object of the friends to a convention, an immediate and unqualified liberation of slaves. . . . All America acknowledges the existence of slavery to be an evil, which while it deprives the slave of the best gift of heaven, in the end injures the master too, by laying waste his lands, enabling him to live indolently, and thus contracting all the vices generated by a state of idleness. If it be this enormous evil, the sooner we attempt its destruction the better. . . .

The next objection which I shall mention to the present constitution, is the senate, a body which to me seems adverse to republican principles, and to be without use. . . . The division of the legislature into two chambers, has been founded upon the principle of two classes of men, whose interests were distinct, living under the same government. It was necessary that the rights of the nobility and commonalty should be guarded and protected by a body of legislators, representing each. These distinctions not existing in America, the use of the senate has ceased. . . .

Is it not against the principles of all just calculation, against the spirit of democracy, to suppose that fifteen men above, are equally well qualified to understand and manage the interests of a nation, with fifty-six below? If it be true that the farther we go from the people, we get men better acquainted with, and more competent to decide upon, the affairs of the republic, why stop at fifteen, why not descend to two or one?

With respect to the check which the senate is supposed to impose upon the impetuosity and precipitancy of the lower house, this scarcely deserves an audience. To it I answer first, the will of the enlightened representatives of a free people should not be checked by any power upon earth, except it be the people themselves. And secondly, that it is not true that the senate [has] men less impetuous and more wise than the other house. . . . Do not these men possess the same passions, the same prejudices with the others? Have not they the same inclinations to gratify? . . .

Having attempted to shew, and I think succeeded in manifesting, in the preceding observations, that there exists no good reason why a convention should not be summoned; that there ought to be a gradual mode of emancipation established, or, at least, that the legislature should be invested with the power of forming one, when the situation of the country should render it necessary; and that the senate should be abolished or at least reformed; I shall conclude by observing to you fellow citizens, that the present is the moment for coming forward.

Since Clay himself became one of the greatest senators of any period in any country, it is ironic in retrospect that he so vigorously attacked the idea of an upper house in the preceding excerpt. Fortunately for the young firebrand's own future, the new Kentucky constitution of 1799 did retain the senate (though by direct, not indirect, election) and that body also continued to flourish in the national Congress. But Clay modified some of his views even before the

Southern planters, accustomed to paying hundreds of dollars for a slave, were easily enticed by a raffle notice (above). For only $1 they stood a chance to win a "guaranteed" slave girl "aged about twenty years" and valued at $900 or, still better in their eyes, a trotting horse that was "warranted sound." A few slave-owners wrote manuals on the feeding and care of slaves—even prescribing medicines for illness. But it was the rare overseer who shared this paternalistic spirit. To slaves toiling beneath his scrutiny (below), he was usually a man with a long whip and short temper.

state constitution was revised. In a document dated February 1799, he qualified his earlier statement, admitting that he did not favor immediate abolition of slavery.

■ The rights of man must always be the same. . . . But, although rights are immutable, cases may be conceived in which the enjoyment of them is improper. That of the present race of negroes is one. Thirty thousand slaves, without preparation for enjoying the rights of a freeman, without property, without principle, let loose upon society would be wretched themselves, and render others miserable. But from the most of these objections will their posterity be exempt. They may receive the education of the poor orphan, which instilling principle, will qualify them for the exercise of the rights of a citizen. So that a man may advocate a gradual and oppose an immediate emancipation (as is actually the case,) upon principle.

Clay's first real success came in law, not politics. While he was involved in some exciting criminal cases (see page 88), the bulk of his early legal practice stemmed from actions involving land, debts, and property (including slaves). In an expanding frontier society, such suits were often lucrative, although payment, as recorded below, was often in goods instead of cash. Clay's correspondence with clients during these years when his shingle was first displayed reflected his businesslike attitude and competence as a lawyer. This excerpt, dated November 1799 when Clay was twenty-two, is addressed to William Taylor, a Baltimore merchant who had retained Clay to collect some outstanding debts. Both Mann Satterwhite and Andrew Holmes were local Lexington merchants.

■ Before this time you must have received my letter acknowleding the receipt of Satterwhites note, and also another letter informing you that by the advice and direction of Mr. Andrew Holmes I had taken a mortgage of Satterwhite upon two houses and lots in this place and a negro fellow to secure your debt and one due to Mr. Holmes himself, and had in consequence thereof extended to Satterwhite a farther credit. And by my last

Early American methods of land survey were often haphazard. Since Clay, as an attorney, frequently handled suits over the ownership of land, he was well versed both in the confusion and the legal jargon that resulted from faulty surveys. In this letter, written at Lexington on August 7, 1805, and addressed to Robert Smith (then Secretary of the Navy), he explains that some controversy might arise over a 9,000-acre tract of land bought some years before by Smith and his brother. Years later the original owner sold what he considered surplus acreage in the tract to another buyer, who now wished to determine whether a certain salt lick was included in his property or if it belonged to the Smiths. The problem of land ownership was prevalent in early nineteenth-century Kentucky because of what Clay here terms "Chimney-corner surveys," then a common practice. Clay defines these as "surveys made without ever going upon the ground and marking corners and boundary." Naturally this led to many squabbles—a situation that did not necessarily dismay the lawyers involved.

In this Country it was frequently practiced by the Surveyors at an early period to make what has been denominated here, Chimney-corner Surveys — that is Surveys made without ever going upon the ground and marking corners and boundary. It sometimes happened that after they had thus returned Surveys, they would go upon the ground and mark corner trees corresponding with le letter I requested of you to inform me whether you would take produce of any description (but more particularly cordage) in payment of your debt, as Satterwhite had a prospect of selling the house for that article; this request I beg leave again to repeat, observing however at the same time that you need not be induced to take it under any apprehension that the debt is insecure, because it is now unquestionably safe, and if he should fail to pay at the times agreed on I shall be able to recover a Judgment and get the money during the next fall in the common course of business. . . .

It is proper for me to inform you that in the collection of all debts, it is customary with the Attos. in this Country to have a commission upon the amount, of 5 P Cent at least.

Clay wrote to Taylor in July 1802 informing his client that he anticipated some troubles with notes owed the merchant. The "light money" referred to are bills and bank notes, which were easier to transport than coins, but uncommon in areas beyond the eastern seaboard.

■ The amount together with a very handsome sum which I expect every day to receive on account of Shepherd shall be remitted the very moment I can procure bankbills; but such has been the demand upon this Country for money lately that it is almost exhausted of all the light money, and I fear I shall meet with great difficulty in procuring notes. . . . I received some mails ago the papers relative to Mr. Wantes' affair—The absence of Mr. Daviess from town ever since they came to hand has prevented me from presenting the order. The answer however I can easily anticipate—It will be that he has no funds & bad prospects.

In November 1800, Clay jotted down a memorandum of court action concerning slaves. A detinue was a legal step taken either to recover personal belongings that had been detained illegally or to obtain a sum equivalent to the value involved. Clearly slaves were regarded—and calmly mentioned in legal parlance—as mere property, not as human beings with feelings of their own.

■ Samuel Willison and Rebecca his wife, Citizens of the Commonwealth of Georgia against Jacob Spier's Detinue for the detention of the following slaves, Kate of the value of $500, Lemerich of the value of $500, Joe of the value of $500, Nero of the value of $500, and Chamont of the value of $500—Damage $3000

In 1801, when John Breckinridge, one of Kentucky's outstanding lawyers, went to the United States Senate, he recommended a number of his clients to twenty-four-year-old Henry Clay. This letter addressed to a surveyor, Nathaniel Massie, on December 11, 1801, reveals Clay's shrewd handling of a client and creditor who is also a debtor. Josias and Patterson Bullock were businessmen of Fayette County, Kentucky. Breckinridge himself did not follow his father's manner of spelling the family name and therefore suffered from having his name frequently misspelled.

John Breckinridge, seventeen years Clay's senior, was a fellow Virginian and Clay's unwitting forerunner. He preceded Clay first as a student of George Wythe, then to Kentucky as a lawyer and legislator, and finally to Washington. His letters to Clay were frank and informative, but at one point he cautioned: "It is very probable that my [recent] letter to you may contain facts or opinions which I ought not to disclose. . . . I have to request that you will consider that letter as well as others you may receive from me as committed to your confidence"—a request Clay honored. Breckinridge resigned from the Senate in 1805 to become Jefferson's Attorney General and died a year later at the age of forty-six.

■ You will recollect that I informed you that Mr. Breckenridge left the balance of his Judgment against you with me for collection, and directed how the money, when received, should be applied; and that you promised if the amount of your Judgment against the Bullocks could not be shortly obtained, to make some other arrangement to pay Mr. Breckenridge—The persons whom he directed the payment of this money to have grown extremely impatient, so much so that I have been compelled to advance out of my own pocket upwards of $100 to one of them. . . .

I beg you will remit the amount to me—For if you do not I fear that the pressing applications of those to whom Mr. Breckenridge gave orders will oblige me to take the disagreeable measure of issuing an execution against your Security, which I assure you would not be more disagreeable to you than to Dr Sir Yr. friend & hble [humble] Servt.

One of Clay's few truly intimate friends was Francis Taliaferro Brooke, a respected Virginia soldier and jurist with whom he maintained a frank correspondence for more than half a century. Francis' elder brother, Robert, had been one of Clay's law teachers, and Clay lived with him for a time in Virginia. In the following letter to Francis, dated December 1801, Clay offered to take Robert's only child, Richard, into his own home in Kentucky and see to his education at nearby Transylvania University, where Clay himself was both a trustee and a law professor.

The last paragraph below, from a letter Clay wrote another friend in 1812, shows not only his continuing interest in Transylvania but also his surprisingly strong views on what was good and bad in architecture. Benjamin Latrobe was the outstanding American architect of his day.

■ I must request the favor of you to execute a small commission for me. The Acts of the Virginia Legislature, passed prior to the separation of this State, are extremely difficult to be procured, even by collecting fugitive Acts, in this country; but few indeed of the public offices possess entire collections. Will you be so obliging as to obtain for me, if you can, the old revisal, which reaches, I believe, to the year 1766, the Chancellor revisal, and the Acts passed since that, in a regular series to the year 1792. The last is most desired, but I could wish to possess all. . . .

What has become of the son of my much regretted friend, your brother? I feel myself under obligation of gratitude to the father, which I should be happy of having an opportunity of discharging to the son. What is the progress he has made in his education? We have in this place an university in a very flourishing condition. Could you not spare him to me in this country for two or three years? I live at a short distance from the buildings, have a small family, and need not add, that from the cheapness of living in this country, his expense to me would be extremely inconsiderable. . . .

I recd your favor on the subject of a building for the University. I immediately addressed a note to Mr. Latrobe to engage him to execute his promise. Owing to the extreme illness of his lady, I have not yet been able to have a personal interview with him. Allow me to entreat the Board not to proceed with the building until they have a judicious design prepared by some architect. I would defer the erection a year, rather than not be in the possession of such a plan. The miserable building put up for a Court House in Lexington—the disgrace of the town and the derision of everybody—ought to admonish us to proceed with more discretion in our public edifices.

By 1806, Clay's ability as a lawyer had earned him a clientele wide enough to attract the attention of Noah Webster, the noted author and lexicographer, who retained him to handle his Western accounts. The first correspondence between the two concerns Webster's contract with Joseph Charless for printing Webster's spelling book; its profits supported Webster for years while he worked laboriously on his famous dictionary. The rival spelling book, which Charless threatened to print instead of Webster's, had first been issued in Philadelphia in 1798.

■ I have received several letters from you and a power of Atto. in relation to a contract with Mr. Charless. Execution of the contract has been delayed in consequence of Mr. Charless not having earlier received the Types. They are now received & the contract is executed. He has struck 5000 Copies of the book, & says he can vend annually 12.000. He i[s] willing to make the purchase yo[. . .] for the Western Country, if you will render the payments less speedy. He will give you the price asked if you will accept of annual payments of $200 each with interest. In the event of your noncurrence he says he will edit the Columbian Spelling book, sales of which he thinks he can effect.

The most famous client to retain Clay while he was a young lawyer was former Vice-President Aaron Burr. Clay twice defended Burr from charges of conspiracy against the United States that had been brought by Joseph Hamilton Daveiss, the federal district attorney for the region. The core of Clay's argument—excerpted here in the third-person version printed in a local newspaper in December 1806—convinced the judge not to allow examination of witnesses, and the jurors threw out the indictment.

■ Mr. Daveiss rose and stated to the grand jury, that they might call on him, if they thought proper, to assist them to examine witnesses; and was proceeding to make some remarks to the foreman, when Mr. Clay interrupted him, and addressing the court, observed, that the privilege contended for by Mr. Daveiss, was a novel one, and he hoped the court would not grant it. . . .

Mr. Clay cared not in what attitude he should be considered as standing; but he would instantly renounce Col. Burr and his cause, did he entertain the slightest idea of his guilt, as to the charges exhibited against him by Mr. Daveiss. You have heard of inquisitions in Europe, (said Mr. Clay) you have heard of the screws and tortures made use of in the

One of the early American methods of publishing such widely admired works as Noah Webster's *Spelling Book* (part of a page is seen below) was to print at various locales. When demand warranted it, the already composed type was simply shipped to a local printer, who then produced finished books. This was cheaper than shipping bound books. The system, however, also necessitated local agents—such as Clay in Lexington—to handle financial and legal matters for the publisher. As Webster (above) wrote in 1808 to Clay: "All I want is, an agent of talents, & fidelity who will attend to my concerns, & from time to time inform me of such facts as may be necessary for me to know."

Cur ri er, a dreſſer of leather
  Deer, a wild animal
  Dear, of great price
Dew, from heaven
Due, owed
  Die, to expire
  Dye, to colour
Doe, a female deer
Dough, bread unbaked
  Dun, brown colour
  Done, performed
Fane, a weather cock
Fain, gladly
Feign, to diſſemble
  Faint, weary
  Feint, a falſe march
Fair, comely

dens of despotism, to extort confession; of the dark conclaves and cau-
cuses, for the purpose of twisting some incoherent expression into evidence
of guilt. Is not the project of the attorney for the United States, a similar
object of terror? But all will not do; all the art of the attorney will not
effect his purpose. I call upon him to produce a single instance where the
public attorney has been accustomed to examine the witnesses before the
grand jury; to sound the jurors and enter into all their secrets.

*Clay's disillusionment with Burr came quickly. Soon after reaching Wash-
ington to serve a brief term in the Senate, he wrote two friends back home—and
seemed relieved that no action was contemplated against himself as Burr's
lawyer!*

■ The Government appear to be confident that Burr is engaged in
treasonable projects. They speak of having received the most unquestion-
able evidence of his designs. . . . And I now enclose you a document
exhibiting the best development of his plans yet presented to the public.
However extensively criminal, I presume they have been frustrated. I do
not believe that any Censure has fallen upon the Judge, or the Counsel
appearing in the defence of Burr, for the result of the prosecution—I mean
censure from the government.

*Clay's first appearance in the corridors of Congress has been described as a
lark by most of his biographers. Part of this reaction is undoubtedly based on
the account given by a contemporary, William Plumer, Senator from New
Hampshire, who noted in his diary on February 13, 1807: "Henry Clay is a
man of pleasure; fond of amusements. He is a great favorite with the ladies;
is in all parties of pleasure; out almost every evening; reads but little; indeed,
he said he meant this session should be a tour of pleasure. He is a man of
talents; is eloquent; but not nice or accurate in his distinctions. He declaims
more than he reasons. He is a gentlemanly and pleasant companion; a man
of honor and integrity."*

*However, Clay was already beginning to formulate some of the ideas he
would later expound. He was not afraid to speak out and was placed on at
least four committees, twice as chairman. He pressed for a canal around the
falls on the Ohio River and supported a bill to forbid further importation of
slaves. John Quincy Adams noted that Clay's speech was "ardent" and that
he was "quite a young man—an orator—and a republican of the first fire."
Much of Clay's seriousness, and a tinge of homesickness, is evidenced in a
letter he wrote his father-in-law, Colonel Thomas Hart, on February 1, 1807:*

■ I am attempting in Congress several things for the good, as I suppose,
of our country. A bill at my instance has passed the Senate to extend to
Kentucky and the other Western States, the circuit court system of the
United States. By this measure, if it passes the other House, Kentucky,
Tennessee and Ohio will have the advantage of two judges upon the
Federal bench instead of one; and the circuit Judge who presides in those

States, will also attend the Supreme bench, and carry with him there a knowledge of the local laws and decisions of each of those States. I have also proposed a resolution to appropriate a quantity of land to assist in opening the canal at the Falls. . . . My reception in this place has been equal, nay superior to my expectations. I have experienced the civility and attention of all whose acquaintance I was desirous of obtaining. Those who are disposed to flatter me say that I have acquitted myself with great credit in several debates in the Senate. But after all that I have seen, Kentucky is still my favorite country. There amidst my dear family, I shall find happiness in a degree to be met with no where else.

Nor was there any evidence of playfulness in Clay's hard-hitting report to the Senate on the need for an Ohio canal. This strong foreshadowing of his passion for internal improvements was delivered on February 24, 1807. At this early date, he advocated a broad interpretation of the Constitution to include such improvements as part of the national concern, thereby permitting use of federal funds for that purpose. The Senate subsequently authorized the President to establish a committee to study the project and to determine if the canal should be built on the Kentucky or Ohio side of the river. The "Saline" referred to consisted of nearby salt springs owned by the federal government.

■ That the work is one of great & national importance is undeniable. The immense Country on the Ohio and its waters, above the rapids, in seeking a market for its surplus products, has to encounter the obstruction in the navigation of that stream which they present. This obstruction, never entirely free from danger, is such as to absolutely preclude the passage of vessels for several months in the year in their descent, and when laden for

Joseph Hamilton Daveiss (above) was a backwoods Virginia lawyer before becoming United States district attorney for Kentucky in 1800. He was removed from office in 1806 for twice failing to indict Aaron Burr, who escaped largely owing to Clay's legal skill in defending him. A year later Burr was rearrested while fleeing (below) to Spanish territory, and tried for treason. Despite his acquittal, few people believed what Burr maintained until death—that he had never been part of any conspiracy. Lawyer Daveiss eventually resumed a pastime of his youth—fighting Indians—and died of a battle wound after Tippecanoe in 1811.

the whole year in their ascent of the river. The rapidity of the current (which averages at the rate of from 10 to 11 miles an hour through the falls) leaves no alternative for a safe voyage up as well as down the river, but in a Canal.

How far it is the policy of the Government to aid in works of this kind, when it has no *direct* interest—whether indeed, in such a case, it has the constitutional power of patronage and encouragement, is not necessary to be decided in the present instance. Being the proprietor of Land bordering upon the Ohio to a greater extent than any individual state, owning too an invaluable Saline near the Wabash, there can be no doubt that both policy and *power* combine in favour of promoting an undertaking by which its property is to be incidentally benefited. If the value and price of land depend, as well upon the facility with which its products find a market, as upon its capacity to produce, there can be no doubt that the public lands will be increased in value, by improvements in the navigation of those streams which water them.

While in Washington in 1807, Clay also interested himself in American foreign policy. Writing to one of his law students at Transylvania, he correctly predicted the effect on the United States of events in Europe. Clay also included some professorial advice, notably a somewhat condescending evaluation of Sir John Strange, whose records of English legal cases were then widely used.

■ The papers inform you of the great events pressing upon the European theater. A measure has been lately taken by Bonaparte of a most gigantic nature, the declaration that the islands of Great Britain are in a state of blockade. It is said that our minister at Paris has written on to Government that our commerce is not to be affected by it; I apprehend, however, that it will subject it to much embarrassment. The session of Congress has not been so interesting as I had anticipated. No questions in relation to our foreign intercourse involving much discussion have been agitated;

Clay wrote finis to the Burr affair in a letter from Lexington on December 5, 1807, to Caesar Rodney, then U.S. Attorney General, who had asked him to prosecute Burr in Ohio. Still bitter about the way Burr had tricked him, Clay categorically refused: "Having deceived me last winter, when I really believed him both innocent and persecuted by Mr. Daveiss, he shall not deceive me again, now that I believe him guilty and meriting punishment." Clearly foreseeing that objections would be raised if he now took the case for the prosecution, Clay also excused himself for political and professional reasons: "Having once appeared for him, it will be supposed, that he imparted to me his projects, etc. The fact is however otherwise, but this may not be known to or thought of by the world." To escape prosecution in several states for treason and for killing Alexander Hamilton in a duel, Burr went into a four-year European exile.

Altho' I have no hesitation as it respects Burr about appearing against him, I have some doubt whether I should not by doing so subject myself to the imputation of violating professional honor. Having once appeared for him, it will be supposed, that he imparted to me his projects &c. The fact is however otherwise, but this may not be known to or thought of by the world. Would it not be everything depends upon the result of pending negotiations, and this will not be known, it is probable, until the session expires. . . . I am glad to find that you have been getting acquainted with Strange. He is a valuable reporter, but occupies a second station only in the grade of merit. I calculate upon finding you much improved in your law knowledge. Two words will make any man of sound intellect a lawyer, industry and application, and the same words with a third, economy, will enable him to make a fortune.

When this one session of the Senate ended, Clay returned to his busy Kentucky routine as gentleman farmer, respected lawyer, and state legislator. But he managed to spend more time on personal affairs than he usually could in later, even busier, years. The four paragraphs below show a variety of the matters with which he concerned himself. The first is a deed of emancipation he executed in 1808 for Daniel, a slave whose brother, James Johnson, a resident of New Orleans, had written Clay asking to purchase Daniel's freedom. The second paragraph is a newspaper advertisement Clay wrote in 1809; dated from Ashland, it is the first recorded time Clay used this name for his farm. The third shows his interest in Lexington's Episcopal church, where he was one of the original pewholders and also helped pay for the steeple. The final sentence is the toast Clay offered at a St. Patrick's Day dinner in 1809.

■ Know all men by these presents that I, Henry Clay a Citizen and resident of Fayette County of Kentucky for divers good considerations me there unto moveing have and by these presents do emancipate, set free and discharge from all manner of servitude a negro slave named Daniel about thirty two or three years of age formerly the property of my Brother John Clay. . . .

Twenty Dollars Reward!

STRAYED or stolen, several weeks ago, from the farm of the subscriber, near Lexington, a sorrel filley, three years old this spring. . . . I will give the above reward to any person who will deliver her to me. . . .

We have this day settled all accounts up to this time except H: Clay's Subscription to the Steeple & a street; and H. Clay has passed his note & others in full. . . .

The genuine Irish character—Frank, brave, and generous.

Not all aspects of Kentucky life, however, were bucolic and peaceful then. Politics were particularly turbulent, and when Dr. Allen Hunn, who had abandoned medicine to edit a newspaper, attacked John Allen (a candidate for governor supported by Clay) and Clay himself as the malevolent power behind Allen, he incurred this retort from Clay in the Lexington Reporter *on June 18, 1808. It is a typical example of the slashing sarcasm (see page 48) Clay liked to use, even to his pun on Hunn's name. Hunn's rather weak reply to this tirade was: "If the card table and punch bowl have left one drop of blood in the face of Mr. Henry Clay, he ought to blush the deepest red." But in a real sense Hunn won out: Allen lost the election.*

The fierce regional pride felt by men of the West gave rise to frequent ridicule in the East. "Half Horse, Half Alligator, with a touch of the Snapping Turtle" was the way an Eastern magazine portrayed one breed of frontiersman in the cartoon above. Clay, though not a backwoods braggart, was undeniably proud of his adopted state. When he went to Washington as a senator in 1806 he presented some Kentucky "wine" to President Jefferson, who served it at a dinner party. Unhappily, the guests found it vile; one man said it tasted like raw corn whiskey. Clay later learned, but never freely admitted, that it *was* raw whiskey—someone in his household had drunk the wine and refilled the bottle! In 1811 Clay sent some Kentucky Madeira to Madison (see page 139), hoping to erase the previous impression.

Thomas Jefferson (above) was perturbed because Clay, though a Republican adherent, did not maintain close ties with him. In September 1807, President Jefferson wrote a friend: "A distance has taken place between Mr. Clay and myself. . . . I had looked to his coming into Congress with an entire belief that he would be cordial with the administration. . . . I feel his loss, therefore, with real concern, but it is irremediable from the necessity of harmony and cordiality between those who are to manage together the public concerns. Not only his withdrawing from the usual civilities of intercourse with me . . . but his open hostility in Congress to the administration, leave no doubt of the state of his mind as a fact." Ironically, within four months came passage of Jefferson's controversial Embargo Act, to which Clay (see opposite page) gave wholehearted support.

■ I have seen some fugitive numbers of the paper edited by you in Lincoln, and . . . the style, the sentiment, and the unprincipled assertions of this print, are such as might be expected from a legitimate descendant of the Goths and Vandals, as you are understood to be. . . . You are an European by birth—a physician by profession; and what you were by practice, may be inferred from the fact of your abandoning the pursuit of medicine, which never fails to reward its meritorious disciples; and commencing the trade of slander and defamation. A temporary success in a limited section of the country, (a success resulting from the honest confidence of the people,) has given to your paper, a momentary eclat; which, however, is now gradually fading away, and will finally leave you to the scorn and contempt of all honest men. It is in vain that you resort to the vile pretext of discharging the contents of your own pistol, in your own hat, for the purpose of creating a belief, that you have been attempted to be assassinated.* It may serve for a time, to awaken the sympathies of a generous people in your behalf; but a detection of the fraud . . . will bring upon you the execrations of the whole community. . . .

For shame, for shame, Doctor, take again to your ancient calling. You have mistaken your powers. Nature never designed you for a statesman. . . . Sooner or later, your press and yourself, will be avoided, as the passing traveller avoids the carrion that annoys him as he journeys on his way. . . . Debased and degraded indeed, would Messrs. Allen and Clay be, if they or their friends paid any attention to your scurrility. This is the *first* and the *last* notice I shall take of you. The world knows, that

Superior virtue and superior sense,
To knaves and fools forever give offence.

*An anecdote of the Doctor not generally known deserves to be told. Riding home one night from Danville, and animated by the laudable ambition of becoming conspicuous, the expedient of raising the cry of assassination suggested itself. . . . The explosion of a pistol was heard. . . . When the *affrighted* Doctor presented himself to some neighbouring family, his head was without its covering, and his mare without her bridle. His hat was sought for, and when found it was discovered to have two corresponding bullet holes, on opposite sides, perforated in such a manner as to render it singular how his head could escape. But upon examining his head critically it was found not to have been penetrated. Now either the Doctor must have discharged the piece himself, or if it were done by another his skull must be impervious, or when the ball came in contact with it, it must have kindly surmounted his head, and passed off quietly on the opposite side.

ACTION AT HOME AND ABROAD

The active role that Clay was soon to play in world affairs began, quietly enough, with a few paragraphs of political rhetoric. President Thomas Jefferson's Embargo Act of 1807 almost wrecked America's foreign trade;

within a year, exports dropped by $85,000,000 and imports by $82,000,000. *Republicans backed their President and party leader; Federalists were furious. In the Kentucky legislature, loyal Jeffersonians proposed a set of resolutions endorsing the embargo. Clay, already beginning to hatch into a War Hawk, rewrote the whole document by adding a much more belligerent amendment that replaced everything after its first word!*

■ Strike out from the word "resolved" in the original resolution, and insert the following in lieu thereof:

"That the administration of the general government, since Thomas Jefferson has been elected to the office of president, has been wise, dignified and patriotic. . . .

Resolved, that the embargo was a measure highly judicious, and was the only honorable expedient to avoid war. . . .

Resolved, That the general assembly of Kentucky would view with the utmost horror a proposition, in any shape, to submit to the tributary exactions of Great Britain, as attempted to be enforced by her orders of council, or to acquiesce in the violation of neutral rights, as menaced by the French decrees; and they pledge themselves to the general government, to spend, if necessary, the last shilling, and to exhaust the last drop of blood, in resisting these aggressions.

Resolved, That whether war, a total non-intercourse, or a more rigid execution of the embargo system be determined on, the general assembly, however they may regret the privations consequent on the occasion, will cordially approve and cooperate in enforcing the measure; for they are sensible that in the present crisis of the nation, the alternatives are—a surrender of liberty and independence, or a *bold* and *manly* resistance.

The embargo was often said to reflect a "terrapin policy," for it made the United States draw into its shell. Cartoonists gleefully pictured the Act as a rather dour turtle (nicknamed "Ograbme"— "embargo" spelled backwards), snapping at the heels of Federalists, or of British and French smugglers. The embargo was justifiably hated; while its purpose had been to protect the United States, its results were devastating, crippling the whole American economy. Jefferson signed a repeal of the embargo shortly before his Presidency ended, but its effect was part of the legacy James Madison inherited. This cartoon, drawn by a well-known portrait artist, John Wesley Jarvis, for publication in the New York *Evening Post*, shows Madison as Ograbme's final victim, trapped in the crushing embrace of a dismembered and dying terrapin.

Resolved, That Thomas Jefferson is entitled to the thanks of his country, for the ability, uprightness and intelligence which he has displayed in the management both of our foreign relations and domestic concerns."

The arguments over this resolution and one that Clay later introduced to enforce it, culminated in a duel between Clay and Humphrey Marshall, the Federalist leader in Kentucky. Before the duel, Clay urgently wrote his brother-in-law, Thomas Hart, Jr.:

■ On this day in the House of Representatives a dispute arose between H. Marshall and myself which terminated by the use of language on his part to which I could not submit, & I attempted to chastise him on the spot, but was prevented by the interference of the House. I have since challenged him, and there is a prospect of his accepting it. Should he do so I shall want a brace of pistols, and know of none that I can get on which I would rely. . . . These I must prevail on you to procure upon any terms, by purchase or otherwise. . . . I must also request the favor of you to procure some of the best powder, adapted to such occasions, which can be had.

Following accepted early nineteenth century formalities with regard to dueling, Clay addressed this cryptic note on January 4, 1809, to Humphrey Marshall (above). "The code of honor" stipulated that if an insult was made in public, the best thing to do was to ignore it at the time. Later, a trusted friend could deliver a formal note, such as this one, with a demand for "explanation." A message that included an insult, however, could be declined, since it indicated that the sender was no gentleman. Written in haste, Clay's note contains deletions and additions that were obvious afterthoughts. Marshall's acceptance was also penned with blotched corrections.

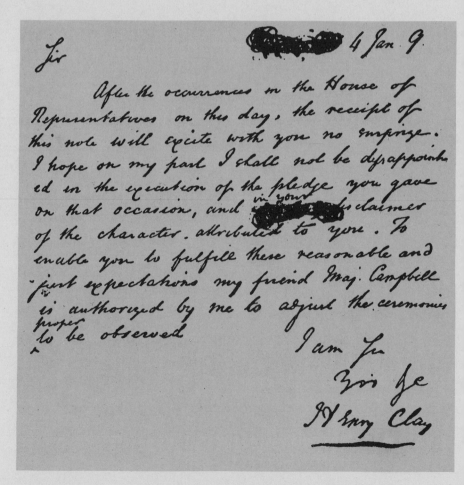

Should the pistols require cleaning I will be obliged to you to get West to put them in proper order. But at any rate let the bearer return with them by tomorrow evening, or in the course of the night. I need not suggest to you the necessity of entire secrecy on this subject.

Neither the duel (see page 18) nor the Kentucky legislature's subsequent censure of its participants detracted from Clay's popularity. His constituents reelected him, while the legislature itself soon chose him to complete another unexpired term in Washington. He addressed his resignation from the state's house of representatives to its speaker, William Logan, who had also been a candidate for the Senate seat:

■ It is in vain . . . to attempt to express my gratitude to a partial country for this new mark of its esteem. No language would do justice to the sensibilities excited on the occasion. I cannot, however, refuse to myself this opportunity of bearing testimony to the frank, liberal, and honorable manner, in which . . . the competition between us has been conducted.

Brash, eager, and fired with the expansionist fever that had engulfed the West, Clay did not waste time nor mince words in taking a stand on vital national issues. He made the following speech to the Senate on February 22, 1810, only seventeen days after reaching Washington. Jefferson's embargo had been replaced by a policy of nonintercourse that was scarcely more successful. When revisions of the Nonintercourse Act were proposed, Clay gave a striking preview of what would become his position on foreign policy.

■ At all times embarrassed when I have ventured to address you, it is with peculiar diffidence I rise on this occasion. The profound respect I have been taught to entertain for this body—my conscious inadequacy to discuss as it deserves the question before you—the magnitude of that question—and the recent seat I have taken in this house, are too well calculated to appal, and would impel me to silence, if any other member would assume the task I propose attempting. But . . . when the regular troops of this house, disciplined as they are in the great affairs of this nation, are inactive at their posts, it becomes the duty of its raw militia, however lately enlisted, to step forth in defence of the honor and independence of the country. . . .

Have we not been for years contending against the tyranny of the ocean? Has not congress solemnly pledged itself to the world not to surrender our rights? Has not the nation, at large, in all its capacities of meetings of the people, state and general governments, resolved to maintain, at all hazards our maritime independence? Your whole circle of commercial restrictions, including the non-importation, embargo and non-intercourse acts, had in view an opposition to the offensive measures of the belligerents, so justly complained of by us. They presented *resistance*—the *peaceful* resistance of the law. When this is abandoned, without effect, I am for resistance by the *sword*.

No man in the nation desires peace more than I. But I prefer the troubled ocean of war, demanded by the honor and independence of the country, with all its calamities, and desolations, to the tranquil, putrescent pool of ignominious peace. If we can accommodate our differences with one of the belligerents only, I should prefer that one to be Great Britain. But if with neither, and we are forced into a selection of our enemy, then am I for war with Britain; because I believe her prior in aggression, and her injuries and insults to us were atrocious in character. . . . Britain stands preeminent, in her outrage on us, by her violation of the sacred personal rights of American freemen, in the arbitrary and lawless impressment of our seamen—the attack on the Chesapeake—the murder. . . . I will not dwell on the long catalogue of our wrongs & disgraces. . . .

We are often reminded that the British navy constitutes the only barrier between us and universal dominion; and warned that resistance to Britain is submission to France. I protest against the castigation of our colonial infancy being applied in the independent manhood of America. . . . I cannot subscribe to British slavery upon the water, that we may escape French subjugation upon land. I should feel myself debased and humbled as an American citizen, if we had to depend upon any foreign power to uphold our independence.

Clay's bellicosity was not limited to tirades against France and England; he was also more than willing to challenge Spain. For some years, settlers from Kentucky and Tennessee had been moving into Spanish-held West Florida between New Orleans and the Perdido River. In October 1810, President James Madison heeded their pleas for annexation and claimed that this area really belonged to the United States because of the Louisiana Purchase. That December, when Congress met, the Federalists attacked Madison's presumptuousness (the region did not actually become part of the United States until

The United States navy, though minuscule, won impressive battles early in the War of 1812—only to receive a severe setback when the frigate *Chesapeake* was vanquished. On June 1, 1813, thirty miles outside Boston harbor, Captain James Lawrence of the *Chesapeake* accepted a challenge from the British frigate *Shannon*. Each ship had thirty-eight guns, but Lawrence thought his larger crew would provide a small advantage. As it happened, the British made up in discipline and training what they lacked in number, and the *Chesapeake* was disabled in fifteen minutes. A boarding party raised the Union Jack over the Stars and Stripes and, escorted by the *Shannon*, sailed to Halifax (right). Lawrence's dying order became a national slogan: "Don't give up the ship."

all of Florida was purchased from Spain in 1819). In the speech excerpted below, Clay stormed against the Federalist fears. Praising the speech, a Republican newspaper editor wrote that it caused Clay to be "hailed as one of the brightest luminaries of his country; when the republick would greet him as one of the most powerful champions of her liberties and independence." The War Hawk was sprouting his wings.

■ It can not be too often repeated, that if Cuba on the one hand, and Florida on the other, are in the possession of a foreign maritime power, the immense extent of country belonging to the United States, and watered by streams discharging themselves into the Gulf of Mexico—that is, one third, nay, more than two thirds of the United States, comprehending Louisiana, are placed at the mercy of that power. The possession of Florida is a guaranty absolutely necessary to the enjoyment of the navigation of those streams. . . .

The gentleman reminds us that Great Britain, the ally of Spain, may be obliged, by her connection with that country, to take part with her against us, and to consider this measure of the president as justifying an appeal to arms. . . . Is the time never to arrive when we may manage our own affairs without the fear of insulting his Britannic majesty? Is the rod of British power to be forever suspended over our heads? Does Congress put on an embargo to shelter our rightful commerce against the piratical depredations committed upon it on the ocean? We are immediately warned of the indignation of offended England. Is a law of non-intercourse proposed? The whole navy of the haughty mistress of the seas is made to thunder in our ears. . . .

I am not . . . in favor of cherishing the passion of conquest. But I must be permitted, in conclusion, to indulge the hope of seeing, ere long, the *new* United States (if you will allow me the expression) embracing, not only the old thirteen States, but the entire country east of the Mississippi, including East Florida, and some of the territories to the north of us also.

The most spectacular switch in position that Clay performed in his whole political career came over the Bank of the United States. When Congress debated the issue of its recharter in 1811, Clay strongly opposed the measure. In the speech excerpted below, Clay poked fun at his fellow-Republican, Senator William B. Giles of Virginia, for being inconsistent on this issue. But in 1816, Clay himself was even more inconsistent—he completely reversed his position on the Bank. The "temporary inconvenience" to the nation's business economy that Clay envisioned here had, meanwhile, developed into an economic depression. So his 1811 speech, though certainly humorous in its shrewd use of a telling anecdote, is a clear case of "the clouded crystal ball."

■ After my honorable friend from Virginia (Mr. Giles) had instructed and amused us with the very able and ingenious argument which he delivered yesterday, I should have still forborne to trespass on the Senate,

Despite his lapdog placidity in the portrait above, William B. Giles maintained a bulldog's belligerence through forty years of public life—in federal and state legislatures and as governor of Virginia. In speeches and papers he assailed men like Washington, Hamilton, the Adamses, Madison, Monroe, Albert Gallatin, John Marshall, and Henry Clay (who cut him down brilliantly in the speech excerpted here). First he was an anti-Federalist more zealous than his Republican party leaders. Then he was a War Hawk demanding government vigor where he had once denounced it. Eventually he became so adamant in defending states' rights that in one speech he called for disunion. People listened to him—Giles was a furious debater—but few took him seriously.

137

James Madison, fourth President of the United States, and Henry Clay held high federal offices simultaneously and worked fairly well together, but possessed completely different personalities. Where Madison was cautious and soft-spoken, Clay was flamboyant and vociferous. On foreign policy the two men could agree; yet, while Madison approached the War of 1812 timidly, Clay strode in with defiance. Dolley Madison (seen above with her husband), who was seventeen years younger than the President, had a flair that fascinated her generation—including Clay. Both Dolley and Clay later gave their blessings to a bizarre marriage that shook Washington society in 1839—between the Baron Bodisco, minister from the Russian court, and the seventeen-year-old daughter of a government clerk, Miss Hattie Williams. Flouting etiquette by ignoring the father, the baron even arranged that Clay, one of his cardplaying cronies, would give the bride away.

but for the extraordinary character of his speech. He discussed both sides of the question, with great ability and eloquence, and certainly demonstrated, to the satisfaction of all who heard him, both that it was constitutional and unconstitutional, highly proper and improper, to prolong the charter of the bank. The honorable gentleman appeared to me in the predicament in which the celebrated orator of Virginia, Patrick Henry, is said to have been once placed. Engaged in a most extensive and lucrative practice of the law, he mistook, in one instance, the side of the cause on which he was retained, and addressed the court and jury in a very masterly and convincing speech, in behalf of his antagonist. His distracted client came up to him, while he was thus employed, and, interrupting him, bitterly exclaimed, "You have undone me! You have ruined me!" "Never mind, give yourself no concern," said the adroit advocate; and turning to the court and jury, continued his argument by observing, "May it please your honors, and you, gentlemen of the jury, I have been stating to you what I presume my adversary may urge on his side. I will now show you how fallacious his reasonings, and groundless his pretensions, are." The skillful orator proceeded, satisfactorily refuted every argument he had advanced, and gained his cause!—success with which I trust the exertion of my honorable friend will on this occasion be crowned. . . .

I conceive, then . . . that we were not empowered by the Constitution, nor bound by any practice under it, to renew the charter of this bank, and I might here rest the argument. But as there are strong objections to the renewal upon the score of expediency, and as the distresses which will attend the dissolution of the bank have been greatly exaggerated, I will ask for your indulgence for a few moments longer. That some temporary inconvenience will arise, I shall not deny; but most groundlessly have the recent failures in New York been attributed to the discontinuance of this bank. . . .

The power of a nation is said to consist in the sword and the purse. Perhaps, at last, all power is resolvable into that of the purse, for with it you may command almost every thing else. The specie circulation of the United States is estimated by some calculators at ten millions of dollars, and if it be no more, one moiety is in the vaults of this bank. May not the time arrive when the concentration of such a vast portion of the circulating medium of the country, in the hands of any corporation, will be dangerous to our liberties?

With the end of the winter session in 1811, Henry Clay left his seat in the Senate. The year before, he had decided to run for what he considered a more exciting post in the House of Representatives. Writing James Monroe on November 13, 1810, Clay explained: "Accustomed to the popular branch of a Legislature, and preferring the turbulence (if I may be allowed the term) of a numerous body to the solemn stillness of the Senate Chamber, it was a mere matter of taste that led me, perhaps injudiciously, to change my station." In his formal appeal for their votes and support, Clay addressed his Kentucky constituents:

■ I tender, fellow citizens, my services to represent you in the 12th Congress. In presenting myself to your notice, I conform to sentiments I have invariably felt, in favor of the station of an immediate representative of the people. I am not vain enough to suppose that, in the event of receiving your approbation, I shall carry with me into the House of Representatives the ability to advance in any material degree the interests of my country. All that I dare promise is, that those political principles, which have hitherto directed me, shall continue to be my guide; and that in honest zeal to promote the welfare of the nation I yield to no one.

In terms of vintage years, 1811 was an excellent one for Clay. He became a father for the sixth time when Henry Junior was born on April 10, and joyously communicated the news to his friend Caesar Rodney. The second paragraph below is the note he sent President Madison with some Kentucky wine he thought was of sufficient vintage quality to rectify an earlier wrong. And in November came the highest honor—Speaker of the House.

■ Our journey out was better than I anticipated. We reached home several weeks ago, and since our return the event which occasioned us so much solicitude, on the way, has occurred & has put me in possession of the stoutest son we ever had, with less inconvenience to Mrs. Clay than she ever before experienced. . . .

H. Clay presents his respects to Mr. Madison, & sends him a bottle of wine made from the grape of the Island of Madeira, which has been cultivated in Kentucky. He regrets that the specimen is not more ample, but it is all that he could have conveniently brought in his carriage. H. C. had the mortification to have been present some years ago at the exhibition at Mr. Jefferson's table of some Kentucky wine which, having been injured in the process of fermentation, was of a most wretched quality. The sample now sent will he flatters himself restore in some degree the credit of the wine of that State.

The Twelfth Congress, which convened in November 1811, was a youthful one. Seventy of the 142 members who composed the House of Representatives were freshmen Congressmen. Believing in a strong and independent nation, many of these young men were ready for a conflict, and considered Britain (because of its support of the Indians on the frontier and its impressment of American seamen) as the chief antagonist. Clay quickly became the leader of this group, the War Hawks, and was elected Speaker. If any single speech sums up the spirit of the War Hawks, it is the long and closely reasoned—but also rather reckless—address that Clay made on December 31, 1811. The House of Representatives was feverishly debating a bill to establish an additional military force. Clay abandoned the Speaker's chair to enter the verbal fray. In those days, few congressional speeches were recorded by a stenographer, so Clay's remarks were recorded in the third person in a number of newspapers at the time, as well as in the first volume of his speeches collected by Calvin Colton.

■ Against this army all our republican jealousies and apprehensions are attempted to be excited. He was not the advocate of standing armies; but the standing armies which excite most his fears, are those which are kept up in time of peace. He confessed he did not perceive any real source of danger in a military force of twenty-five thousand men in the United States, provided for a state only of war. . . . The diffusion of political information among the great body of the people constituted a powerful safeguard. . . . Such a people, consisting of upward of seven millions, affording a physical power of about a million of men capable of bearing arms, and ardently devoted to liberty, could not be subdued by an army of twenty-five thousand men. . . .

Mr. Clay proceeded, more particularly, to inquire into the object of the force. That object he understood distinctly to be war, and war with Great Britain. It had been supposed by some gentlemen, improper to discuss publicly so delicate a question. He did not feel the impropriety. It was a subject in its nature incapable of concealment. . . .

What are we to gain by war? has been emphatically asked. In reply, he would ask, what are we not to lose by peace? Commerce, character, a nation's best treasure, honor! If pecuniary considerations alone are to govern, there is sufficient motive for the war. Our revenue is reduced, by the operation of the belligerent edicts, to about six millions of dollars, according to the Secretary of the Treasury's report. The year preceding the embargo it was sixteen. Take away the orders in council, it will again mount up to sixteen millions. By continuing, therefore, in peace (if the mongrel state in which we are deserve that denomination), we lose annually in revenue alone ten millions of dollars. . . .

He had no disposition to magnify or dwell upon the catalogue of injuries we had received from England. He could not, however, overlook the impressment of our seamen—an aggression upon which he never reflected without feelings of indignation. . . . England is said to be fighting for the world, and shall we, it is asked, attempt to weaken her exertions? . . . What are we required to do by those who would engage our feelings and wishes in her behalf? To bear the actual cuffs of her arrogance, that we may escape a chimerical French subjugation! We are invited, conjured to drink the potion of British poison, actually presented to our lips . . . to submit to debasement, dishonor, and disgrace; to bow the neck to royal insolence, as a course of preparation for manly resistance to Gallic invasion! What nation, what individual, was ever taught, in the schools of ignominious submission, these patriotic lessons of freedom and independence? . . .

The career of encroachment is never arrested by submission. It will advance while there remains a single privilege on which it can operate. Gentlemen say that this government is unfit for any war but a war of invasion. What, is it not equivalent to invasion, if the mouths of our harbors and outlets are blocked up, and we are denied egress from our own waters? . . .

He contended, that the real cause of British aggression was, not to distress an enemy, but to destroy a rival. . . . She sickens at your pros-

By the expiration of the Embargo the Hornet will have returned with good or bad news, and of course the question of War may then be fairly decided.

The acceptance of such a Corps of Volunteers as is described, will get rid of all constitutional embarrassment, furnish a force in itself highly useful, and leave a certain quarter of the Country disposed to fly off without even a pretext for dereliction.

Yr friend
H. Clay

perity, and beholds, in your growth—your sails spread on every ocean, and your numerous seamen—the foundations of a power which, at no very distant day, is to make her tremble for her naval superiority. He had omitted before to notice the loss of our seamen, if we continued in our present situation. What would become of the one hundred thousand (for he understood there was about that number) in the American service? Would they not leave us and seek employment abroad, perhaps in the very country that injures us? He was fully persuaded, now that war was the only alternative left to us, by the injustice of one of the powers, that the support and confidence of the people would remain undiminished. He was one, however, who was prepared (and he would not believe that he was more so than any other member . . .) to march on in the road of his duty, at all hazards. What! shall it be said that our *amor patricae* [love of country] is located at these desks; that we pusillanimously cling to our seats here, rather than boldly vindicate the most inestimable rights of the country?

On June 18, 1812, the day President Madison signed a declaration of war between the United States and Great Britain, Clay wrote a friend in Kentucky:

■ By the next mail an account of our doings will be transmitted. *We shall have War, and, as I think it ought to be at present, War with England alone.* France has done us much injury, but she has foreborne, except as to her tariff, which we cannot complain of as an infraction of the public law. The balance with her is struck; tho' not paid. England has a running account with us, which every passing moment swells with the most enormous items. The blows of the one, tho' heavy and severe, are at least intermitted. With regard to the other, behind and before us is exhibited but one boundless prospect of wrong & of insult. Let us give, in return for the insolence of British cannon, the peals of American thunder. Silencing her, we can then speak to the hushed batteries of French aggression.

War fever was running high in the United States when Clay wrote this letter on March 15, 1812, to Secretary of State James Monroe. In it he proposed that the Secretary ask for an embargo of at least thirty days against British and French products, and that a declaration of war against either or both of the countries follow its termination. He also recommended that a provision be made for the recruitment of ten thousand men for a military force. Clay felt that although an embargo might hurt sales in America, it would also allow time for war preparation and for arousing public interest in the war. In addition, it would give time for the United States warship *Hornet*, which had been detained in a French port by the American minister Joel Barlow, to return bearing a commercial treaty; this might at least avoid war with France. The *Hornet*, however, returned empty-handed on May 22; there was to be no Franco-American treaty of commerce.

Clay's dissatisfaction with the President's inability to handle the war grew rapidly. On December 29, 1812, he wrote Caesar Rodney:

■ It is in vain to conceal the fact—at least I will not attempt to disguise with you—Mr. Madison is wholly unfit for the storms of War. Nature has cast him in too benevolent a mould. Admirably adapted to the tranquil scenes of peace—blending all the mild & amiable virtues, he is not fit for the rough and rude blasts which the conflicts of Nations generate. Our hopes then for the future conduct of the War must be placed upon the vigor which he may bring into the administration by the organization of his new Cabinet. And here again he is so hesitating, so tardy, so far behind the National sentiment, in his proceedings towards his War Ministers, that he will lose whatever credit he might otherwise acquire by the introduction of suitable characters in their places.

Opposition to the war was especially strong in New England, and the Federalists continued to counter the war effort. Thus Massachusetts Congressman Josiah Quincy attacked the war policy and its supporters when the bill to reinforce the army was debated in 1813. Challenging Clay and cohorts, Quincy railed: "Those must be very young politicians, their pin-feathers not yet grown, and, however they may flutter on this floor, they are not yet fledged for any high or distant flight." Quincy also charged that the Republican objective throughout the administrations of both Jefferson and Madison had been to promote a war with England while overlooking degradations caused by France. Clay answered Quincy's attack in a two-day speech eloquent in its passages defending Jefferson.

■ Gentlemen appear to me to forget, that they stand on American soil; that they are not in the British House of Commons, but in the chamber of the House of Representatives of the United States; that we have nothing to do with the affairs of Europe, the partition of territory and sovereignty there, except so far as these things affect the interests of our country. . . . I look at the political transactions of Europe, with the single exception of their possible bearing upon us, as I do the history of other countries, or other times. I do not survey them with half the interest that I do the movements in South America. Our political relation with them is much less important than it is supposed to be. I have no fears of French or English subjugation. If we are united we are too powerful for the mightiest nation in Europe, or all Europe combined. . . .

Next to the notice which the opposition has found itself called upon to bestow upon the French emperor, a distinguished citizen of Virginia formerly President of the United States, has never for a moment failed to receive their kindest and most respectful attention. An honorable gentleman from Massachusetts (Mr. Quincy), of whom I am sorry to say it becomes necessary for me, in the course of my remarks, to take some notice, has alluded [to him] in a remarkable manner. Neither his retirement from public office, his eminent services, nor his advanced age, can exempt this patriot from the coarse assaults of party malevolence. . . . In 1801, he snatched from the rude hands of usurpation the violated Constitution of his country, and that is his crime. He preserved that instrument in form, and substance, and spirit, a precious inheritance for generations to come, and for this he can never be forgiven. How vain and impotent is party rage directed against such a man! He is not more elevated by his lofty residence upon the summit of his own favorite mountain, than he is lifted, by the serenity of his mind and the consciousness of a well-spent life, above the malignant passions and bitter feelings of the day. No! his own beloved Monticello is not more moved by the storms that beat against its sides, than is this illustrious man by [these] howlings. . . . When the gentleman, to whom I have been compelled to allude . . . shall have been consigned to oblivion . . . the name of Jefferson will be hailed with gratitude, his memory honored and cherished as the second founder of the liberties of the people.

Clay's obvious discomfort with the peace terms agreed upon at Ghent is conveyed in the entry John Quincy Adams made in his diary two days before the peace treaty was signed: "Mr. Clay came to my chamber and on reading the British note [on fisheries and navigation of the Mississippi] manifested some chagrin. He still talked of breaking off the negotiation. In the evening we met, and Mr. Clay continued in his discontented humor. He was for taking time to deliberate upon the British note. . . . He was sounding all round for support in making another stand of resistance at this stage of the business. At last he turned to me and asked me whether I would not join him now and break off the negotiation. I told him, No, there was nothing now to break off on." On Christmas Day, Clay wrote a private letter to Secretary of State James Monroe disclosing his reluctant acceptance of the treaty—and his typical American interest in sightseeing:

During the second half of 1814, five Americans, including Clay, were at Ghent (seen below in a contemporary print) to negotiate peace with the British. An article by Emily Stone Whiteley in *The Virginia Quarterly Review* of January 1929 vividly describes the proceedings: "The Americans felt terribly depressed. . . . The ideas of the two [sides] were so far apart that it seemed no compromise could ever bridge the gulf. . . . Only Henry Clay took a contrary view. Clay was a great card player. . . . He suspected that the British . . . would retreat from their position. . . . The Americans always had great discussions over every paper they drew up. . . . One of the fiercest battles they had was about an article relating to the fisheries . . . tangled up with another article regarding the navigation of the Mississippi. . . . Years afterwards Henry Clay was dining with John Quincy Adams in Washington. A large fish was brought on the table. 'What is that?' Clay inquired. . . . 'A codfish from my constituents in Marblehead,' replied his host; 'shall I send you a bit of it?' Clay remembered their ancient quarrel, 'Not the least bit,' he replied. . . . 'The bones would stick in my throat like a Mississippi snag.' "

■ The terms of this instrument are undoubtedly not such as our Country expected at the commencement of the War. Judged of however by the actual condition of things, so far as it is known to us, they cannot be pronounced very unfavorable. We lose no territory, I think no honor. If we lose a particular liberty in the Fisheries, on the one hand, (which may be doubted), we gain, on the other, the exemption of the Navigation of the Mississippi from British claims. We gain also the right of exemption from the British practice of trading with the Indians. . . . I observe that I am again returned to Congress, and as I presume it will become necessary to have an Extra Session in the Spring to make the arrangements belonging to a state of peace, I am anxious to reach home, to be at my post. . . . I intend to employ the three months before me at Paris and in England to see whatever is curious or instructive.

Clay's plans for returning to the United States during the spring of 1815 went a bit awry when the Administration asked him to help negotiate a commercial treaty with the British. The day after he arrived in London in March 1815, he wrote some comment on the cowardice of certain Kentuckians at the battle of New Orleans, also disclosing effusive admiration for Napoleon.

■ The loss of the British in their New Orleans expedition is estimated at 4000. Jackson's account of the assault of the 8th. of Jan. does not essentially vary from that of the British. But for the cowardice of the Militia (and I am mortified to add a portion of my Countrymen) on the right bank of the Mississippi, Jackson states that the whole of Thornton's Corps would have been captured.

Although Clay disapproved of Napoleon's monarchical traits, he heartily approved of some results that the French emperor obtained. When it was to his partisan political advantage, Clay employed Napoleon's example to make a point. In 1818, while Napoleon was held in exile by the British, Clay remarked in a speech pressing for internal improvements: "If there were no other monument remaining of the sagacity, and of the illustrious deeds of the unfortunate captive of St. Helena, the internal improvements which he made, the road from Hamburg to Basle, would perpetuate his memory to future ages. In making these allusions, let me not be misunderstood. I do not desire to see military roads established for the purpose of conquest, but of defence; and as a part of that preparation which should be made in a season of peace for a season of war." In an engraving done after a painting by Carle Vernet, Napoleon is pictured here on the morning of the battle of Austerlitz, one of the pinnacles of his military career.

If we are to credit the papers of this morning the denoument [*sic*] of the astonishing scenes began [*sic*] in France before I left it has occurred, and Napoleon is again quietly seated on the throne. Wonderful age! wonderful man! wonderful nation! The mind is not sufficiently tranquillized to speculate on the consequences of this great event. European peace is out of the question, but who will be the parties to the new War? Will they make war upon him, or he on them? Is the same career to be run of Blockades, decrees, orders in Council, captures, confiscations, and burnings?

In the fall of 1815, Clay returned to Kentucky from the only trip he ever made to Europe. At a Lexington banquet in his honor, he replied to a toast to "our able negotiators at Ghent—their talents for diplomacy have kept pace with the valor of our arms" by showing pride in America and confidence that it had gained in world prestige:

■ Another point which appears to me to afford the highest consolation is, that we fought the most powerful nation, perhaps, in existence, single-handed and alone, without any sort of alliance. More than thirty years has Great Britain been maturing her physical means, which she had rendered as efficacious as possible, by skill, by discipline, and by actual service. Proudly boasting of the conquest of Europe, she vainly flattered herself with the easy conquest of America also. Her veterans were put to flight or defeated—while all Europe—I mean the governments of Europe—was gazing with cold indifference, or sentiments of positive hatred of us, upon the arduous contest. Hereafter no monarch can assert claims of gratitude upon us, for assistance rendered in the hour of danger. . . . The effects of the war are highly satisfactory. Abroad, our character, which at the time of its declaration was in the lowest state of degradation, is raised to the highest point of elevation. It is impossible for any American to visit Europe, without being sensible of this agreeable change, in the personal attentions which he receives, in the praises which are bestowed on our past exertions, and the predictions which are made as to our future prospects. At home, a government, which, at its formation, was apprehended by its best friends, and pronounced by its enemies to be incapable of standing the shock, is found to answer all the purposes of its institution. In spite of the errors which have been committed (and errors have undoubtedly been committed), aided by the spirit and patriotism of the people, it is demonstrated to be as competent to the objects of effective war, as it has been before proved to be to the concerns of a season of peace. Government has thus acquired strength and confidence.

Campaigning for reelection in 1816, Clay was nearly ousted by a perennial problem haunting legislators—how to justify a pay raise to cover rising costs and expenses. Congress had just increased its members' salary from about $900 to $1,500 a year. Clay had favored the bill, and if his opponent had not been against the War of 1812 (a conflict then still popular in the West), Clay might have lost his seat in the House. In a somewhat defensive speech to the voters, Clay explained his stand in logic a Congressman could well use today.

Clay was at his best, as a man and certainly as a diplomat, when ladies were around. He went out of his way to charm them, though he found it no effort at all if the ladies themselves were attractive. A handsome woman, well-turned-out, knew that when Clay was present her appearance would be properly appreciated, for he was quick to commend a fashionable gown or a new hair style. Here is part of an 1817 fashion plate that featured Empire gowns with high waists and low necklines, as well as coiffures heavy with curls and plumes—all of these reflecting an unmistakably French influence.

■ It has been said, that this measure was adopted at an improper time, when the people were burdened with taxes. What is the fact? During this same session of Congress almost every tax to which the people are subject, was either diminished or repealed. The tax on manufactures and on furniture was repealed—the tax on whiskey has been lessened, and the direct tax reduced one half. It is therefore not true, that the people are burdened with taxes—their taxes are now but trifling. And how much more do my constituents pay in consequence of this bill? I believe, on my conscience not more than one hundred dollars. . . . Yet for this paltry sum you would quarrel with your representative, a man, who has thro' a long course of years been a *faithful* if not an able servant. Did I ever neglect your interests? Have I not done all in my power to serve you? When the wide ocean separated us, when far from my wife, children, friends, and country, did I forget you, or neglect your interest? . . .

If you would quarrel with me, I beg you to select for that purpose some great and important act of my life, which is worthy of you, and not descend to a measure so trifling and so pitiful. I voted for the war. . . . I sacrificed much in its progress. . . . Go, then censure me for this, for the war, for the peace, or some other great act of my life, but do not quarrel with me for the mean, pitiful consideration of my tavern-bills at Washington.

The seeds of Andrew Jackson's future hostility toward Clay were planted in 1818–1819 with the former's swashbuckling raid into Spanish-held Florida and the latter's effort to censure him for it. According to biographer Carl Schurz, Clay made "a fine speech . . . brilliant in diction; statesmanlike in reasoning; full of stirring appeals; also undoubtedly right in its general drift of argument. But it had some very weak points. . . . Such flaws were exposed, and thus the impression was created that he had been rather quick in making his assault without having taken the trouble of thoroughly studying his case." In any case, Clay's oratory did not avail; the House of Representatives refused to censure Jackson's acts.

■ I am far from attributing to General Jackson any other than the very slight degree of blame that attaches to him as the negotiator of the treaty of Fort Jackson, and will be shared by those who subsequently ratified and sanctioned that treaty. . . . The first circumstance which, in the course of his performing that duty, fixed our attention, has filled me with regret. It was the execution of the Indian chiefs. How, I ask, did they come into our possession? Was it in the course of fair, and open, and honorable war? No; but by means of deception—by hoisting foreign colors on the staff from which the stars and stripes should alone have floated. Thus insnared, the Indians were taken on shore, and without ceremony, and without delay, were hung. . . . On the 25th of March, 1818, the President of the United States communicated a message to Congress in relation to the Seminole war, in which he declared, that although, in the prosecution of it, orders had been given to pass into the Spanish territory, they were so guarded as that the local authorities of Spain should be respected. . . . And yet on the same 25th day of March (a most singular concurrence of dates), when the representatives of the people received this solemn message, announced in the presence of the nation and in the face of the world, and in the midst of a friendly negotiation with Spain, does General Jackson write from his head-quarters, that he shall take St. Marks as a necessary dépôt for his military operations! . . .

On the 23d of May, on [General Jackson's] way home, he receives a letter from the commandant of Pensacola, intimating his surprise at the invasion of the Spanish territory, and the acts of hostility performed by the American army, and his determination, if persisted in, to employ force to repel them. . . . Could the governor have done less than write some such letter? We have only to reverse situations, and suppose him to have been an American governor. General Jackson says that when he received that letter he no longer hesitated. No . . . he did no longer hesitate. He received it on the 23d, he was in Pensacola on the 24th, and immediately after set himself before the fortress of San Carlos de Barancas, which he shortly reduced. *Veni, vidi, vici.* Wonderful energy! Admirable promptitude! Alas! that it had not been an energy and a promptitude within the pale of the Constitution. . . . It was open, undisguised, and unauthorized hostility.

THE FIRST COMPROMISE

Clay's dramatic role in the Missouri Compromise has been described on pages 31–32. Yet his own words on the subject are very revealing. Clay, while favoring the admission of Maine as a free state to balance that of Missouri as a slave state, nevertheless made a speech on the House floor on December 30, 1819, questioning the extent to which state sovereignty could be limited by the federal government. Clay's own dilemma as a slaveholder who on moral grounds was opposed to slavery but represented a slaveholding state is obvious. The speech was reported in the third person.

■ Mr. Clay (Speaker) said . . . he was not opposed to the admission of the state of Maine into the Union. . . . But, before it was finally acted on, he wished to know . . . whether certain doctrines of an alarming character . . . with respect to a restriction on the admission into the Union of states West of the Mississippi, were to be sustained on this floor. . . . Heretofore, when the population and extent of a territory had been such as to entitle a territory to the privilege of self-government and the rank of a state, the single question had presented itself to admit or reject it, without qualification. But new doctrines had sprung up on this subject; and, said he, before we take a single step to change the present relations of the members of the confederation, there should be distinct understanding between the Representatives from the various parts of the country, as to the extent to which they are to be carried. If beyond the mountains Congress can exert the power of imposing restrictions on new states—can they not also on this side of them? If, there, they can impose hard conditions—conditions which

Although Andrew Jackson was hardly partial to Indians and sometimes executed them out of hand (see opposite), he showed uncommon leniency toward William Weatherford, the half-breed depicted above who became a Creek chieftain. After the 1813 Indian massacre of five hundred whites at Fort Mims (in the Mississippi Territory), in which Weatherford took part, Jackson led a retaliatory force, and Weatherford was forced to surrender. He expected death as his due but asked that consideration be given to Creek women and children. Jackson, impressed by Weatherford's courage, spared his life, allowed him to maintain property rights, and even welcomed him as his own guest.

strike vitally at the independence and power of the states—can they not also here? If, said he, the states of the West are to be subject to restrictions by Congress, whilst the Atlantic states are free from them, proclaim the distinction at once; announce your privileges and immunities: let us have a clear and distinct understanding of what we are to expect. . . .

He thought . . . that Maine *ought* to be admitted into the Union: he thought the same of Missouri; and although he might be forced to withhold his assent to the admission of Maine, if a majority of this House should (which he trusted they would not) impose unconstitutional restrictions on the admission of Missouri, he should do it with great reluctance.

The nation's tensions over the Missouri-Maine situation is evident in two letters of early 1820 that Clay wrote his old friend Adam Beatty. The first paragraph is dated January 22. The second, dated March 4, gives some hint of the various parliamentary maneuvers needed to take the bill through the congressional labyrinth.

■ At present Spanish affairs, manufactures, and every other matter of public concern, have given way to the Missouri question, which engrosses the whole thoughts of the members, and constitutes almost the only topic of conversation. It is a most unhappy question, awakening sectional feelings, and exasperating them to the highest degree. The words, civil war, and disunion, are uttered almost without emotion, and a Senator of the United States . . . said the other day that he would rather have both than fail in the resolution. . . .

I am happy to inform you that an arrangement has been made of the Missouri subject. . . . I gave my consent to and employed my best exertions to produce this settlement of the question, and I shall be rejoiced if the community will sanction it. The question thus put at rest will I hope leave no bad consequences.

Later that same month of March 1820, under personal financial difficulties, Clay decided to retire the next year from political life until his losses had been recouped somewhat. He explained the situation in two letters written on the same day to Langdon Cheves, then president of the Bank of the United States and Clay's former War Hawk associate. First he accepts employ as the Bank's counsel. In a missive marked "private"—the second paragraph below—Clay then elaborates on the troubles confronting him:

■ I received the letter which you did me the favor to write on the 11th. inst. communicating the wish of the Bank of the U. States to engage my professional services. . . . I will engage, in its service, in the case in question, with great pleasure; and I beg you to inform the Board that I am very sensible of the honor which it does me by this manifestation of its confidence. In reference to any duty, which is likely to be incident to my appearing in behalf of the Bank, the compensation which is proposed is liberal and perfectly satisfactory. . . .

The native-born son of a Revolutionary War officer, James Tallmadge served only one term as a congressman from New York. However, just before leaving Washington he presented his anti-slavery amendment to Missouri's petition for admission to the United States. This in turn precipitated the long, angry debate that was settled only by the Missouri Compromise. Clay strongly opposed the amendment, but it was not Tallmadge who answered him. Instead, John W. Taylor, also of New York, made this sarcastic retort: "I have often admired the liberality of his [Clay's] sentiments. He is governed by no vulgar prejudices; yet with what abhorrence did he speak of the performance, by our wives and daughters, of those domestic offices which he was pleased to call servile! What comparison did he make between the 'black slaves' of Kentucky and the 'white slaves' of the north; and how instantly did he strike a balance in favor of the condition of the former."

It is my intention to resign my seat in Congress, after my return home, upon the close of the present Session. . . . I have not escaped the ravages of the pressure of the times. Some connexions of Mrs. Clay's, in whom I had great confidence, which is yet unimpaired, have involved me, by indorsing for them, in a considerable sum. . . . The obligations, imposed on me by this unexpected creation of debt and by the relations in which a parent and a husband stands, have determined me to recommence the practice of the Law. . . . I have made these explanations to you, because I am persuaded you will take some interest in what so intimately concerns me, and because they have a connexion with my engagement for the Bank, which has proceeded in some measure from your friendly regard for me.

On February 26, 1821, Clay introduced in the House the resolution to admit Missouri to the United States. His remarks on the occasion rang with pragmatic idealism.

■ I wish that my country should be prosperous, and her Government perpetual. I am in my soul assured that no other can ever afford the same protection to human liberty, and insure the same amount. Leave the North to her laws and her institutions. Extend the same conciliating charity to the South and West. Their people, as yours, know best their wants—know best their interests. Let them provide for their own—our system is one of compromises—and in the spirit of harmony come together, in the spirit of brothers compromise any and every jarring sentiment or interest which may arise in the progress of the country. There is security in this; there is peace, and fraternal union. . . . To the unrestrained energies of an intelligent and enterprising people, the mountains shall yield their mineral tribute, the valleys their cereals and fruits, and . . . millions of contented and prosperous people shall demonstrate to an admiring world . . . that man is capable of self-government.

The Missouri controversy was temporarily settled. But Clay, like many others, envisioned that the problem of slavery would plague the nation until a final solution had been attained. Langdon Cheves also was convinced that a complete answer had not yet been found. In a complimentary letter to Clay dated March 3, 1821, he wrote: "The Missouri question has done, irremediably, much evil, and the disease can never be Completely eradicated. But you have accomplished all that was Practicable & so much as leaves the Patient a whole Constitution. . . . The Constitution of the Union was in danger & has been Saved." Clay's answering letter, written two days later, shows both his determination to preserve the Union and his farsighted fear of future crises.

■ No human being could have anticipated all the tremendous consequences of the exclusion from the Union of Missouri, for any length of time. . . . Wisdom and prudence may keep us united a long time, I hope for ever. But there are natural causes, tending towards disseverance, which ought to be counteracted by an enlightened policy. There may be oc-

A German-born butcher's son who found the wilderness of America to be a source of tremendous wealth, John Jacob Astor often bailed Clay out of financial straits (such as the one described on these two pages) by lending him money. In amassing his fortune, Astor never found his lack of English spelling and grammar to be any hindrance. In an 1820 letter to Clay from Italy, Astor commented: "In Europe the Revolution is addord & admired. by all who are not in government pay in Naples it has excited much feare So much So that Several persons have been privetly excuted & I rather think that in less than 12 months the Spirit of Liberty will again Show itself on this Continent, & Should not bee Surprizd to see A genral excitement which may be beneficial to our Country. where I understand bussiness is prety bade, & every artcil exept mony receeding in value." Astor died in 1848, the richest man in the United States, leaving an estate valued at approximately $20,000,000.

casions when it is necessary even to risk a rupture of the cord which binds us together. But they ought to be occasions worthy of such a risk.

Unabashed by the embarrassment that might be caused the Administration in its negotiations with Spain over Florida, Clay kept pleading for recognition of the newly independent governments of South America and the exchange of diplomatic personnel. His speech in the House of Representatives on May 10, 1820, was a forerunner of the Monroe Doctrine and presented some of the classic arguments in favor of a new policy toward the emerging Latin nations.

Through his magnificent paintings of birds, Audubon—highly praised by Clay here—has become a patron saint of conservationists. Paradoxically, he was an ardent hunter in frontier Kentucky, where, as a twenty-three-year-old, he brought his wife in 1808. Some of his most vivid writing attests to the appeal of the Kentucky landscape and the geniality of the people: "The country was settled by planters and farmers of the most benevolent nature; and my young wife, who possessed talents far above par, was received by them all with the greatest pleasure. All the sportsmen and hunters were fond of me, and I became their companion. . . . The simplicity of those days I cannot describe; man was man, and each, one to another, a brother."

■ It is in our power to create a system of which we shall be the center and in which all South America will act with us. In respect to commerce, we shall be most benefited; this country would become the place of deposit of the commerce of the world. . . . From the character of our population, we must always take the lead in the prosecution of commerce and manufactures. Imagine the vast power of the two countries, and the value of the intercourse between them, when we shall have a population of forty millions, and they of seventy millions! In relation to South America, the people of the United States will occupy the same position as the people of New England do to the rest of the United States. Our enterprise, industry, and habits of economy, will give us the advantage in any competition which South America may sustain with us. . . .

Was there not another view of the subject, infinitely more gratifying? We should become the center of a system which would constitute the rallying-point of human freedom against all the despotism of the old world. Did any man doubt the feelings of the South toward us? In spite of our coldness toward them, of the rigor of our laws, and the conduct of our officers, their hearts still turned toward us, as to their brethren; and he had no earthly doubt, if our government would take the lead and recognize them, that they would become yet more anxious to imitate our institutions, and to secure to themselves and to their posterity the same freedom which we enjoy. . . . Let us become real and true Americans, and place ourselves at the head of the American system.

Spain, hoping to delay recognition of the Latin American republics by the United States, continued to procrastinate over the ratification of the Adams-Onís Treaty signed in 1819. On February 19, 1821, the treaty finally became effective. It provided for the establishment of the Louisiana Territory's western boundary and transferred Florida to the United States. Tangential to the acquisition of the new area was provision for a pictorial recording of the wildlife in it. Although he misspelled his candidate's name, Clay recommended John James Audubon for this job to John Quincy Adams, in a letter of 1821 from Louisville. Though dead, Alexander Wilson, a Scot who had settled near Philadelphia, was still regarded as America's foremost ornithologist.

■ I presume that the line between us and the possessions of Spain . . . on the South of us will be run in conformity to the late Treaty; and that arrangements for that purpose will be shortly made. The Government will most probably avail itself of that occasion to ascertain the natural productions &c. of the Country. Should it think proper to adopt measures for that object, I have great pleasure in recommending John Audibun Esq. of this place as a fit person to compose a part of the suite. Mr. Audibun is a French Gentleman of remarkable attainments, who has resided some fifteen or sixteen years in this State, and whose connexions by marriage and otherwise are highly respectable. He has an uncommon talent for drawing, and some of his sketches of birds &c. which I have seen greatly excel those beautiful ones taken by the late Mr. Wilson.

Clay returned to Congress in 1823 and was promptly reelected Speaker. When the bill for surveys of roads and canals was reported to the House in January 1824, he took the opportunity to enter the debate. He had some very definite and some amazingly forward-looking ideas about the federal government's need to take part in the construction and maintenance of national roads, canals, and other internal improvements. In answer to Philip P. Barbour of Virginia, Clay was foresighted and to the point.

■ The gentleman from Virginia sought to alarm us by the awful emphasis with which he set before us the total extent of post roads in the Union. Eighty thousand miles of post roads! exclaimed the gentleman; and will you assert for the general government jurisdiction, and erect turnpikes on such an immense distance? Not today, nor to-morrow; but this government is to last, I trust, forever; we may at least hope it will endure until the wave of population, cultivation, and intelligence, shall have washed the Rocky mountains and mingled with the Pacific. And may we not also hope that the day will arrive when the improvements and the comforts of social life shall spread over the wide surface of this vast continent? All this is not to be suddenly done. Society must not be burthened or oppressed. Things must be gradual and progressive. The same species of formidable array which the gentleman makes, might be exhibited in reference to the

Ever eager to press for internal improvements such as national highways, Clay took any opportunity to gain his ends. From Wheeling on April 12, 1822, he wrote to Richard M. Johnson (see picture, page 112), then senator from Kentucky, urging him to "suggest to the President [Monroe] the propriety of making" repairs on the Cumberland Road "the subject of a special message." Johnson had already introduced a bill to pay for such repairs —it was enacted but Monroe then vetoed it. Johnson had gained notoriety from the jingle—"Rumpsey, Dumpsey, Colonel Johnson killed Tecumsey"—which credited him with the death of the famed Indian, Tecumseh, during the battle of the Thames in 1813. Though this feat was never proved, it did help Johnson become Vice-President under Van Buren in 1837.

As this specimen shows, Clay had unusually neat and regular script for a busy man in public life, and his papers are easier to read today than those of most of his contemporaries. Much writing then was in a heavy hand, but Clay—probably because of his youthful years spent in copying documents for Chancellor Wythe in Virginia—used a fine goose quill. He raised geese at Ashland and had his pens made there under his personal supervision.

Can you do nothing for the Cumberland road? It is going to decay with a much greater rapidity than it was erected? Suppose you were to suggest to the President the propriety of making its reparation the subject of a special message? It would have good effect in Congress and good effect upon him. He might take that occasion to make the promised exposition of his views on the question of Internal improvements construction of a navy, or any other of the great purposes of government. We might be told of the fleets and vessels of great maritime powers which whiten the ocean; and triumphantly asked if we should vainly attempt to cope with or rival that tremendous power? And we should shrink from the effort, if we were to listen to his counsels, in hopeless despair. Yes . . . it is a subject of peculiar delight to me to look forward to the proud and happy period, distant as it may be, when circulation and association between the Atlantic and the Pacific and the Mexican Gulf, shall be as free and perfect as they are at this moment in England, or in any . . . highly improved country on the globe. In the mean time, without bearing heavily upon any of our important interests, let us apply ourselves to the accomplishment of what is most practicable and immediately necessary.

Another cornerstone of Clay's program was the protective tariff. By 1824 the man who had once argued merely for the protection of local Kentucky products such as hemp and homespun had become the complete protectionist who championed all American manufactures and believed the tariff was the best means of augmenting the nation's economic strength. The tariff proposed in January 1824, unlike the one of 1816, was designed to protect the whole manufacturing segment of the economy and not just individual products. In March, Clay spoke for two days in a lucid, persuasive, forceful argument on the principles involved. It was a full-fledged exposition of his credo, a fine example of his ability to reconcile different—somewhat clashing—interests and concerns. Defenders of the tariff have been using his contentions ever since. In this address, Clay also employed the fine overall phrase, "the American System," by which his entire program soon came to be known.

■ The greatest want of civilized society is, a market for the sale and exchange of the surplus of the produce of the labor of its members. . . . It is most desirable that there should be both a home and a foreign market. But . . . the home market is first in order, and paramount in importance. The object of the bill under consideration, is, to create this home market, and to lay the foundations of a genuine American policy. It is opposed; and it is incumbent upon the partisans of the foreign policy (terms which I shall use without any invidious intent), to demonstrate that the foreign market is an adequate vent for the surplus produce of our labor. But is it so? First, foreign nations can not, if they would, take our surplus produce. If the source of supply, no matter of what, increases in a greater ratio than the demand for that supply, a glut of the market is inevitable, even if we suppose both to remain perfectly unobstructed. . . .

It is the solemn duty of government to apply a remedy to the evils which afflict our country, if it can apply one. Is there no remedy within the reach of the government? Are we doomed to behold our industry languish and decay yet more and more? But there is a remedy, and that remedy consists in modifying our foreign policy, and in adopting a genuine AMERICAN SYSTEM. We must naturalize the arts in our country . . . by the only means which the wisdom of nations has yet discovered to be effectual;

Eleuthère Irénée du Pont de Nemours not only backed Clay's attempts to protect American manufactured goods but even advocated raising the low duties on fine cloths that were included in this tariff of 1824. He also joined Clay in supporting the efforts of the American Colonization Society to settle emancipated slaves in Africa. Du Pont came to America in 1800—along with his father, brother, and other relatives—as a French political refugee. In 1801 he returned to France to obtain machinery and plans for gunpowder mills. Founder of the famous company that still bears his name, he headed it from 1802 to 1834, building textile and gunpowder mills in the area near Wilmington, Delaware. By 1805 his munitions were being used by American warships against the Barbary pirates, and he greatly expanded his plant to meet the nation's demand for powder in the War of 1812. Du Pont himself served as an officer in the Delaware volunteer army during that conflict.

by adequate protection against the otherwise overwhelming influence of foreigners. This is only to be accomplished by the establishment of a tariff. . . .

And what is this tariff? It seems to have been regarded as a sort of monster, huge and deformed—a wild beast, endowed with tremendous powers of destruction, about to be let loose among our people, if not to devour them, at least to consume their substance. But let us calm our passions, and deliberately survey this alarming, this terrific being. The sole object of the tariff is to tax the produce of foreign industry, with the view of promoting American industry. The tax is exclusively leveled at foreign industry. . . . If it subjects any part of American industry to burdens, that is an effect not intended, but is altogether incidental, and perfectly voluntary. . . .

Our confederacy comprehends, within its vast limits, great diversity of interests: agricultural, planting, farming, commercial, navigating, fishing, manufacturing. No one of these interests is felt in the same degree, and cherished with the same solicitude, throughout all parts of the Union. Some of them are peculiar to particular sections of our common country. But all these great interests are confided to the protection of one government—to the fate of one ship—and a most gallant ship it is, with a noble crew. . . .

If the promotion of these interests would not injuriously affect any other section, then every thing should be done for them, which would be done if it formed a distinct government. If they come into absolute collision with the interests of another section, a reconciliation, if possible, should be attempted, by mutual concession, so as to avoid a sacrifice of the prosperity of either to that of the other. In . . . devising the measure, the good of each part and of the whole, should be carefully consulted. This is the only mode by which we can preserve, in full vigor, the harmony of the whole Union. . . .

Here then is a case for mutual concession, for fair compromise. The bill under consideration presents this compromise. It is a medium between the absolute exclusion and the unrestricted admission of the produce of foreign industry. It sacrifices the interest of neither section to that of the other; neither, it is true, gets all that it wants, nor is subject to all that it fears. But it has been said that the South obtains nothing in this compromise. Does it lose any thing? is the first question. I have endeavored to prove that it does not, by showing that a mere transfer is effected in the source of the supply of its consumption from Europe to America. . . . But does the South really gain nothing in this compromise? The consumption of the other sections, though somewhat restricted, is still left open by this bill, to foreign fabrics purchased by southern staples. So far its operation is beneficial to the South, and prejudicial to the industry of the other sections, and that is the point of mutual concession. . . .

Even if the benefits of the policy were limited to certain sections of our country, would it not be satisfactory to behold American industry, wherever situated, active, animated, and thrifty, rather than persevere in a course which renders us subservient to foreign industry? But these benefits are twofold, direct, and collateral, and, in the one shape or the other, they will diffuse themselves throughout the Union. All parts of the Union will participate, more or less, in both. As to the direct benefit, it is probable that the North and the East will enjoy the largest share. But the West and the South will also participate in them. . . .

To the friends of the tariff I would also anxiously appeal. Every arrangement of its provisions does not suit each of you, you desire some further alterations; you would make it perfect. You want what you will never get. Nothing human is perfect. . . .

I call, therefore, upon the friends of the American policy, to yield somewhat of their own peculiar wishes, and not to reject the practicable in the idle pursuit after the unattainable. Let us imitate the illustrious example of the framers of the Constitution, and always remembering that whatever springs from man partakes of his imperfections, depend upon experience to suggest, in future, the necessary amendments. . . . But the cause is the cause of the country, and it must and will prevail. It is founded in the interests and affections of the people. It is as native as the granite deeply imbosomed in our mountains. And, in conclusion, I would pray God, in His infinite mercy, to avert from our country the evils which are impending over it, and, by enlightening our councils, to conduct us into that path which leads to riches, to greatness, to glory.

FIRST TRY FOR THE PRESIDENCY

While Clay was evolving his political philosophy and developing his domestic and foreign policies, he was also shrewdly edging himself into position as a potential candidate for President. One of the first written proofs that he was aiming at the White House is a letter—marked "confidential"—that he wrote to General Peter B. Porter, a prominent New York politician, on April 14, 1822:

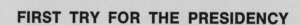 I regretted much that I did not see you as you passed, on your return from Virginia, through Washington City. I was not aware of your being in the City until after you left it. I wished to have consulted with you on a subject of great interest to me personally, and respecting which I am persuaded you do not feel altogether indifferent. Two or three years ago I thought that if the State of New York could present to the Nation a suitable Citizen to succeed Mr. Monroe, her claims were very strong, and that it would promote good feeling and the general harmony to elect him. From the present state of things it is extremely unlikely that she will bring forward any one of her own Citizens. Nor is it likely that Pennsa., which also has strong claims, will ask the general suffrage in behalf of any of her sons. For myself, if I dared indulge the hope of attaining, at any time, the Chief Magistracy, I was content to wait the termination of the period of Mr. Monroes successor, if a Northern Candidate arose who was likely to

Like Clay, Peter B. Porter was a congressional War Hawk—and so determined to see America do battle with Britain that instead of running for a third term in Congress in 1812, he joined the army. He returned to Congress two years later but resigned within a few months to pursue political interests in New York. From the tone of the letters to him printed here, it is clear that even after Porter left Washington, Clay continued to value his opinions and rely on his support. Porter's response to the first letter told Clay what he wanted to hear: "There is not a man in the U. States whom I should be more gratified to see in the presidential chair than yourself." Porter was later rewarded for his fidelity. At Clay's suggestion, President Adams appointed him Secretary of War in 1828.

unite, in any considerable degree, the general confidence. I think no such Northern Candidate will appear. In the mean time, in the South, there are springing up several candidates, my juniors in years and in the duration of the terms of our respective service. Under these circumstances my friends think that there are no public considerations which should restrain them from bringing forward my name; and I frankly confess that I do not feel myself required to discountenance or repress the exertion which they are disposed to make in my behalf. Their calculation, as to the chances of my success, is sanguine and plausible, if not solid. It is assumed that the Western States, from Ohio to the Gulph of Mexico, will be firmly and ardently united in my support. Of that I entertain no doubt. This, it is thought, will give me broader, firmer and more commanding ground than any other competitor can occupy. And, upon the supposition that there is no candidate in that portion of the union which extends from New York to North Carolina inclusive, we think that, guided by liberal & national considerations, it will, in the sequel, unite with the West.

But Clay's exclusivity as the West's candidate was short-lived. Another aspirant, General Jackson, was soon being trumpeted by his followers. Yet Clay's confidence in his own popularity is still manifest in a second "confidential" letter he wrote Porter in August 1822:

■ You will also have noticed another event, the recommendation of Genl. Jackson, by the Legislature of Tennessee, as the next President. It has excited some surprize with us, because it is believed to have been only recently thought of even in that quarter. . . . I think it may be asserted very confidently that no other Western State will lend its support to him. My friends in Tennessee continue to assure me that, if the General be out of the way, I shall receive its undivided support; and they think that it will not persist in bringing him forward, without probability of a considerable support in other States. All the information which is received from other Western States, and particularly Ohio, continues to be encouraging in the highest degree.

During this preelection period, Clay thought that his earlier clash with Jackson had been forgotten. He wrote Porter in 1823: "General Jackson has buried the hatchet and we are again on good terms." However, this did not signify that Jackson was out of the race; it just meant the differences between the two men were less evident than before. Their dispute would surface again. Meanwhile, Clay had no Vice-President to accompany him on the ticket. On February 15, 1824, in a "strictly confidential" and rather oily missive to Porter, he proposed that a New Yorker join him—hoping thus to win that influential state's numerous electoral votes.

■ The affair of the Vice-Presidency becomes one of much interest, as time elapses. My friends are desirous of running some one from your State. . . . Your unfortunate deafness forms an objection to you, and besides there is another place in which I think you can render more service to the public. Will you turn this matter over in your mind, and advise us? And I pray you to throw this note into the fire. What I have said in respect to yourself is more than I ever said in relation to any other person whatever. I trust I need not apologize to you for saying it. *You* can never misconceive the *purity* of *my* motives.

However, Clay himself was not eager to be a nominee for the Vice-Presidency. When approached for that post in August 1824, he duly replied in two letters dated September 3 and 10, excerpts from which appear in the respective paragraphs below.

■ Eight months ago, I supposed there would be no difficulty in my election as Vice-President, if my friends had thought it advisable to press me for that office. It would now be extremely difficult, if not impracticable, to effect that object, if it were desirable. My friends in the West do not attach any very great, perhaps not sufficient, importance to that station; and it would be, I apprehend, nearly impossible now to induce them to divert their support of me from the first to the second office. And if they could be prevailed on to do it, the electoral colleges would hardly be induced, by any possible exertion, to unite their individual suffrages on any other candidate for the Presidency. . . . If my Eastern friends think proper to bring me forward for the office of Vice-President . . . it is their own movement, unprompted by me. . . . It would not look well, in any respect, if it were supposed that I was instrumental in the attempt to elect me. It is certainly a high and dignified office, such as no American citizen could readily decline. . . .

Most undoubtedly the office of Vice-President is one of high respectability and great dignity, preferable, in my opinion, to any place in the cabinet. If the acceptance of it were offered to me (I mean by the public having the right to tender it), I could not decline it; but I can not seek it, much less make any sacrifices of honor or duty to obtain it.

With four strong candidates—Andrew Jackson, John Quincy Adams, William H. Crawford, and Henry Clay—aspiring to the Presidency in 1824, it was almost inevitable that the final balloting would be thrown into the House of Representatives. No one man could hope to win a clear majority. Intrigues and whispering campaigns were rampant in the country; it was rumored that Clay would withdraw in favor of Crawford. As the election approached, Clay's spirits were not dampened. He was confident that he would place at least third and thus be eligible for selection by the House. Then even this hope vanished, and Clay's disappointment is apparent in the letter he wrote to Peter Porter on December 7, 1824:

■ The event at Albany has not realized the well founded expectations of yourself and other faithful friends. Had the vote there been given to me, as you had every reason to anticipate, my entry into the H. of R. would have been secured. . . . But the causes which were nigh losing to us the vote of Ohio, and occasioned the loss of those of Illinois and Indiana—the discouragement of my friends—the power of the Atlantic press—the influence of Governmental patronage—the fabrication of tales of my being withdrawn, propagated so late as to accomplish their object before they could be contradicted—will probably transfer the vote of Louisiana from me. Thankful to my friends and especially to yourself, for their zeal, firmness and fidelity, I shall bear with great fortitude the result.

Clay displayed his bitterness more clearly to his son-in-law on December 13, writing that the commiserations he was receiving resembled "the eulogiums which are pronounced upon a man after his death. I cannot tell you who will be elected, most probably it will be either Genl. Jackson or Mr. Adams. And what an alternative that is!" However unpleasant the alternative, Clay soon made up his mind. The first paragraph below is from a letter dated December 28, 1824, that Clay wrote to George McClure, who was not a particularly close friend. The remainder of this passage is from a January 8 letter to a much closer friend, Francis P. Blair, in which Clay ironically relates the interplay of political factions in Washington. Blair, a Kentucky journalist, was a Clay supporter until he switched his allegiance to Jackson in 1825. His reward was a summons to Washington, after Jackson became President in 1829, to edit the pro-Administration newspaper, the Globe.

■ I have no hesitation in saying, that I have long since decided in favor of Mr. Adams, in case the contest should be between him and General Jackson. What I would ask, should be the distinguishing characteristic of an American statesman? Should it not be a devotion to civil liberty? Is it then compatible with that principle, to elect a man, whose sole recommendation rests on military pretensions? . . .

My position in relation to the friends of the three returned candidates is singular enough, and often to me very amusing. In the first place they all believe that my friends have the power of deciding the question, and then that I have the power of controlling my friends. Acting upon this supposition, in the same hour, I am sometimes touched gently on the shoulder by a friend, for example, of General Jackson, who will thus address me, "My dear Sir, all my dependence is upon you, don't disappoint us, you know our partiality was for you next to the hero; and how much we want a Western President." Immediately after a friend of Mr. Crawford will accost me, "The hopes of the Republican party are concentrated on you, for God's sake preserve it. If you had been returned, instead of Mr. Crawford, every man of us would have supported you to the last hour. We consider him and you as the only genuine Republican candidates." Next a friend of Mr. Adams comes with tears in his eyes, "Sir, Mr. Adams has always had the greatest respect for you, and admiration of your talents. There is no station to which you are not equal. Most undoubtedly you are the second choice of New England, and I pray you to consider seriously whether the public good and your own future interests do not

The only foreigner to be individually given dual citizenship by an American legislative body until Congress conferred it on Winston Churchill in 1963, the Marquis de Lafayette also received gifts of nearly $25,000 and a township during his triumphal tour of the United States in 1824 and 1825. Speaker Clay welcomed the sixty-seven-year-old hero (with whom he often corresponded) to Congress in December 1824 in his usual felicitous manner: "During the recent convulsions of Europe, amid, as after the dispersion of, every political storm, the people of the United States have beheld you, true to your old principles, firm and erect, cheering and animating, with your well-known voice, the votaries of liberty." Lafayette later visited Ashland, where he left as a memento the Masonic apron he had worn during a ceremony at Boston's Bunker Hill Monument. At Lexington's own celebration for Lafayette, a special ode was recited, which began:

"Our nation's great Champion
   has come to the West;
O meet him and greet him with
   hearts of devotion!
As the shades of our sires
   from the land of the blest
Would visit their sons, *he*
   has traversed old ocean.
Ye illustrious dead, can we
   e'er pay the debt
Of grateful affection to You
   and *Fayette*."

point most distinctly to the choice which you ought to make." How can one withstand all this disinterested homage and kindness? Really the friends of all three gentlemen are so very courteous and affectionate that I sometimes almost wish that it was in my power to accommodate each of them, but that being impossible, we are beginning to think seriously of the choice which we must finally make. . . . I shall, therefore, with great regret on account of the dilemma in which the people have placed us, support Mr. Adams.

When the supporters of Jackson and Crawford realized Clay was favoring Adams in the upcoming election by the House, threats and abuse replaced their cordiality described just above. Before January ended, the charges of "bargain and corruption" began (see page 39). In another letter to Francis Blair, dated January 29, a somewhat chagrined Clay reiterated his reasons for selecting Adams—but his last sentence reveals at least some doubt that even so good a friend as Blair will wholly believe him. After Clay became Adams' Secretary of State, Blair did turn Jacksonite.

■ My last letter informed you of the unction that was unceasingly applied to me by all the returned candidates for the Presidency, or rather their friends. Since then I have avowed my intention to support Mr. Adams, under actual circumstances, and thereupon the oil has been instantly transformed into vinegar. The friends of the other two have turned upon me, and with the most amiable unanimity agree to vituperate me. . . . The knaves can not comprehend how a man can be honest. They can not conceive that I should have solemnly interrogated my conscience and asked it to tell me seriously what I ought to do. That it should have enjoined me not to establish the dangerous precedent of elevating, in this early stage of the Republic, a military chieftain, merely because he has won a great victory? . . . Mr. Adams you know well I should never have selected, if at liberty to draw from the whole mass of our citizens for a President. But there is no danger in his elevation now, or in time to come. Not so of his competitor, of whom I can not believe that killing two thousand five hundred Englishmen at New Orleans, qualifies for the various, difficult, and complicated duties of the chief magistracy. I perceive that I am unconsciously writing a sort of defense, which you may possibly think implies guilt.

The balloting to determine which of the three candidates should wear the presidential mantle took place on February 9, 1825. Since many of his Kentucky constituents remained irate at his not backing Jackson, Clay issued a lengthy address to them on March 26, rationalizing in detail his vote for Adams. This document not only listed all the reasons given in the foregoing excerpts but also included a classic argument for the rights of a minority.

■ The first inquiry which it behooved me to make was, as to the influence which ought to be exerted on my judgment, by the relative state of the

Known for the lash of his biting tongue, John Randolph of Roanoke devoted more than thirty years to public life—as representative and senator from Virginia, and as envoy to Russia. He was a fighter but not a coarse man, and his venomous retaliation was often memorable because it was so colorful. Randolph once said of Edward Livingston: "Like rotten mackerel by moonlight, he shines and stinks." He was Clay's bitter enemy and fought both the American System and the Adams Administration at every opportunity, but he was at a disadvantage in the fields of economics and geography where Clay excelled. One rumor of the time had it that Randolph was buried facing the west so he could keep an eye on Henry Clay.

electoral votes which the three returned candidates brought into the House. . . . General Jackson obtained ninety-nine, Mr. Adams eighty-four, and Mr. Crawford forty-one. Ought the fact of a plurality being given to one of the candidates to have any, and what, weight? If the Constitution had intended that it should have been decisive, the Constitution would have made it decisive, and interdicted the exercise of any discretion on the part of the House of Representatives. The Constitution has not so ordained. . . . Thus a discretion is necessarily invested in the House; for choice implies examination, comparison, judgment. The fact, therefore, that one of the three persons was the highest returned, not being, by the Constitution of the country, conclusive upon the judgment of the House . . . what is the true degree of weight belonging to it? . . .

Is the fact, then, of a plurality to have no weight? Far from it. . . . The expression of the will of ninety-nine out of two hundred and sixty-one electors, is entitled to very great attention, but that will can not be considered as entitled to control the will of one hundred and sixty-two electors who have manifested a different will. To give it such controlling influence, would be a subversion of the fundamental maxim of the republic—that the majority should govern. . . . It may be an argument, a persuasion, addressed to all and each of them, but it is binding and obligatory upon none. It follows, then, that the fact of a plurality was only one among the various considerations which the House was called upon to weigh, in making up its judgment. And the weight of the consideration ought to have been regulated by the extent of the plurality. As between General Jackson and Mr. Adams, the vote standing in the proportions of ninety-nine to eighty-four, it was entitled to less weight; as between the general and Mr. Crawford, it was entitled to more, the vote being as ninety-nine to forty-one. . . .

With these views of the relative state of the vote with which the three returned candidates entered the House, I proceeded to examine the other considerations which belonged to the question. For Mr. Crawford . . . I have ever felt much personal regard. But I was called upon to perform a solemn public duty, in which my private feelings, whether of affection or aversion, were not to be indulged, but the good of my country only consulted. It appeared to me that the precarious state of that gentleman's health, although I participated with his best friends in all their regrets and sympathies on account of it, was conclusive against him, to say nothing of other considerations of a public nature, which would have deserved examination if, happily, in that respect he had been differently circumstanced. He had been ill near eighteen months. . . . He may, and I ardently hope will, recover; but I did not think it became me to assist in committing the executive administration of this great republic, on the doubtful contingency of the restoration to health of a gentleman who had been so long and so seriously afflicted. . . .

It appeared to me, then, that, sooner or later, we must arrive at the only practical issue of the contest before us, and that was between Mr. Adams and General Jackson. . . . In considering this only alternative, I was not unaware of your strong desire to have a western president; but I thought

Francis P. Blair had the fighting spirit of a Kentucky frontiersman, though he battled more fiercely with pen than with sword. Poor health forced his withdrawal from the War of 1812, but political acumen and journalistic skill won him an influential stake in national and state affairs. By the time of Clay's letter to him (opposite page), Blair not only had a thriving plantation but was also serving on Kentucky's supreme court and editing an influential newspaper, the *Argus*. Disappointed in 1824 when Clay failed to reach the presidential run-off, he was even more distressed when Clay chose to support Adams. Eventually, Blair cast his lot with Jackson, deciding that the Adams Administration was not doing enough for the West. Blair later moved to Washington, becoming one of Clay's harshest political opponents and a leading member of Jackson's "kitchen cabinet." The American government now maintains Blair House, his Washington home diagonally across Pennsylvania Avenue from the White House, as a residence for high-ranking official visitors to the capital.

When William H. Crawford was Monroe's Secretary of the Treasury, some observers in Washington felt that Crawford's oft-indulged desire to do justice to a well-spread table would bring about his untimely end, yet he lived to be sixty-two. He did have a paralytic stroke in 1823, but he recovered enough to continue his campaign for the Presidency. Van Buren, the mastermind of Crawford's campaign, thought, however, that his candidate's case would be strengthened if a coalition were struck with either Clay or Calhoun. Both men quickly refused. Van Buren was doubtless aware that Crawford's talents were no match for the statesmanship of John Quincy Adams, for the popularity of Andrew Jackson, or for Clay's ability to make real and lasting friendships.

that I knew enough of your patriotism and magnanimity, displayed on so many occasions, to believe that you could rise above the mere gratification of sectional pride, if the common good of the whole required you to make the sacrifice of local partiality. I solemnly believe it did, and this brings me to the most important consideration which belonged to the whole subject—that arising out of the respective fitness of the only two real competitors, as it appeared to my best judgment.

In speaking of General Jackson, I am aware of the delicacy and respect which are justly due to that distinguished citizen. . . . I did not believe him so competent to discharge the various, intricate, and complex duties of the office of chief magistrate, as his competitor. He has displayed great skill and bravery, as a military commander. . . . But to be qualified to discharge the duties of President of the United States, the incumbent must have more than mere military attainments—he must be a STATESMAN. An individual may be a gallant and successful general, an eminent lawyer, an eloquent divine, a learned physician, or an accomplished artist; and doubtless the union of all these characters in the person of a chief magistrate would be desirable, but no one of them, nor all combined, will qualify him to be president, unless he superadds that indispensible requisite of being a statesman. . . . If General Jackson has exhibited, either in the councils of the Union, or in those of his own State, or in those of any other State or Territory, the qualities of a statesman, the evidence of the fact has escaped my observation. . . .

It did not seem to me to be wise or prudent, if, as I solemnly believe, General Jackson's competency for the office was highly questionable, that he should be placed in a situation where neither his fame nor the public interests would be advanced. General Jackson himself would be the last man to recommend or vote for any one for a place for which he thought him unfit. . . .

Whether Mr. Adams would or would not have been my choice of a president, if I had been left freely to select from the whole mass of American citizens, was not the question submitted to my decision. I had no such liberty; but I was circumscribed, in the selection I had to make, to one of the three gentlemen whom the people themselves had thought proper to present to the House of Representatives. Whatever objections might be supposed to exist against him, still greater appeared to me to apply to his competitor. Of Mr. Adams it is but truth and justice to say, that he is highly gifted, profoundly learned, and long and greatly experienced in public affairs, at home and abroad. Intimately conversant with the rise and progress of every negotiation with foreign powers, pending or concluded; personally acquainted with the capacity and attainments of most of the public men of this country, whom it might be proper to employ in the public service; extensively possessed of much of that valuable kind of information which is to be acquired neither from books nor tradition, but which is the fruit of largely participating in public affairs; discreet and sagacious, he would enter upon the duties of the office with great advantages. I saw in his election the establishment of no dangerous example. I saw in it, on the contrary, only conformity to the safe precedents which had been established in the instances of Mr. Jefferson, Mr. Madison, and Mr. Monroe, who had respectively filled the same office. . . .

If it be unnatural in the western States to support a citizen of New England, it must be equally unnatural in the New England States to support a citizen of the West. And, on the same principle, the New England States ought to be restrained from concurring in the election of a citizen of the southern States, or the southern States from cooperating in the election of a citizen of New England. . . .

The tendency of such reasoning would be to denationalize us, and to contract every part of the Union within the narrow, selfish limits of its own section. It would be still worse; it would lead to the destruction of the Union itself. For if it be unnatural in one section to support a citizen in another, the Union itself must be unnatural; all our ties, all our glories, all that is animating in the past, all that is bright and cheering in the future, must be unnatural. . . .

The names of both the general and myself had been before the American public for its highest office. We had both been unsuccessful. . . . I never gave General Jackson nor his friends any reason to believe that I would, in any contingency, support him. He had, as I thought, no public claims, and, I will now add, no personal claims, if these ought to be ever considered, to my support. No one, therefore, ought to have been disappointed or chagrined that I did not vote for him. . . .

General Jackson fights better than he reasons. . . . Why this denunciation of those who have not repelled an invading foe, or led our armies to victory? At the very moment when he is inveighing against an objection to his election to the presidency, founded upon the exclusive military nature of his merits, does he not perceive that he is establishing its validity by proscribing every man who has not successfully fought the public enemy; and that, by such a general proscription, and the requirement of successful military service as the only condition of civil preferment, the inevitable effect would be the ultimate establishment of a military government? . . .

Fellow-citizens, I am sensible that, generally, a public officer had better abstain from any vindication of his conduct, and leave it to the candor and justice of his countrymen, under all its attending circumstances. . . . This is the first, as I hope it may be the last, occasion of my thus appearing before you. The separation which has just taken place between us, and the venom . . . of the late onsets upon my public conduct, will, I hope, be allowed in this instance to form an adequate apology.

One of the few pleasant interludes during the bitter election and the arguments over it, which raged for years afterward, came in a friendly response from Clay to Crawford in 1828:

■ I do, my dear sir, know you too well to suppose that you ever countenanced the charge of corruption against me. No man of sense and candor—at least none that know me—ever could, or did countenance it. Your frank admission that you would have voted as I did, between Mr. Adams and General Jackson, accords with the estimate I have always made of your intelligence, your independence, and your patriotism. . . . I have always entertained a lively solicitude for your welfare, and availed myself of every opportunity to inquire particularly about your health and situation. I have heard with unaffected pleasure of the improvement of your health. That it may be perfectly reestablished, and that you may be long spared for the benefit of your family, and the good of your country, is the sincere wish of your faithful friend and obedient servant.

"NO BED OF ROSES"

President-elect Adams promptly chose Clay as his Secretary of State. Knowing he would lose something whatever he did, Clay took nearly a week to accept. A letter he wrote on February 18, 1825, to one of his oldest friends, Francis T. Brooke, vividly displays the anxiety and apprehension Clay suffered while slowly reaching his decision. Brooke had become a soldier in the American Revolution at the tender age of sixteen and served as a judge in Virginia from 1804 until his death in 1851. Brooke knew him from the time Clay was a mere lad, and Clay probably trusted Brooke more than he did any other man. George Kremer, mentioned here, was a Pennsylvania congressman who made the first public charge that Adams had bribed Clay to back him by the offer of a Cabinet post.

■ When the subject of the offer of the Department of State to me was first opened to my congressional friends, there existed among them some diversity of opinion as to the propriety of my accepting it. On the one hand, it was said that, if I took it, that fact would be treated as conclusive evidence of the justice of the imputations which have been made against me; that the House of Representatives was my theater; that the administration would want me there, if it should prove itself worthy of support, more than in the cabinet; and that my own section would not like to see me translated from the legislative hall to the executive departments.

On the other hand, it was urged that, whether I accepted or declined the office, I should not escape severe animadversion; that, in the latter contingency, it would be said that the patriotic Mr. Kremer, by an exposure of the corrupt arrangement, had prevented its consummation; that the very object of propagating the calumny would be accomplished; that, conscious of my own purity of intentions, I ought not to give the weight of a feather to Mr. Kremer's affair; that there would be much difficulty in filling the administration without me; that either of the other candidates, if he had been elected, would have made me the same offer; that it would be said of me that, after having contributed to the election of a President, I thought so ill of him, that I would not take the first place under him; that he was now the constitutional head of the Government, and, as such,

I ought to regard him, dismissing any personal objections which I might have heretofore had to him; that I had, perhaps, remained long enough in the House of Representatives; and that my own section could not be dissatisfied with seeing me placed where, if I should prove myself possessed of the requisite attainments, my services might have a more extended usefulness. . . .

From the first, I determined to throw myself into the hands of my friends, and if they advised me to decline the office, not to accept it, but if they thought it was my duty, and for the public interest, to go into it, to do so. I have an unaffected repugnance to any executive employment, and my rejection of the offer, if it were in conformity to their deliberate judgment, would have been more compatible with my feelings, than its acceptance. But as their advice to me is to accept, I have resolved accordingly.

After assuming his new post, Clay wrote Francis Brooke: "I find my office no bed of roses. . . . Twelve hours work per day are almost too much for my physical frame." Clay never enjoyed desk work the way he did the lively and more variegated labors of a legislator, and thus he found the State Department very wearing compared to Congress. Carl Schurz aptly describes him as "a lion in a cage" and adds that Clay was so often sick that "he could only with difficulty be persuaded by President Adams to remain in office." But after eighteen months in the Cabinet, Clay not only was eager to justify his presence there but also ardently defended the Administration's policy on Latin America and its hedging on slavery:

■ With some, condemnation, right or wrong, is the order of the day. No matter what prudence and wisdom may stamp the measures of the administration, no matter how much the prosperity of the country may be advanced, or what public evils may be averted, under its guidance, there are persons who would make general, indiscriminate, and interminable opposition. . . . But . . . what measure of domestic policy has been proposed or recommended by the present executive, which has not its prototype in previous acts or recommendations of administrations at the head of which was a citizen of Virginia? Can the liberal and high-minded people of this State condemn measures emanating from a citizen of Massachusetts, which, when proposed by a Virginian, commanded their express assent or silent acquiescence, or to which, if in any instance they made opposition, it was respectful, limited, and qualified? The present administration desires only to be judged by its measures. . . .

What should have been the course taken with the very respectful invitation which was given to the United States to be represented at Panama? Haughtily folding your arms, would you have given it a cold and abrupt refusal? Or would you not rather accept it, send ministers, and in a friendly and respectful manner, endeavor to satisfy those who are looking to us for counsel and example, and imitating our free institutions, that there is no necessity for such an alliance; that the dangers which alone could, in the opinion of any one, have justified it, have vanished, and that it is not good for them or for us? . . . All candid and reflecting men must admit that we have great interests in connection with the southern republics, independent of any compacts of alliance. Those republics . . . comprising within their limits the most abundant sources of the precious metals, offer to our commerce, to our manufactures, to our navigation, so many advantages, that none can doubt the expediency of cultivating the most friendly relations with them. . . .

There are persons who would impress on the southern States the belief that they have just cause of apprehending danger to a certain portion of their property from the present administration. . . . However much the president and the members of his administration may deprecate the existence of slavery among us, as the greatest evil with which we are afflicted, there is not one of them that does not believe that the Constitution of the general government confers no authority to interpose between the master and his slave, none to apply an adequate remedy, if indeed there be any remedy within the scope of human power. Suppose an object of these alarmists were accomplished, and the slaveholding States were united in the sentiment, that the policy of this government, in all time to come, should be regulated on the basis of the fact of slavery, would not union on the one side lead to union on the other? And would not such a fatal division of the people and States of this confederacy produce perpetual mutual irritation and exasperation, and ultimately disunion itself? The slaveholding States can not forget that they are now in a minority.

During the last two years of Adams' Presidency, it became increasingly apparent that the Jacksonians were gaining ground. Sniped at by various factions—Southerners who hated the tariff and feared a strong central government; Northerners who wanted high tariffs; states rights' advocates and those opposing internal improvements undertaken by the federal government—Clay tried to recruit the National Republican party to support Adams. To this end, he wrote a number of letters to leading Republicans defending the Administration. The one below went to Colonel Henry Rutgers of New York, a Republican patriarch who contributed so generously to Queen's College in New Jersey that the institution demonstrated its gratitude in 1825 by changing its name to Rutgers College.

■ Long accustomed to regard you as one of the fathers of the Republican church, to which we both belong, I hope I shall be excused from that circumstance, if I am not authorized by our acquaintance, in taking the liberty of addressing this letter to you. . . .

During the administration of the father [John Adams] of our present Chief Magistrate, I was too young and too poor to take any part in the public councils; but I, nevertheless, had very decided opinions, to which I gave all the effect I could in private circles, against some of the prominent measures of that administration, and what I believed to be its tendency, if not the ultimate aim of some of its principal supporters. But I could not

A devout supporter of the Dutch Reformed Church as well as an ardent Republican and philanthropist, Colonel Henry Rutgers is said to have given one fourth of his income to charitable causes. He served in the American Revolution, helped to raise funds for the original Tammany Hall, remained active in politics, and was often the recipient of such Clay correspondence as the letter on this page. His home on the Lower East Side of New York City was thronged every New Year's Day, when Rutgers passed out cakes and books to each boy who called on him. A street in the neighborhood and a housing project next to the Manhattan Bridge now bear the family name. (Another project, La Guardia Houses, stands on the actual site of the Rutgers home.)

allow myself to transfer my dislike of the Administration of the father to the person and public character of the son, who, I firmly believe, after an acquaintance with him of more than twenty years, to be sincerely attached to our free institutions, and to the general cause of liberty. . . .

If there be one characteristic which, more than any other, distinguishes the Republican party, and of which, more than any other, they may be justly proud, it is their devotion to liberty and to the guarantees for its preservation which experience and reason demonstrate to be necessary. Does not the history of all nations and of all times prove, that the greatest danger to freedom is from mere military men? With this light before them, can [Republicans elect] a chief magistrate, who possesses no other qualification than that of being a successful military commander? I thought they could not, and yet believe that they can not.

The accusation of "bargain and sale" continued to haunt Clay throughout his years as Secretary of State. In the spring of 1827, Jackson even claimed that a Clay emissary had approached him offering the Presidency if he would not appoint Adams as Secretary of State. According to Jackson the offer was declined, and two days later Clay came out in favor of Adams. On July 12, 1827, in a speech to his constituents at Lexington, Clay both denied any such arrangement and insisted that Jackson produce evidence of his charges, which Jackson never did.

As this excerpted letter clearly demonstrates, being Secretary of State did not diminish Clay's political bent. Despite his heavy load of correspondence, he still found time for politicking. Here he writes to a New York politician, hoping to obtain a useful exchange of information. Undoubtedly overclassified as "Private and Confidential," the letter also chides the leaders of the Republican party in New York for trying to win favor for Jackson. Clay expresses here his amazement that the party "which has always been animated by a love of liberty" would "lend itself to the establishment of a principle which has subverted all Republics"— namely, choosing a military man as President.

Washington 29ᵗ Oct. 1827

Sir

(Private and Confidential)

Your favor of the 26ᵗ inst. is received. A common friend had suggested the utility of a correspondence with you, to which I urged no other objection than that of the very great extent of the correspondence by which I am already oppressed. I shall nevertheless always receive any communication from you with pleasure, and I shall be happy to transmit from this place any information which I can, with propriety, communicate.

The attempt to enlist the Republican party in your State in favor of Genl. Jackson is the most extraordinary of all the political incidents of the day. The Republican party! Which has always been animated by a love of liberty to lend itself to the establishment of a principle which has subverted all Republics.

■ For nearly two years and a half I have been assailed with a rancor and bitterness which have few examples. . . . A portion of the press devoted to the cause of General Jackson has been teeming with the vilest calumnies against me . . . a thousand times repeated. Up to this time I have in vain invited investigation, and demanded evidence. None, not a particle, has been adduced.

The extraordinary ground has been taken, that the accusers were not bound to establish by proof the guilt of their designated victim. In a civilized, Christian, and free community, the monstrous principle has been assumed, that accusation and conviction are synonymous; and that the persons who deliberately bring forward an atrocious charge are exempted from all obligations to substantiate it! And the pretext is, that the crime, being of a political nature, is shrouded in darkness, and incapable of being substantiated. But is there any real difference, in this respect, between political and other offenses? Do not all the perpetrators of crime endeavor to conceal their guilt and to elude detection? If the accuser of a political offense is absolved from the duty of supporting his accusation, every other accuser of offense stands equally absolved. Such a principle, practically carried into society, would subvert all harmony, peace, and tranquillity. None—no age, nor sex, nor profession, nor calling—would be safe against its baleful and overwhelming influence. . . .

Of all the properties which belong to honorable men, not one is so highly prized as that of character. General Jackson can not be insensible to its value, for he appears to be the most anxious to set forth the loftiness and purity of his own. How has he treated mine? During the dispensation of the hospitalities of the Hermitage, in the midst of a mixed company of individuals from various States, he permits himself to make certain state-

ments respecting my friends and me, which, if true, would forever dishonor and degrade us. The words are hardly passed from his mouth, before they are committed to paper by one of his guests . . . published in a newspaper, and thence circulated throughout the Union. And now he pretends that these statements were made "without any calculation that they were to be thrown into the public journals." . . .

What apology can be made for his failure to discharge his sacred duty as an American senator? More than two months after the alleged overture, my nomination to the office which I now hold, was made to the Senate of the United States, of which General Jackson was then a sworn member. On that nomination he had to deliberate and to act in the most solemn manner. If I were privy to a corrupt proposal to General Jackson, touching the recent election; if I had entered into a corrupt bargain with Mr. Adams to secure his elevation, I was unworthy of the office to which I was nominated; and it was the duty of General Jackson, if he really possessed the information which he now puts forward, to have moved the Senate to appoint a committee of inquiry, and by establishing my guilt, to have preserved the national councils from an abominable contamination. . . .

How can General Jackson justify to his conscience or to his country this palpable breach of his public duty? It is in vain to say that he gave a silent negative vote. He was in possession of information which, if true, must have occasioned the rejection of my nomination. It does not appear that any other senator possessed the same information. Investigation was alike due to the purity of the national councils, to me, and, as an act of strict justice, to all the other parties implicated. It is impossible for him to escape from the dilemma that he has been faithless as a senator of the United States, or has lent himself to the circulation of an atrocious calumny.

After the election, General Jackson was among the first who eagerly pressed his congratulations upon his successful rival. If Mr. Adams had been guilty of the employment of impure means to effect his election, General Jackson ought to have disdained to sully his own hands by touching those of his corrupt competitor.

In 1828, Adams ran for reelection against Jackson. Clay campaigned with his usual gusto, warmly supporting Adams. Initially, he thought Adams might be reelected. By October, however, he had his doubts and on November 14 he wrote his son, Henry Junior, then a cadet at West Point, that Jackson would "obtain the votes of Kentucky and Ohio, and perhaps of Indiana also. I consider the question as decided." A day earlier he had glumly written the first paragraph below to Adam Beatty. On November 18, hearing of a plot hatched by the editors of the National Intelligencer *to engineer Jackson's defeat, he indignantly wrote Francis Brooke the second paragraph.*

■ There is reason to apprehend that the vote of Kentucky has been given to General Jackson. . . . There is but too much probability of his election. . . . As a lover of liberty, I shall ever deeply deplore it. And the course

Amos Kendall, here seen in a later portrait, tutored Clay's children while Clay was abroad (see page 28). A New Englander, Kendall was strict where Clay might have been lax—he wrote tartly in his diary while at Ashland: "I have, I think, learned the way to be popular in Kentucky, but do not, as yet, put it in practice. Drink whiskey and talk loud, with the fullest confidence, and you will hardly fail of being called a clever fellow." Kendall's discipline was obviously needed, and Clay was pleased in 1815 with the change he saw in his sons. Writing to the tutor that December, he said: "Scarcely any circumstance upon my return to Kentucky gave me so much gratification as the improvement, both in manners and education, which my sons had made, in my absence; and I am sure that they will owe much of any success they may hereafter attain, to the impulse given by you."

Some months after Kendall left the Clay household, he was stricken with illness and Mrs. Clay sent her carriage to bring him to Ashland, where she nursed him back to health. This act of mercy won for her Kendall's deep gratitude, but he later sided with Jackson in the feud with Clay and was rewarded with a Cabinet post—Postmaster General—which he held from 1835 until 1840. In the anti-Jackson cartoon opposite, one of a series based on the nursery rhyme "The House that Jack Built," Kendall is portrayed as a rat greedily devouring government funds.

Again and again, like recurrent thunder, came the charge that Clay supported Adams only after Adams promised to make him Secretary of State. Yet Senator Thomas Hart Benton of Missouri (above), though a Jacksonian, affirmed his belief that Clay would not make a "corrupt bargain." In 1828, as hope dimmed for Adams' reelection, his supporters circulated a newspaper article suggesting that despite the "voluntary and faithful testimony" of Benton's letter to Clay, the Senator had done an about-face when addressing his constituents. An uproar ensued—but that was common enough in Clay-Benton relations. Both were slaveholders and both opposed the war with Mexico, yet for thirty years they fought each other on almost every major issue. Benton had once brawled with Jackson before becoming his chief supporter in the Senate, and Clay taunted him in Congress about this. Benton replied: "It is true, sir, that I had an affray with General Jackson. . . . We fought, sir; and we fought, I hope, like men. When the explosion was over, there remained no ill will, on either side. No vituperation or system of petty persecution was kept up between us." Because of Benton's ardent support of metal coinage over paper money—a subject on which Clay opposed him—he was nicknamed "Old Bullion." The gold coins that resulted, a great political asset for the Jacksonians, were known as "Benton's mint drops."

of my own State, should it be what I have reason to apprehend it has been, will mortify and distress me. I hope, nevertheless, that I shall find myself able to sustain with composure the shock of this event, and every other trial to which I shall be destined. . . .

A most wild and reprehensible suggestion has been made by some anonymous correspondent of the Editors of "The Intelligencer," whose letter is published in their paper of this day, to defeat the election of General Jackson, by the Electoral Colleges, or some of them, taking up a new candidate. Nothing could be more exceptionable. . . . Calamitous as I regard the election of General Jackson, I should consider the defeat of his election, at this time, by any such means, as a still greater calamity.

President-elect Jackson chose Governor Martin Van Buren of New York as his Secretary of State. Since the latter was unable to be in Washington at once, Jackson—who did not want Clay in office for even one extra hour—gave Colonel James A. Hamilton of New York a letter stating: "Sir—you are appointed to take charge of the Department of State . . . until Governor Van Buren arrives in this city." Carl Schurz dryly notes: "Colonel Hamilton did as directed, and . . . the danger that Clay might still exercise any influence was averted from the country."

The first two paragraphs below are from Clay's official statement of March 7, 1829, after retiring from office; they refer acidly to the military dictatorships then springing up in Latin America. The third paragraph, from a letter he wrote Francis Brooke on March 12, is noteworthy both for its vivid description of the atmosphere during the first few days of Jackson's "spoils system" and for its indication that Clay often had the recipients of his letters pay the mailing rates, a common practice until stamps were first used late in the 1840's. The last paragraph excerpted below—written to another friend on April 1— indicates that Clay's return to Kentucky was a triumphal tour.

■ I deprecated the election of the present President of the United States, because . . . I thought I beheld in his election an awful foreboding of the fate which, at some future (I pray to God that, if it ever arrive, it may be some far distant) day, was to befall this infant republic. All past history has impressed on my mind this solemn apprehension. Nor is it effaced or weakened by contemporaneous events passing upon our own favored continent. . . .

A majority of my fellow-citizens, it would seem, do not perceive the dangers which I apprehend from the example. Believing that they are not real, or that we have some security against their effect, which ancient and modern republics have not found, that majority . . . have chosen for chief magistrate a citizen who brings into that high trust no qualification other than military triumphs. That citizen has done me much injustice . . . inflicted, as I must ever believe, for the double purpose of gratifying private resentment and promoting personal ambition. . . . But my relations to that citizen by a recent event are now changed. He is the chief magistrate of my country. . . . Patriotism enjoins as a duty, that while he is in that exalted station, he should be treated with decorum. . . . Suppressing, as far as I can, a sense of my personal wrong; willing even to forgive him, if his own conscience and our common God can acquit him . . . I most anxiously hope, that under his guidance the great interests of our country, foreign and domestic, may be upheld, our free institutions be unimpaired, and the happiness of the nation be continued and increased. . . .

I have not written you . . . lately, because, having nothing to communicate which the papers did not contain, I did not wish to make you pay postage for the thousand rumors with which this city has been filled. Among the official corps here there is the greatest solicitude and apprehension. The members of it feel something like the inhabitants of Cairo when the plague breaks out; no one knows who is next to encounter the stroke of death; or which, with many of them is the same thing, to be dismissed from office. You have no conception of the moral tyranny which prevails here over those in employment. It is, however, believed that the work of expulsion will not begin till after [Senate] adjournment. . . .

My journey has been marked by every token of warm attachment and cordial demonstrations. I never experienced more testimonies of respect and confidence, nor more enthusiasm. Dinners, suppers, balls, etc. I have had literally a free passage. Taverns, stages, toll-gates have been generally thrown open to me, free from all charge. Monarchs might be proud of the reception with which I have been everywhere honored.

SECOND ATTEMPT TO BE PRESIDENT

Clay was ready to renew his life as country squire when he reached his residence near Lexington in April 1829. Yet the master of Ashland could never really divorce himself from politics. The classic expression of how he was torn between his two passions is a paragraph he wrote his good friend Francis Brooke as spring was brightening the Kentucky bluegrass in 1830: "I assure you, most sincerely, that I feel myself more and more weaned from public affairs. My attachment to rural occupation every day acquires more strength, and if it continues to increase another year as it has the last, I shall be fully prepared to renounce forever the strifes of public life. My farm is in fine order, and my preparations for the crop of the present year are in advance of all my neighbors. I shall make a better farmer than statesman. And I find in the business of cultivation, gardening, grazing, and the rearing of the various descriptions of domestic animals, the most agreeable resources."

But though Clay truly enjoyed cultivating his garden—and agreed with Alexander Hamilton's dictum that "a garden, you know, is a very useful refuge of a disappointed politician"—his presidential hopes kept burgeoning even higher than the lushest of his crops. Into his seventies, he dreamed of the White House. A series of three letters he wrote in 1829 to another Kentucky farmer-politician, Adam Beatty (who became a state senator in 1836), contains an ironic mixture of Clay's two prime concerns at that point: a shipment of Merino sheep—and politics. The first letter is dated June 2:

■ I have lately purchased in Washington County, Pennsylvania, fifty full-blooded Merino ewes, the choice out of three hundred, part of one of the finest flocks in the country. . . . It is my intention to let a few of my particular friends have about a dozen of them, at reasonable prices. If you wish any of them you may have your choice of an ewe with the ram lamb belonging to her, at $25 for both. . . .

Is there not danger, my dear sir, of an adverse result to the Congressional election in your district? I fear it, and I hear perhaps some things that you do not. There is much dissatisfaction among our friends in Bourbon, as I regret to learn. They think that they are entitled to the member. Can you not devise some plan to collect and concentrate public opinion in behalf of one candidate of the party of our friends? There is no one in the district that I should be more happy to see elected than yourself; and I hope, if you continue to offer, that you may be.

Clay feared that a split among the National Republicans would hand Kentucky's Second Congressional District over to his hated Jacksonian rivals for the indefinite future. But since the internecine Republican strife was continuing, he was less optimistic in his letter of July 9:

■ I view with inexpressible regret the state of things in your district, and I should be most happy to learn that any mode had been adopted to concentrate on yourself, or any other friend, the votes of those who concur in their political principles. . . . Of what avail to the present candidates on the same side, can it be to persevere, with the certainty of defeat before them all? How will the honor of any one of them be vindicated by such a

Male jackasses such as Clay's Magnum Bonum, depicted here, were used for breeding with full-sized mares to produce mules. Clay imported Achilles, the Maltese jack that sired Magnum Bonum; his dam was a jennet (female jackass) descended from the stock of George Washington, who introduced the breeding of mules to the United States. Mules, highly favored as draft animals in America and abroad, are not only cheaper to feed and maintain than horses but also are sturdier in hot climates. Even when he was aged and feeble, Clay loved to feed his livestock in person; one visitor to Ashland was startled to overhear through a partition a heated discussion between Clay and his Negro valet, Charles, who begged the elderly statesman to stay in bed on such a rainy morning, and finally persuaded him to do so by solemnly promising to go right out and feed the stock himself!

course? Defeat can neither gratify friends nor the candidate himself. . . .
The existing state of things can afford pleasure to none but our opponents.
They alone will profit by it. And I fear that it may lead, in your district,
to pernicious consequences permanently. . . . But I must leave this painful
subject, fearing, I confess, that owing to the unhappy divisions among
friends, we are destined to add another to the long catalogue of defeats,
from the same cause, which we have sustained within a few years.

I have been disappointed in not receiving the Merino sheep, which, I
presume, have been kept to be sent when the weather is somewhat cooler.
You shall be advised of their arrival.

*On September 5, Clay wrote Beatty a third letter. The arrival of the sheep
was imminent; the election had been lost.*

■ My friend . . . informs me that he sent my sheep on the 26th ultimo,
from his residence, near Washington, in Pennsylvania, in the care of a man
whose name he has omitted to mention. They were to proceed by land,
and were expected to travel at the rate of about fifteen miles per day. If
no accident has happened, they ought to be at Maysville about the time
this letter reaches you. I will thank you to take measures to secure a
knowledge of their arrival, so that you [may select those] which I have
reserved for . . . you. Should you prefer not to take the dams of the particular lambs which you may choose, you are at liberty to take other ewes,
without lambs, in lieu of them. As the weaning-time is at hand, I thought
this option might be agreeable to you. . . .

I received your favor in regard to the unfortunate issue of the election.
You have no friend who more sincerely regrets it than I do; but as that is
now unavailing, I hope, with you, that it may lead to no lasting consequences of a nature to be deprecated.

*Actually, Clay had begun planning his campaign against Jackson within
days of returning to Kentucky, hoping to lead his party to victory in 1832. He
would defend a protective tariff for American industry and urge a program of
internal improvements. At a public dinner in Lexington on May 16, 1829,
Clay started his drive by launching an all-out attack, excerpted here, on the
spoils system. One of the prime objects of his outrage was Jackson's appointment in April of Samuel Swartwout as Collector of the Port of New York, then
the most lucrative of all federal positions. Clay's vindication came ten years
later when it was discovered that Swartwout had embezzled more than a
million dollars of public funds.*

■ Government is a trust, and the officers of government are trustees; and
both the trust and the trustees are created for the benefit of the people.
Official incumbents are bound, therefore, to administer the trust, not for
their own private or individual benefits, but so as to promote the prosperity of the people. This is the vital principle of a republic. . . . In a
monarchy, all power and authority, all offices and honors, proceed from

the monarch. His interests, his caprices, and his passions, influence and control the destinies of the kingdom. In a republic, the people are every thing, and a particular individual nothing. In a monarchy, the monarch is every thing, and the people nothing. . . . If . . . the chief magistrate, as soon as he is clothed with power, proceeds to exercise it . . . upon the principle of devotion and attachment to him, and not according to the ability and fidelity with which the people are or may be served, that chief magistrate . . . is in fact, if not in form, a monarch. . . .

The president is invested with the tremendous power of dismission, to be exercised for the public good, and not to gratify any private passions or purposes. . . . But it never was in the contemplation of Congress, that the power would or could be applied to the removal of competent, diligent, and faithful officers. Such an application of it is an act of arbitrary power, and a great abuse. . . . I will not dwell on the injustice and individual distress which are the necessary consequences of these acts of authority. . . . One of the worst consequences . . . will be . . . to substitute for a system of responsibility, founded upon the ability and integrity with which public officers discharge their duties to the community, a system of universal rapacity. Incumbents, feeling the instability of their situations, and knowing their liability to periodical removals, at short terms, without any regard to the manner in which they have executed their trusts, will be disposed to make the most of their uncertain offices while they hold them. And hence we may expect innumerable cases of fraud, peculation, and corruption. . . .

I will not impute to President Jackson any design to subvert our liberties. . . . But I must say, that if an ambitious president sought the overthrow of our government, and ultimately to establish a different form, he . . . would dismiss all from public employment who did not belong to the true faith. He would stamp upon the whole official corps of government one . . . uniform principle of action. He would scatter, with an open and liberal hand, offices among the members of Congress, giving the best to those who had spoken . . . most in his behalf. He would subsidize the press. It would be his earnest and constant aim to secure the two greatest engines of operation upon public opinion—Congress and the press. . . . And when all this powerful machinery was put in operation, if he did not succeed in subverting the liberties of his country, and in establishing himself upon a throne, it would be because some new means or principle of resistance had been discovered, which was unknown in other times. . . .

The consequence of these principles would be to convert the nation into one perpetual theater for political gladiators. There would be one universal scramble for the public offices. The termination of one presidential contest would be only the signal for the commencement of another. And on the conclusion of each we should behold the victor distributing the prizes and applying his punishments, like a military commander, immediately after he had won a great victory. Congress corrupted, and the press corrupted, general corruption would ensue, until the substance of free government [would disappear].

There are a few cases of recent removal of such flagrant impropriety, as I sincerely think, that I can not forbear alluding to them. Under no administration prior to the present, from the commencement of the government, have our diplomatic representatives been recalled from abroad, on account of the political opinions they entertained in regard to a previous presidential election. . . . President Jackson has ordered home two of our foreign ministers, one filling the most important European mission, and the other the most important of our missions on this continent. In both cases the sole ground of recall is, that they were opposed to his election as president. . . .

At the most important port of the United States, the office of collector was filled by Mr. Thompson, whose removal was often urged upon the late administration by some of its friends, upon the ground of his alleged attachment to General Jackson. But the late president was immovable in his resolution to deprive no man of his office, in consequence of his political opinions or preferences. Mr. Thompson's removal was so often and so strongly pressed, for the reason just stated, that an inquiry was made of the Secretary of the Treasury, into the manner in which the duties of the office were discharged. The secretary stated that there was no better collector in the public service; and that his returns and accounts were regularly and neatly rendered, and all the duties of his office ably and honestly performed, as he knew or believed. This meritorious officer has been removed to provide a place for Mr. Swartwout, whose association with Colonel Burr is notorious throughout the United States. I put it to the candor of all who are here, to say if such a change can be justified in the port of New York, the revenue collected at which amounts to about ten millions of dollars, or more than one third of the whole revenue of the United States.

An enthusiastic political campaigner, Clay made frequent trips during his so-called retirement, to keep himself before his public. On October 5, 1829, he wrote to Josiah Johnston, then a senator from Louisiana, of such a trip.

■ I have just returned from my . . . tour to the southern part of this State. I went as far as Hopkinsville. . . . The tour was full of gratification. Every sort of enthusiastic demonstration of friendship and attachment, on the part of the people, was made toward me. Barbecues, dinners, balls, etc., etc., without number. I have been really in danger of that gout with which I have been threatened by some of the Jackson party. And tell Mrs. J. that if I had a younger heart, that also would have been in danger amid the blaze of beauty. . . . I thought the men, and women too, would devour me. I devoured many of their good dishes at their numerous festivals.

In spite of all my prudence, which nobody, I am sure, will question, I was forced to speak often and long. At Russellville, and Hopkinsville, I spoke upward of three hours together, to at least three thousand persons at each place. My addresses were never better received by all parties, nor were they ever more satisfactory to myself.

From his youth onward, Senator Johnston, to whom this exuberant letter was addressed, was Clay's close friend. He graduated from Transylvania University in 1802 when only eighteen, and became a lawyer. Unlike many Westerners of his day, Johnston did not merely keep out of brawls but actively helped settle those of others, and thus was nicknamed "the Peacemaker." Chairman of the Senate's committee on commerce, he joined Clay's strenuous fight on nullification. He was killed on May 19, 1833, by an explosion aboard the steamboat *Lioness* on the Red River, not far from Alexandria, Louisiana.

Explosions were a frequent and terrible hazard on early riverboats. Here is a contemporary account of an 1838 accident on the Ohio River similar to the one in which Johnston perished: "With a tremendous roar three of the four boilers exploded. Spectators at a distance saw a great cloud of steam and smoke mushroom several hundred feet into the air. Fragments of the boilers, pieces of timber, parts of the machinery and other debris, bodies, and fragments of bodies described great arcs through the sky and rained down on the river and adjacent shore over a considerable area. . . . Altogether there appear to have been on board some 280 persons, and . . . 150 of these lost their lives."

Robert Young Hayne, the outstanding spokesman for states' rights in the famous senatorial debates of 1830 with Webster, was described by one who knew him as "lucid, logical, with a well-balanced mind, graceful, and impassioned." Though brilliant, the South Carolinian's argument, contending that state sovereignty was not subject to judicial review, was overshadowed by Webster's answering rhetoric. Later, when Hayne, as Governor of South Carolina, joined other nullifiers in declaring that the tariffs of 1828 and 1832 would not be enforced in the state after February 1, 1833, he earned the execration of President Jackson. Old Hickory declared that Hayne was little better than Calhoun, who he thought was insane. Actually, Hayne was a relative moderate who did much to lessen South Carolina's bitterness after the state lost its nullification struggle. Hayne also clashed with Clay on the subject of protective tariffs, bitterly observing: "The manufacturers will never be satisfied."

As the unofficial leader of the National Republicans, Clay was never far removed from national politics. By the start of 1830, the Webster-Hayne debate was rocking the country and nullification rapidly became a subject of violent argument. Joining Webster—and agreeing with Jackson himself that any partition of the Union was to be avoided—Clay made a speech in Mississippi in 1830, on the benefits of the tariff to the cotton growers. The state's legislature had protested the imposition of the 1828 tariff.

■ I am aware that the people of this quarter of the Union conscientiously believe, that the tariff bears heavily on them. . . . But while claiming no immunity from error, I feel the most sincere, the deepest conviction, that the tariff . . . has been eminently beneficial. I ask leave to put two questions. . . . Has the operation of the tariff lowered the price of what you sell? . . . No, [the consumption of cotton] has increased, greatly increased; and why? Because the protection extended by this policy, has created a new customer in the American manufacturer, who takes two hundred thousand bales, without having lessened the demand for the European market. . . . Again, has the tariff increased the price of what you buy? Take the article of domestic cotton, for example; has not the American manufacturer, since the adoption of this system, afforded you a better article and at less price than before? Take [an item] manufactured in my own State. . . . Take any period, say six years before and six years since the tariff of 1824; has the average price of cotton bagging increased or diminished, in that period? I think I can appeal confidently to those around me, for the reply. We afford you a better article than the European, and at a greatly reduced price.

THE MAYSVILLE ROAD

By the summer of 1830, even partial retirement was at an end; Clay was campaigning far beyond Kentucky's borders. South Carolina, assaulting the tariff principle, was threatening the nullification it would later enact (see page 52); Jackson had struck a deadly blow at internal improvements by vetoing any federal funds for one of Clay's pet projects, the Maysville Road. In a major speech in Ohio, Clay deplored the undermining of his American System:

■ I do not march at the head of any military force. . . . I travel with my friend Charles (a black boy, residing in my family, for whom I feel the same sort of attachment that I do for my own children), without sword, pistol, or musket! . . .

With respect to the American system . . . its great object is to secure the independence of our country, to augment its wealth, and to diffuse the comforts of civilization throughout society. . . . It has increased the wealth, and power, and population of the nation. It has diminished the price of articles of consumption, and has placed them within the reach of a far greater number of our people than could have found means to command them, if they had been manufactured abroad instead of at home. . . . Cotton fabrics have diminished in price, and been improved in their texture, to an extent that it is difficult for the imagination to keep pace with. Those partly of cotton and partly of wool are also better and cheaper supplied. The same observation is applicable to those [products] which are exclusively wrought of wool, iron, or glass. . . . There is not one item of the tariff inserted for the protection of native industry, which has not fallen in price. The American competition has tended to keep down the European rival . . . and the European has tended to lower the American. Of what then can the South Carolina planter justly complain in the operation of this system? What is there in it which justifies the harsh and strong epithets which some of her politicians have applied to it? . . .

She is oppressed by a great reduction in the price of manufactured articles of consumption. She is oppressed by the advantage of two markets for the sale of her valuable staple, and for the purchase of objects required by her wants. She is oppressed by better prices for that staple than she could command, if the system to which they object did not exist. She is oppressed by the option of purchasing cheaper and better articles, the produce of the hands of American freemen, instead of dearer and worse articles, the produce of the hands of British subjects. She is oppressed by the measures of a government in which she has had, for many years, a larger proportion of power and influence, at home and abroad, than any State in the whole Union, in comparison with the population. . . .

Yet her situation has been compared to that of a colony which has no voice in the laws enacted by the parent country for its subjection! And to be relieved from this cruel state of vassalage, and to put down a system which has been established by the united voice of all America, some of her politicians have broached . . . a novel doctrine . . . that it is competent to that State to annul, within its limits, the authority of an act deliberately passed by the Congress of the United States. They do not appear to have looked much beyond the simple act of nullification, into the consequences which would ensue, and have not distinctly announced, whether one of them might not necessarily be, to light up a civil war. . . .

But nullification and disunion are not the only nor the most formidable means of assailing the tariff. Its opponents opened the campaign at the last session of Congress, and, with the most obliging frankness, have since publicly exposed their plan of operations. It is, to divide and conquer; to attack and subdue the system in detail. . . . The American system of protection should be regarded, as it is, an entire and comprehensive system, made up of various items, and aiming at the prosperity of the whole Union, by protecting the interests of each part. Every part, therefore, has a direct interest in the protection which it enjoys of the articles which its agriculture produces, or its manufactories fabricate, and also a collateral interest in the protection which other portions of the Union derive from their peculiar interests. Thus, the aggregate of the prosperity of all is constituted by the sums of the prosperity of each. . . .

The stratagem which has been adopted by the foes of the system, to destroy it, requires the exercise of constant vigilance and firmness, to prevent the accomplishment of the object. They have resolved to divide and conquer—the friends of the system should assume the revolutionary motto of our ancestors, "United we stand, divided we fall." . . . If any thing could be considered as settled, under the present Constitution of our government, I had supposed that it was its authority to construct such internal improvements as may be deemed by Congress necessary and proper to carry into effect the power granted to it. For nearly twenty-five years, the power has been asserted and exercised by the government. . . . This power, necessary to all parts of the Union, is indispensable to the West. Without it, this section can never enjoy any part of the benefit of a regular disbursement of the vast revenues of the United States. . . . Yet we are told that this power can no longer be exercised without an amendment of the Constitution. . . .

If I could believe that the executive message, which was communicated to Congress upon the application of the veto to the Maysville road, really expressed the opinion of the President of the United States . . . I would forbear to make any observation upon it. It has his name affixed to it; but it is not every paper which bears the name of a distinguished personage, that is his, or expresses his opinions. . . . The veto message proceeds to insist, that the Maysville and Lexington road is not a national but a local road, of sixty miles in length, and confined within the limits of a particular State. . . . The Maysville road was undoubtedly national. It connects the

largest body perhaps, of fertile land in the Union, with the navigation of the Ohio and Mississippi rivers, and with the canals of the States of Ohio, Pennsylvania, and New York. It begins on the line which divides the States of Ohio and Kentucky, and, of course, quickens trade and intercourse between them. Tested by the character of other works, for which the president, as a senator, voted, or which were approved by him only about a month before he rejected the Maysville bill, the road was undoubtedly national.

But this view of the matter, however satisfactory it ought to be, is imperfect. It will be admitted that the Cumberland road is national. It is completed no further than Zanesville, in the State of Ohio. On reaching that point two routes present themselves for its further extension, both national, and both deserving of execution. One leading north-westwardly, through the States of Ohio, Indiana, and Illinois, to Missouri, and the other south-westwardly, through the States of Ohio, Kentucky, Tennessee, and Alabama, to the Gulf of Mexico. Both have been long contemplated. Of the two, the south-western is the most wanted, in the present state of population, and will probably always be of the greatest use. But the north-western route is in process of execution beyond Zanesville, and appropriations toward part of it were sanctioned by the president at the last session. National highways can only be executed in sections, at different times. So the Cumberland road was and continues to be constructed. Of all the parts of the south-western route, the road from Maysville to Lexington is most needed, whether we regard the amount of transportation and traveling upon it, or the impediments which it presents in the winter and spring months. It took my family four days to reach Lexington from Maysville, in April, 1829.

The same scheme which has been devised and practiced to defeat the tariff, has been adopted to undermine internal improvements. They are to be attacked in detail. . . . But is this fair? Ought each proposed road to be viewed separately and detached? Ought it not to be considered in connection with other great works which are in process of execution, or are projected? The policy of the foes indicates what ought to be the policy of the friends of the power. . . .

Another mode of destroying the system . . . which its foes have adopted, is to assail the character of its friends. Can you otherwise account for this spirit of animosity with which I am pursued? A sentiment this morning caught my eye, in the shape of a 4th of July toast, proposed at the celebration of that anniversary in South Carolina, by a gentleman whom I never saw, and to whom I am a total stranger. With humanity, charity, and Christian benevolence, unexampled, he wished that I might be driven so far beyond the frigid regions of the northern zone, that all hell could not thaw me! Do you believe it was against me, this feeble and frail form, tottering with age, this lump of perishing clay that all this kindness was directed? No, no, no. It was against the measures of policy which I have espoused, against the system which I have labored to uphold, that it was aimed.

The need for a strong and capable leader in the United States Senate to marshal the growing opposition to Jackson became obvious by mid-1831. Even Daniel Webster put forth a plea to Clay. On October 5, 1831, he wrote from Boston: "You must be aware of the strong desire manifested in many parts of the country that you should come into the Senate: the wish is entertained here as earnestly as anywhere. We are to have an interesting and arduous session. Everything is to be attacked. . . . Not only the tariff, but the Constitution itself, in its elementary and fundamental provisions, will be assailed with talent, vigor, and union. Everything is to be debated as if nothing had ever been settled. It would be an infinite gratification to me to have your aid, or rather your lead. I know nothing so likely to be useful. Everything valuable in the government is to be fought for, and we need your arm in the fight." This is a noble tribute from one political leader to another. Clay, too, felt the time was ripe for his reentry into the national forum, but he feared he would jeopardize his hoped-for presidential candidacy if he served in the Senate. Nevertheless, he outlined his program in a letter to Francis Brooke on October 4, 1831.

■ I agree with Mr. Calhoun, that the next session of Congress is a suitable time for such a modification of the Tariff as is called for by the near approach of the payment of the public debt. . . . I think the principle of protection should be preserved unimpaired, in its application to our domestic industry; but, at the same time, that no more revenue should be collected than is necessary to an economical Administration. . . . An arrangement of the Tariff upon the principles stated, would be in conformity with what was always admitted by Southern statesmen, that is, that protection might be incidentally afforded in the collection of revenue. . . .

In regard to internal improvements, I never have thought or contended, that a single cent of duty ought to be laid or continued for their promotion. I believe the power is possessed by the general Government. In any prudent adjustment of the Tariff . . . sound policy requires that a deficit should be guarded against by laying duties enough. In some years, owing to the fluctuations of commerce, there may be a surplus. . . . Such an occasional surplus, I would apply to . . . internal improvements.

But the great resource on which I think we should rely for that object, after the payment of the public debt, is the proceeds of the sales of the public lands. There is an obvious fitness in such an appropriation. And I think that a more liberal application to the Western States ought to be made, of this fund, than to the others, for two reasons; 1st. That the public domain is there situated, and improvements in that quarter have a tendency to enhance the value of the unsold residue; 2nd. As a sort of counter-balance to the expenditures on a navy and fortifications, which are for the more immediate benefit of the maritime frontier. . . .

I think the Charter of the Bank of the United States ought to be renewed upon equitable conditions.

Clay came to Washington in December 1831 as both a Senator and a candidate for President. The tariff was the first item on Clay's agenda. During the years since 1828, the nation had prospered—and the rates of duties were amassing a surplus of revenue in the Treasury. The "Tariff of Abominations" (as it was known in the Southern states) could accordingly be reduced. Early in February 1832, Clay delivered an eloquent, three-day oration in defense of protection and against the free-trade theories of former Secretary of the Treasury Albert Gallatin, who was foreign-born himself and had sometimes clashed with Clay at Ghent. Clay's version of conditions for women working in the cotton mills was rather different from contemporary reports urging organization of the working class into labor parties as a bulwark against the sweatshop.

■ If the term of seven years were to be selected, of the greatest prosperity which this people have enjoyed since the establishment of their present Constitution, it would be exactly that period of seven years which immediately followed the passage of the tariff of 1824. This transformation of the condition of the country from gloom and distress to brightness and prosperity, has been mainly the work of American legislation, fostering American industry. . . .

The question . . . we are now called upon to determine, is not, whether we shall establish a new and doubtful system of policy, just proposed, and for the first time presented to our consideration, but whether we shall break down and destroy a long established system, patiently and carefully built up and sanctioned, during a series of years, again and again, by the nation and its highest and most revered authorities. . . .

Its beneficial effects, although they may vary in degree, have been felt in all parts of the Union. To none, I verily believe, has it been prejudicial. In the North, everywhere, testimonials are borne to the high prosperity which it has diffused. There, all branches of industry are animated and flourishing. . . . The gentleman from South Carolina has supposed that we in the West derive no advantages from this system. He is mistaken. Let him visit us, and he will find . . . the most rapid and gratifying advances. . . .

Nor has the system which has been the parent source of so much benefit to other parts of the Union, proved injurious to the cotton-growing country. . . . If cotton-planting is less profitable than it was, that is the result of increased production; but I believe it to be still the most profitable investment of capital of any branch of business in the United States. . . .

When gentlemen have succeeded in their design of an immediate or gradual destruction of the American system, what is their substitute? Free trade! Free trade! The call for free trade is as unavailing, as the cry of a spoiled child in its nurse's arms, for the moon, or the stars that glitter in the firmament of heaven. . . . We may break down all barriers to free trade on our part, but the work will not be complete, until foreign powers shall have removed theirs. . . .

Gentlemen deceive themselves. It is not free trade that they are recommending to our acceptance. It is, in effect, the British colonial system that we are invited to adopt; and, if their policy prevail, it will lead substan-

Clay's sharp attack on Gallatin excerpted here demonstrated an unpleasant facet of his character. Joseph Rogers, whose biography of Clay is quite favorable to him, says of the episode: "It was the great misfortune of Clay that he never could avoid personalities in debate. . . . He made an assault upon the aged and revered Albert Gallatin which is one of the most indefensible acts of his life. . . . When Clay made the war [of 1812] without means or men, it was Gallatin who had the terrible task of going to a poverty-stricken country, and to sections which were opposed to the war, to raise the money. . . . Moreover, Gallatin had sat with Clay . . . at Ghent, and none knew better than Clay how Gallatin's suavity and good humor had prevented a rupture among the American members. . . . This speech . . . did no credit to Clay, because it was . . . demagogy to which he seldom stooped, and never without lowering himself and injuring his own cause."

179

tially to the recolonization of these States under the commercial dominion of Great Britain. And whom do we find some of the principal supporters, out of Congress, of this foreign system? . . . There are some foreigners who always remain exotics, and never become naturalized in our country; while happily, there are many others who readily attach themselves to our principles and our institutions. . . . The gentleman to whom I am about to allude, although long a resident of this country, has no feelings, no attachments, no sympathies, no principles, in common with our people. Nearly fifty years ago, Pennsylvania took him to her bosom, and warmed, and cherished, and honored him, and how does he manifest his gratitude? By aiming a vital blow at a system endeared to her by a thorough conviction that it is indispensable to her prosperity. He has filled, at home and abroad, some of the highest offices under this government, during thirty years, and he is still at heart an alien. The authority of his name has been invoked, and the labors of his pen, in the form of a memorial to Congress, have been engaged, to overthrow the American system, and to substitute the foreign. Go home to your native Europe, and there inculcate upon her sovereigns your Utopian doctrines of free trade, and when you have prevailed upon them to unseal their ports, and freely admit the produce of Pennsylvania and other States, come back, and we shall be prepared to become converts, and to adopt your faith. . . .

The United States, at this time, manufacture one half the quantity of cotton which Great Britain did in 1816! We possess three great advantages: first, the raw material; second, water-power instead of that of steam, generally used in England; and, third, the cheaper labor of females.

Female labor in the United States was becoming commonplace by the 1830's just as Clay had opined in his speech of February 1832 (this page and next). "Lowell girls," as the women workers shown here were called, operated complex textile machinery in a former rural village of Massachusetts that was renamed after Francis Lowell. He founded the first American mill to combine all the operations needed to manufacture fabrics—carding, spinning, and weaving—under one roof. The girls, most of them drawn from New England farm families, were relatively well paid for that period—and were most watchfully chaperoned.

In England, males spin with the mule and weave; in this country, women and girls spin with the throstle, and superintend the power-loom. And can there be any employment more appropriate? Who has not been delighted with contemplating the clock-work regularity of a large cotton manufactory? I have often visited them at Cincinnati and other places, and always with increased admiration. The women, separated from the other sex, work in apartments, large, airy, well warmed, and spacious. Neatly dressed, with ruddy complexions, and happy countenances, they watch the work before them, mend the broken threads, and replace the exhausted balls or broaches. At stated hours they are called to their meals, and go and return with light and cheerful step. At night they separate, and repair to their respective houses, under the care of a mother, guardian, or friend. . . . Manufacturers have brought into profitable employment a vast amount of female labor, which, without them, would be lost to the country. . . .

Gentlemen have allowed to the manufacturing portions of the community no peace; they have been constantly threatened with the overthrow of the American system. . . . Nothing is more prejudicial to the great interests of a nation than unsettled and varying policy. . . . Let the country breathe, let its vast resources be developed, let its energies be fully put forth, let it have tranquillity, and my word for it, the degree of perfection in the arts which it will exhibit, will be greater than that which has been presented, astonishing as our progress has been. . . .

The great principle which lies at the foundation of all free governments, is, that the majority must govern; from which there is or can be no appeal but to the sword. That majority ought to govern wisely, equitably, moderately, and constitutionally, but govern it must, subject only to that terrible appeal. If ever one or several States, being a minority, can, by menacing a dissolution of the Union, succeed in forcing an abandonment of great measures, deemed essential to the interests and prosperity of the whole, the Union from that moment is practically gone. It may linger on, in form and name, but its vital spirit has fled forever!

THE LITTLE MAGICIAN

An early "victory" for the Clayites in their struggle with Jackson came in connection with Martin Van Buren. While Secretary of State, Van Buren was caught in Jackson's shuffle of his Cabinet after the Eaton affair; he was named minister to Britain (replacing the thoroughly competent Louis McLane of Delaware) and sent to London prior to approval by the Senate. The forces of Clay, Calhoun, and Webster succeeded in rejecting the nomination; after the Senate vote was tied, Vice-President Calhoun cast a deciding ballot in the negative. Calhoun exclaimed: "It will kill him, sir, kill him dead." Senator Benton's retort turned out to be correct: "You have broken a minister, and elected a Vice-President." Clay himself told the Senate:

■ I regret that I find myself utterly unable to reconcile with the duty I owe to my country a vote in favor of this nomination. . . . My main objec-

Louis McLane may have been more involved than any other man in the frequent abrupt changes among President Jackson's high officials. In 1829 he resigned from the Senate to become American envoy in London—and soon was compelled to yield that post to Van Buren. Later he became Secretary of the Treasury. but had to leave rather quickly when he dared to urge Jackson to recharter the Bank of the United States even though Jackson was already calling it "the Monster." In 1833 he became Secretary of State, but stepped down when Jackson overruled him on his policy toward France. (It may have been just an excuse, for McLane aspired to a vacancy on the Supreme Court.) Writing about this last episode, Margaret Bayard Smith—who had already commented pungently on more than three decades of the capital city's goings-on—moralized: "When the highest place is attained, is the successful occupant happier? For no sooner is it obtained than he becomes the object of abuse, and feels himself tottering in place and reputation. . . . Poor Mr. McLane, after all the sacrifices of private and domestic comfort, after all his labors and strivings, to retain his hard-earned place for so short a time!"

tion to the confirmation of his appointment arises out of his instructions to the late minister of the United States at the court of Great Britain. . . . On our side, according to Mr. Van Buren, all was wrong; on the British side, all was right. . . . We erred in too tenaciously and too long insisting upon our pretensions, and not yielding at once to the force of their just demands. And Mr. McLane was commanded to avail himself of all the circumstances in his power to mitigate our offense, and to dissuade the British government from allowing their feelings, justly incurred by the past conduct of the party driven from power, to have an adverse influence toward the American party now in power. . . . Was this becoming language from one independent nation to another? Was it proper, in the mouth of an American minister? . . . Was it not, on the contrary, the language of an humble vassal to a proud and haughty lord? Was it not prostrating and degrading the American eagle before the British lion? . . .

I have another objection to this nomination. I believe, upon circumstances which satisfy my mind, that to this gentleman is principally to be ascribed the introduction of the odious system of proscription [with] the dismission of clerks in his department, known to me to be highly meritorious. . . . It is a detestable system, drawn from the worst periods of the Roman republic, and if it were to be perpetuated—if the offices, honors, and dignities of the people were to be put up to a scramble, and to be decided by the results of every presidential election—our government and institutions, becoming intolerable, would finally end in a despotism as inexorable as that at Constantinople. . . .

The necessity under which we are placed is painful. But it is no fault of the Senate, whose consent and advice are required by the Constitution, to consummate this appointment, that the minister has been sent out of the United States without their concurrence. I hope that the public will not be prejudiced by his rejection, if he should be rejected.

The Senate's rejection of Van Buren's nomination did indeed backfire. Jackson groomed Van Buren, also nicknamed the "Little Magician," as his protégé and heir apparent—much to Clay's scorn. An overly smug letter to Francis Brooke in February 1832 observed:

■ Every thing is going on well. Van Buren, old Hickory, and the whole crew, will, I think, in due time, be gotten rid of. The attempt to excite public sympathy in behalf of the Little Magician has totally failed; and I sincerely wish that he may be nominated as Vice-President. That is exactly the point to which I wish to see matters brought. Do urge our Jackson friends (if there be any that you can approach) to nominate him on the 28th. It will be so consistent that they should support him who is, or at least pretends to have been, for the Tariff, and oppose all others who are for it.

By April, Clay was far less smug. Another intimate letter to his devoted friend Brooke betrays his annoyance with the incessant intrigues of the nation's capital as well as some worry about his health. The form of tobacco that he wished to "quit" was probably the pipe, though it may have been chewing; Clay's close associate, John Crittenden, chewed—and even spat on the floor at dinner parties. Clay continued to use snuff for many more years.

■ I have received your affectionate letter of the 23d instant, and the interest which it manifests in my health and prosperity has affected me sensibly. Among the many circumstances to disgust me with life and my fellow man, the warmth, fidelity, and duration of your friendship have ever been a source of cheering satisfaction. You have described, I believe correctly, the true causes of my indisposition; and your advice is full of wisdom. Naturally ardent, perhaps too ardent, I can not avoid being too much excited and provoked by the scenes of tergiversation, hypocrisy, degeneracy, and corruption which are daily exhibited. I would fly from them, and renounce forever public life, if I were not restrained by a sentiment of duty, and of attachment to my friends. I shall endeavor to profit by your kindness, and to avoid as much as possible, in future, all causes of irritation. I have quit the use of tobacco, in one of the two forms to which I had been accustomed, and will gradually discontinue the other.

Another major issue in 1832 concerned the public lands. Clay's enemies in the Senate devised a maneuver to hamper his campaign for President. They had the Committee on Manufactures, in which Clay was prominent, consider lowering the price of these lands. This committee report was then countered by one from the Committee on Public Lands, where the matter should have gone in the first place. In a Senate speech on June 20, 1832, Clay assailed the procedure. A rather remarkable address, it is nonetheless amusing to present-day readers because the prognostications he made for America's growth are so far from what has actually occurred. Unfortunately for Clay, his opposition to cheap lands did lose him many Western votes.

■ It may not be amiss again to allude to the extraordinary reference of the subject of the public lands . . . to the committee on manufactures—a committee than which there is not another standing committee of the Senate, whose prescribed duties are more incongruous with the public domain. . . . I could not be insensible to the embarrassment in which the committee on manufactures was placed, and especially myself. Although any other member of that committee could have rendered himself, with appropriate researches and proper time, more competent than I was to understand the subject of the public lands, it was known that, from my local position, I alone was supposed to have any particular knowledge of them. Whatever emanated from the committee was likely, therefore, to be ascribed to me. If the committee should propose a measure of great liberality toward the new States, the old States might complain. If the measure [leaned] toward the old States, the new might be dissatisfied. . . .

No subject which had presented itself to the present, or perhaps any preceding Congress, was of greater magnitude than that of the public

An American phenomenon, tobacco was a mainstay of the nation's agricultural economy and a cash crop in Virginia as early as 1612. A tall, large-leaved plant (above), it is usually cultivated as an annual and transplanted as a small plant to the field after being nurtured in hotbeds from seeds. When tobacco is fully mature, the leaves are harvested, or gathered along with the stalk, and cured, fermented, and aged so that the harsh taste of the fresh leaves develops into an agreeable aroma. Requiring a warm climate and amply watered but adequately drained soil, tobacco is grown successfully in the southeastern United States. About 60 percent of the one billion tons now produced in the country is grown in North Carolina and Kentucky. As Clay notes in this letter, the noxious effects of tobacco on the human system have long been apparent, though only in recent years has tobacco's direct link to lung cancer and other dread ailments been scientifically corroborated.

lands. . . . There is public land enough to found an empire; stretching across the immense continent, from the Atlantic to the Pacific ocean, from the Gulf of Mexico to the northwestern lakes, the quantity, according to official surveys and estimates, amounting to the prodigious sum of one billion and eighty millions of acres! . . . During the past year, when the greatest quantity was sold that ever, in one year, had been previously sold, it amounted to less than three millions of acres. . . . [At that rate] it would require three hundred years to dispose of them. But the sales will probably be accelerated from increased population, and other causes. We may safely, however, anticipate that long, if not centuries, after the present day, the representatives of our children's children may be deliberating in the halls of Congress, on laws relating to the public lands. . . .

In a national point of view, one of the greatest advantages which these public lands in the West, and this system of settling them, affords, is the resource which they possess against pressure and want, in other parts of the Union, from the vocations of society being too closely filled, and too much crowded. They constantly tend to sustain the price of labor, by the opportunity which they offer, of the acquisition of fertile land at a moderate price, and the consequent temptation to emigrate from those parts of the Union where labor may be badly rewarded.

The progress of settlement, and the improvement in the fortunes and condition of individuals, under the operation of this beneficent system, are as simple as they are manifest. Pioneers of a more adventurous character, advancing before the tide of emigration, penetrate into the uninhabited regions of the West. They apply the axe to the forest, which falls before them, or the plow to the prairie, deeply sinking its share in the unbroken wild grasses in which it abounds. They build houses, plant orchards, enclose fields, cultivate the earth, and rear up families around them. Meantime, the tide of emigration flows upon them, their improved farms rise in value, a demand for them takes place, they sell to the new comers, at a great advance, and proceed further west, with ample means to purchase from government, at reasonable prices, sufficient land for all the members of their families. Another and another tide succeeds, the first pushing on westwardly the previous settlers, who, in their turn, sell out their farms, constantly augmenting in price, until they arrive at a fixed and stationary value. In this way thousands, and tens of thousands, are daily improving their circumstances, and bettering their condition. I have often witnessed this gratifying progress. . . . What other nation can boast of such an outlet for its increasing population, such bountiful means of promoting their prosperity, and securing their independence?

To the public lands of the United States, and especially to the existing system by which they are distributed with so much regularity and equity, are we indebted for these signal benefits in our national condition. And every consideration of duty, to ourselves, and to posterity, enjoins that we should abstain from the adoption of any wild project that would cast away this vast national property, holden by the general government in sacred trust for the whole people of the United States, and forbids that we should rashly touch a system which has been so successfully tested by experience . . .

There are good men in different parts, but especially in the Atlantic portion, of the Union, who have been induced to regard lightly this vast national property; who have been persuaded that the people of the West are dissatisfied with the administration of it; and who believe that it will, in the end, be lost to the nation, and that it is not worth present care and preservation. But these are radical mistakes. The great body of the West are satisfied, perfectly satisfied, with the general administration of the public lands. They would indeed like, and are entitled to, a more liberal expenditure among them of the proceeds of the sales. For this, provision is made by the bill to which I will hereafter call the attention of the Senate . . . but the great body of the West have not called for, and understand too well their real interest to desire, any essential change in the system of survey, sale, or price of the lands. There may be a few, stimulated by demagogues, who desire change; and what system is there, what government, what order of human society, in which a few do not desire change?

The bill proposes a division of the net proceeds of the sales of the public lands, among the several States composing the Union, according to their federal representative population, as ascertained by the last census; and it provides for new States that may hereafter be admitted into the Union. The basis of the distribution, therefore, is derived from the Constitution itself, which has adopted the same rule, in respect to representation and direct taxes. None could be more just and equitable. . . .

The States, each judging for itself, will select among the objects enumerated in the bill, that which comports best with its own policy. There is

Clay's long speech on the public lands, here excerpted, included a passage printed on these two pages paying deserved tribute to the intrepid pioneers who steadily kept penetrating their nation's still unsettled wilderness. This old engraving, which originally accompanied an article in a German magazine narrating the rigors of the early American West, vividly illustrates Clay's description of how such adventuresome souls "apply the axe to the forest, which falls before them." A settler's small clearing encourages another pioneering family, complete with covered wagon, to take a repose before continuing west. Scattered about are stumps of trees cut down before the planting of crops can begin. The rude log cabin's lean-to affords some nighttime protection from the wild animals of the forest for the cattle, pigs, and poultry seen grubbing about for nourishment in haphazard fashion.

185

no compulsion in the choice. Some will prefer, perhaps, to apply the fund to the extinction of debt, now burdensome, created for internal improvement; some to new objects of internal improvement; others to education; and others again to colonization. It may be supposed possible that the States will divert the fund from the specified purposes. But against such a mis-application we have, in the first place, the security which arises out of their presumed good faith; and, in the second, the power to withhold subsequent, if there has been any abuse in previous, appropriations. . . .

Whatever may be the fate of the particular proposition now under consideration, I sincerely hope that the attention of the nation may be attracted to this most interesting subject; that it may justly appreciate the value of this immense national property; and that preserving the regulation of it by the will of the whole, for the advantage of the whole, it may be transmitted, as a sacred and inestimable succession, to posterity, for its benefit and blessing for ages to come.

The most important round of Clay's political bout with Jackson in 1832 came over renewal of the charter for the national Bank (see page 51). Passed by Congress, the bill was vetoed by Jackson in July. Reiterating Clay's own arguments of 1811 against the Bank, Old Hickory pulled a tremendous political coup by contending that the Bank was extracting money from the pockets of the poor to fill the pockets of the rich. Falsely confident that Jackson's act would split the Democratic party between proponents and adversaries of the Bank, Clay spoke as follows against the President's use of the veto, also justifying his 1811 position and asserting that Jackson's interpretation of the Constitution would lead to anarchy.

■ A bill to re-charter the bank, has recently passed Congress, after much deliberation. . . . Not withstanding this state of things, the president has rejected the bill, and transmitted to the Senate an elaborate message, communicating at large his objections. . . .

I voted, in 1811, against the old bank of the United States, and I delivered, on that occasion, a speech, in which, among other reasons, I assigned that of its being unconstitutional. . . . During a long public life (I mention the fact not as claiming any merit for it), the only great question on which I have ever changed my opinion, is that of the bank of the United States. . . . In 1816, being Speaker of the House of Representatives, it was perfectly in my power to have said nothing and done nothing, and thus have concealed the change of opinion my mind had undergone. But I did not choose to remain silent and escape responsibility. I chose publicly to avow my actual conversion. The war and the fatal experience of its disastrous events had changed me. Mr. Madison . . . and almost all the public men around me . . . changed their opinions from the same causes.

At the commencement of this session, in his annual report, the Secretary of the Treasury stated his reasons at large, not merely in favor of a bank, but in support of the renewal of the charter of the existing bank. Who could have believed that that responsible officer was communicating to

Congress opinions directly adverse to those entertained by the president himself? When before has it happened, that the head of a department recommended the passage of a law which, being accordingly passed and presented to the president, is subject to his veto? What sort of a bank it is, [that the president has in mind as a substitute], with a project of which the president would have deigned to furnish Congress, if they had applied to him, he has not stated. In the absence of such statement, we can only conjecture that it is his famous treasury bank, formerly recommended by him, from which the people have recoiled with the instinctive horror excited by the approach of the cholera. . . .

There are some parts of this [veto] message that ought to excite deep alarm; and that especially in which the president announces, that each public officer may interpret the Constitution as he pleases. His language is, "Each public officer, who takes an oath to support the Constitution, swears that he will support it as he understands it, and not as it is understood by others. . . . The opinion of the judges has no more authority over Congress than the opinion of Congress has over the judges; and on that point the president is independent of both." Now . . . all men are bound to obey the laws, of which the Constitution is the supreme; but must they obey them as they are, or as they understand them? If the obligation of obedience is limited and . . . if the party is bound to obey the Constitution only *as he understands it;* what would be the consequence? . . . We should have nothing settled, nothing stable, nothing fixed. There would be general disorder and confusion throughout every branch of administration, from the highest to the lowest officers—universal nullification.

The Jackson ground swell, however, could not be halted by any of Clay's tirades. The President's veto of the Bank's recharter increased his popularity, and Clay lost to him by a landslide. In December 1832, with all the returns in, a disgruntled Clay wrote the ever-faithful Francis Brooke: "It is useless to dwell on the issue of the presidential election, respecting which we were so greatly disappointed. From whatever causes it proceeded, it is now irrevocable." A letter to Brooke on January 17, 1833, disclosed the extent of his private despair and lack of self-assurance. Clay presented a far better front when he was in the public eye.

■ As to politics, we have no past, no future. After forty-four years of existence under the present Constitution, what single principle is fixed? The Bank? No. Internal Improvements? No. The Tariff? No. Who is to interpret the Constitution? We are as much afloat at sea as the day when the Constitution went into operation. There is nothing certain but that the will of Andrew Jackson is to govern; and that will fluctuates with the change of every pen which gives expression to it. As to the Tariff, now pending before the House, whether it will pass or no in that body depends upon his command. . . . Any plan that I might offer would be instantly opposed, because I offered it. Sometimes I have thought that, considering how I have been and still am treated by both parties (the Tariff and the

For thirteen years (1823–1836) Nicholas Biddle was president of the second Bank of the United States. Acclaimed as a financier, Biddle was also a shrewd editor and a bookworm; his slightly edited 1814 journal of the Lewis and Clark expedition was a first-rate travelogue. One critic, however—the young and irreverent nineteen-year-old George Templeton Strong, whose diaries are a prime source of nineteenth-century social history—even found fault with Biddle's love of books. After a visit to Appleton's Bookstore in New York, Strong jotted in his diary: "I noticed a gigantic basket full of [books], and it turned out to be an assortment selected last night by the distinguished Mr. Nick Biddle—about as trashy as the rest. . . . If Mr. B. has no more skill as a financier than as a collector of books, he's very little of a loss to the U.S. bank." When the Bank lost its federal charter in 1836, a new one was acquired from the state of Pennsylvania. Biddle retired in 1839 and the Bank failed two years later. A trial on a criminal charge and the loss of his personal fortune left Biddle a disheartened, disillusioned man at the end of his life.

Anti-Tariff), I would leave them to fight it out as well as they can. The lingering hopes for my country prevail over these feelings of a just resentment, and my judgment tells me, that disregarding them, I ought to the last to endeavor to do what I can to preserve its institutions and re-establish confidence and concord. I shall act in conformity with this judgment, but I am far from being sanguine that I have the power to effect any thing.

THE COMPROMISE OF 1833

The shining proof of Clay's continuing statesmanship, despite his inner doubts, came within weeks of the discouraged letter printed just above. He rose magnificently to the occasion when crisis gripped the nation. By its defiant Ordinance of Nullification, South Carolina had refused to comply with the tariffs of 1824 and 1832. So recently and decisively rejected at the polls, Clay could simply have sat back and enjoyed his victorious rival's embarrassment. Instead, he made an impassioned Senate speech on February 12, not only offering a workable compromise on the tariff but imploring the states to remain at peace. It was one of his finest hours.

■ In presenting the modification of the tariff laws, which I am now about to submit, I have two great objects in view. My first object looks to the tariff. I am compelled to express the opinion, formed after the most deliberate reflection, and on full survey of the whole country, that . . . the tariff stands in imminent danger. The sudden repeal of the tariff policy

Seated before a door opening on a porch bordered by palmetto trees (from which South Carolina acquired its nickname—the Palmetto State), this Southern lady actively expresses her protest of the "Tariff of Abominations" by stitching away gracefully at a blue cockade fastened to a gentleman's hat by a palmetto button. Wearing such a cockade expressed militant support for the doctrine of nullification. Other Southerners, antipathetic to the separatist cause, festooned themselves with American eagles to symbolize their unshaken loyalty to the Union.

would bring ruin and destruction on the whole people of this country. There is no evil, in my opinion, equal to the consequences which would result from such a catastrophe. . . .

I will now take up some of the objections which will be made to [my] bill. It may be said that the act is prospective, that it binds our successors, and that we have no power thus to bind them. It is true that the act is prospective, and so is almost every act which we ever passed, but we can repeal it the next day. It is the established usage to give all acts a prospective operation. . . . In the next place, it will be objected to the bill, by the friends of the protective policy, of whom I hold myself to be one . . . that it abandons the power of protection. . . . There are four modes by which the industry of the country can be protected.

First, the absolute prohibition of rival foreign articles. . . . Second, the imposition of duties in such a manner as to have no reference to any object but revenue. . . . The third mode was attempted last session . . . and . . . finally passed both Houses. This was to raise as much revenue as was wanted to the use of the government, and no more, but to raise it from the protected and not from the unprotected articles. . . . I regret most deeply that the greater part of the country will not suffer this principle to prevail. It ought to prevail; and the day . . . will come, when it will be adopted as . . . permanent policy. . . . Shall we legislate for our own wants or that of a foreign country? To protect our own interests in opposition to foreign legislation was the basis of this system. The fourth mode . . . is to admit free of duty every article which aided the operations of the manufacturers. . . . To those who say the bill abandons the power of protection, I reply, that . . . the fourth mode . . . is extended and upheld by the bill. . . .

All parties may find in this measure some reasons for objection. And what human measure is there which is free from objectionable qualities? . . . It may be true that there will be loss and gain in the measure. But how is this loss and gain distributed? Among our countrymen. . . . The distribution is founded on that great principle of compromise and concession which lies at the bottom of our institutions, which gave birth to the Constitution itself, and which has continued to regulate us in our onward march, and conducted the nation to glory and renown. . . .

When I came to take my seat on this floor, I had supposed that a member of this Union had taken an attitude of defiance and hostility against the authority of the general government. I had imagined that she had arrogantly required that we should abandon at once a system which had long been the settled policy of this country. . . . But . . . I find that South Carolina does not contemplate force. . . . She disclaims it; and asserts that she is merely . . . endeavoring by her civil tribunals to prevent the general government from carrying the laws of the United States into operation within her limits. . . . Her appeal is not to arms, but to another power; not to the sword, but to the law. . . . Her purposes are all of a civil nature. She thinks she can oust the United States from her limits. . . . I venture to predict that [South Carolina] must ultimately fail in her attempt. . . . Nullification has been put down, and put down in a manner more effectually than by a thousand wars or a thousand armies—by the irresistible force, by the mighty influence of public opinion. Not a voice beyond the single State of South Carolina has been heard in favor of the principle of nullification, which she has asserted by her own ordinance; and I will say, that she must fail in her lawsuit. . . . I wish to see war of no kind; but, above all, I do not desire to see civil war. When war begins, whether civil or foreign, no human sight is competent to foresee when, or how, or where it is to terminate. But when a civil war shall be lighted up in the bosom of our own happy land, and armies are marching, and commanders are winning their victories, and fleets are in motion on our coast, tell me, if you can, tell me, if any human being can tell its duration. God alone knows where such a war would end. In what a state will our institutions be left? In what a state [afterward will we find] our liberties? I want no war; above all, no war at home. . . .

I think South Carolina has been rash, intemperate, and greatly in the wrong; but I do not want to disgrace her, nor any other member of this Union. . . . Has not the State of South Carolina been one of the members of this Union in "days that tried men's souls?" Have not her ancestors fought alongside our ancestors? If we had to go into a civil war with such a State, how would it terminate? Whenever it should have terminated, what would be her condition? If she should ever return to the Union, what would be the condition of her feelings and affections? what the state of the heart of her people? She has been with us before, when her ancestors mingled in the throng of battle, and as I hope our posterity will mingle with hers, for ages and centuries to come, in the united defense of liberty, and for the honor and glory of the Union, I do not wish to see her degraded or defaced as a member of this confederacy.

In conclusion, allow me to intreat and implore each individual member of this body to bring into the consideration of this measure which I have had the honor of proposing, the same love of country which, if I know myself, has actuated me, and the same desire of restoring harmony to the Union, which has prompted this effort. If we can forget for a moment—but that would be asking too much of human nature—if we could suffer, for one moment, party feelings and party causes—and, as I stand here before my God, I declare I have looked beyond those considerations, and regarded only the vast interests of this united people—I should hope that under such feelings, and with such dispositions, we may advantageously proceed to the consideration of this bill, and heal, before they are yet bleeding, the wounds of our distracted country.

Another telling blow had been aimed at the American System. First, internal improvements; then, the Bank; and now, the protective tariff had been undermined. Clay, however, was philosophical and willing to sacrifice part of his own aims for the sake of the Union. A letter to Francis Brooke two days after he had submitted his legislation is evidence of his political reappraisal. Within three weeks, his Compromise Tariff was enacted, and the country rang with praise for him as the Great Pacificator.

You will see in the papers that I have presented [my plan] to the Senate in the shape of a bill. I was fully aware of all the personal consequences, and personal risks to which I exposed myself; but "what is a public man worth that will not sacrifice himself, if necessary, for the good of his country?" The measure has been well secured. Still every contrivance will be resorted to by the Van Buren men, and by some of the Administration party, to prostrate or defeat the project. That, you know, I anticipated. What will be the final issue of the plan, I can not certainly say. I hope for success.

The summer respite from congressional duties afforded Clay the opportunity of returning annually to his beloved Ashland. In a May 1833 letter to Francis Brooke, he showed his delight in his livestock, and outlined a trip north, planning to visit his son James, then a clerk in a Boston mercantile house. Certain that Jackson's successor would be unbeatable, he also expressed his lack of interest in running for President in 1836.

Since my return from Washington, I have been principally occupied with the operations of my farm, which have more and more interest for me. . . . I have the Maltese ass, the Arabian horse, the merino and Saxe merino sheep, the English Hereford and Durham cattle, the goat, the mule, and the hog. The progress of these animals from their infancy to maturity, presents a constantly-varying subject of interest. . . . Then, our fine green sward, our natural parks, our beautiful undulating country, every where exhibiting combinations of grass and trees, or luxuriant crops, all conspire to render home delightful. Notwithstanding, I shall leave it early in July, to make a journey which I have long desired to perform. I

These two icehouses with conical roofs, built under Clay's supervision, still stand only a few yards from his mansion at Ashland (see pages 116–117). The icehouses and the other immediate surroundings (including the stable, with a handsome carriage presented by businessmen of Newark, New Jersey, who warmly appreciated Clay's work for protective tariffs), now form part of a memorial shrine to Clay almost as reflective of his varied interests as Monticello is of Jefferson's. From the open door a flight of steps leads down into the cool earth heaped up around the thick walls. Ice was cut in blocks on neighboring ponds during the coldest days of winter, then insulated here with plenty of sawdust to keep melting at a minimum even on the hottest days of summer. The doors were opened only when some ice was needed. Thus Clay and his guests could enjoy heavily frosted mint juleps and other chilled drinks.

Roger B. Taney's appointment as Attorney General in 1831 was a surprise to many, for he was a rather unprepossessing Maryland lawyer. His name rhymed with "scrawny," and no more fitting adjective exists to describe him. His eyes squinted from near-sightedness, his voice was flat, his clothing was rumpled, but he fought so ably in Jackson's war on the Bank of the United States that he was named Secretary of the Treasury in 1833 (a calculated move described here). The Senate rejected him, and subsequently turned down his appointment to the Supreme Court. But before long, the Jacksonians won a Senate majority and Taney's appointment to succeed John Marshall as Chief Justice was then confirmed. During his tenure of twenty-eight years, he aroused the ire of Republicans by supporting slavery laws in the Dred Scott case. Taney's decision against Scott, however, was based on his view that Negroes could not be citizens. He, nevertheless, disapproved of slavery, set his own slaves free, and as a Roman Catholic often waited in line behind Negroes at confession.

shall go through Ohio to Lake Erie, thence to Buffalo, Niagara, Montreal, Quebec, Saratoga, and toward September, to Boston, where I have a young son of sixteen. The papers have attributed to me an intention of visiting New England, as if it were the principal object of my excursion. It is the least important one, and I should not go there but for the sake of my son. I intend traveling with as much privacy as practicable, and absolutely to decline every species of public entertainment. . . .

I doubt very much whether any successful opposition can be made against General Jackson's designated successor. The press, patronage, and party, will probably carry him triumphantly through. I have borne the taunts of the Jackson party and principles long enough. The country has not thought proper to sustain my exertions. Distinguished men, who could not possibly have viewed things differently from me, have stood by with a cold indifference, without lending any helping hand. What can one man do alone against a host? . . . I want repose. I have reached a time of life when all men want it. I shall not neglect the duties which belong to one who has aimed to be a good citizen, and a patriot, even in retirement; but the country had better try other sentinels, not more devoted or zealous, but who may be more successful than I have been.

The cholera epidemic that ravaged Kentucky in the summer of 1833 caused Clay to cancel his northern trip. Reluctant to leave home, he explained the situation in a letter dated July 22 to Edward Everett, then a Massachusetts congressman and later governor of the state, president of Harvard, and widely considered the finest orator of his time.

■ We have indeed had a terrible time of it at Lexington, and in other parts of Kentucky, with the cholera. The accounts which have reached you are probably not much exaggerated. But I have reason to be thankful for the signal exemption from loss with which we have been blessed. In a family of about sixty, white and black, we have had no death; and the connections, both of Mrs. Clay and myself, have been generally equally fortunate. . . . The apprehension that the cholera might visit my family in my absence, determined me to abandon my northern journey, from which I had anticipated so much satisfaction. I regret it extremely, but you will readily conceive how painful my situation would have been if, when distant from my residence, I had heard that it was here.

CONTINUED CLASH OVER THE BANK

The conflict with Jackson over the Bank continued to rage during the 1833–1835 period. Hoping to destroy the institution completely, the President decided to withdraw all the public funds on deposit there. But since Secretary of the Treasury Louis McLane favored the Bank, Jackson shuffled his Cabinet again in 1833 and replaced him with William J. Duane. When Duane also proved obstinate in bending to Jackson's will, he was removed and Roger B.

Taney was shifted from Attorney General to the Treasury in the fall of 1833. The public deposits were duly transferred, and Congress met in December in a spirit of rebellion. Clay, Webster, and Calhoun jointly challenged Old Hickory's action. The acrimonious Senate debate centered not so much on the Bank's constitutionality as on the extension of the President's power over the Treasury. In the first part of the nineteenth century, many Americans still clung to the theory that the Constitution placed the Departments of State and War under direct authority of the President, while the Treasury was more under the jurisdiction of Congress. Agreeing with this interpretation—one which Jackson soon made dead as a dodo by demonstrating that the Chief Executive had far more power than any of his predecessors in the office had ever dreamed of using—Clay addressed the Senate as follows:

■ We can now deliberately contemplate the vast expansion of executive power, under the present administration, free from embarrassment. And is there any real lover of civil liberty, who can behold it without great and just alarm? . . . Instead of having a balanced government with three coordinate departments, we have but one power in the State. . . . All the officers concerned in the administration of the laws are bound to obey the president. . . . The will of the president, even in opposition to their own deliberate sense of their obligations, is to prevail, and expulsion from office is the penalty of disobedience! . . .

The basis of this overshadowing superstructure of executive power is, the power of dismission, which it is one of the objects of the bill under consideration somewhat to regulate. . . . The practical exercise of this power, during this administration, has reduced the salutary co-operation of the Senate, as approved by the Constitution, in all appointments, to an idle form. Of what avail is it, that the Senate shall have passed upon a nomination, if the president, at any time thereafter, even the next day, whether the Senate be in session or in vacation, without any known cause, may dismiss the incumbent? . . . Is not a power so exercised essentially a despotic power? It is adverse to the genius of all free governments, the foundation of which is responsibility. Responsibility is the vital principle of civil liberty, as irresponsibility is the vital principle of despotism. . . . But is not the president absolutely irresponsible in the exercise of this power? How can he be reached? By Impeachment? It is a mockery. . . .

The power of removal, as now exercised, is nowhere in the Constitution expressly recognized. The only mode of displacing a public officer, for which it does provide, is by impeachment. But it has been argued, on this occasion, that it is a sovereign power, an inherent power, and an executive power; and, therefore, that it belongs to the president. . . . Sovereign power is supreme power; and in no instance whatever is there any supreme power vested in the president. Whatever sovereign power is, if there be any, conveyed by the Constitution of the United States, is vested in Congress, or in the president and Senate. The power to declare war, to lay taxes, to coin money, is vested in Congress; and the treaty-making power in the president and Senate. . . .

Educator, editor, politician, statesman, and cabinet minister, Edward Everett, to whom Clay addressed the letter opposite, had frequent contact and correspondence with the Kentuckian. When Everett was editor of *The North American Review*, a nominally Whig publication, he occasionally took issue with the party. The protective tariff, for instance, was a Clay measure Everett criticized. Clay and Everett also disagreed about interpretation of the Constitution, causing Clay to write: "The government can not go out of the Constitution, and appeal to our existence as a Nation for a source of power. If the Union were dissolved, the Nation would [exist only] in the shape of the 24 Sovereign states which compose it." Everett was asked to give the principal address when the Gettysburg cemetery was dedicated, while Lincoln was merely requested to speak briefly. But after the ceremony, Everett assessed it shrewdly and promptly; he told the President that his two-hour speech had not got as close to the heart of the occasion as Lincoln's address had in the space of only two minutes.

As President, Jackson combined the steel-ribbed authority of a troop commander with the spirit of a backwoodsman lusting to fight. The power of the presidential office was notably expanded by the thrust of his energy. His temper could be fierce. Provoked by Clay, he was heard to exclaim: "Oh, if I live to get these robes of office off me, I will bring that rascal to a dear account." Jackson never carried out this threat—though just after he left the White House he expressed sorrow that he had not shot Clay or hanged Calhoun.

Inherent power? That is a new principle to enlarge the powers of the general government. Hitherto it has been supposed, that there are no powers possessed by the government of the United States, or any branch of it, but such as are granted by the Constitution; and, in order to ascertain what has been granted, that it was necessary to show the grant, or to establish that the power claimed was necessary and proper to execute some granted power. In other words, that there are no powers but those which are expressed or incidental. But it seems that a great mistake has existed. The partisans of the executive have discovered a third and more fruitful source of power. Inherent power! Whence is it derived? The Constitution created the office of president, and made it just what it is. It had no powers prior to its existence. It can have none but those which are conferred upon it by the instrument which created it, or laws passed in pursuance of that instrument. Do gentlemen mean, by inherent power, such power as is exercised by the monarchs or chief magistrates of other countries? If that be their meaning, they should avow it.

It has been argued, that the power of removal from office is an executive power; that all executive power is vested in the president; and that he is to see that the laws are faithfully executed, which, it is contended, he can not do, unless, at his pleasure, he may dismiss any subordinate officer. The mere act of dismission or removal may be of an executive nature, but the judgment or sentence which precedes it is a function of a judicial, and not executive nature. Impeachments, which, as has been already observed, are the only mode of removal from office expressly provided for in the Constitution, are to be tried by the Senate, acting as a judicial tribunal. . . .

The president's oath obliges him to do no more than every member of Congress is also bound by official oath to do; that is, to support the Constitution of the United States, in their respective spheres of action. In the discharge of the duties specifically assigned to him by the Constitution and laws, he is forever to keep in view the Constitution; and this every member of Congress is equally bound to do, in the passage of laws. To step out of his sphere: to trench upon other departments of the government, under the notion that they are about to violate the Constitution, would be to set a most pernicious and dangerous example of violation of the Constitution. . . .

The power of removal from office not being one of those powers which are expressly granted and enumerated in the Constitution, and having I hope successfully shown that it is not essentially of an executive nature, the question arises, to what department of the government does it belong, in regard to all offices created by law, or whose tenure is not defined in the Constitution? . . . It is the legislative authority which creates the office, defines its duties, and may prescribe its duration. I speak, of course, of offices not created by the Constitution, but the law. The office coming into existence by the will of Congress, the same will may provide how, and in what manner the office and the officer shall both cease to exist. It may direct the conditions on which he shall hold the office, and when and how he shall be dismissed. . . . It would be unreasonable to contend that, although Congress, in pursuit of the public good, brings the office and officer into being, and assigns their purposes, yet the president has a control over the officer which Congress can not reach or regulate; and this control, in virtue of some vague and undefined implied executive power, which the friends of executive supremacy are totally unable to attach to any specific clause in the Constitution. . . .

The principal object of the bill, is, to require the president, in cases of dismission, to communicate the reasons which have induced him to dismiss the officer; in other words, to make an arbitrary and despotic power a responsible power. . . . And yet this mild regulation of the power is opposed by the friends of the administration! They think it unreasonable that the president should state his reasons. If he has none, perhaps it is. . . .

It is contended, that the president can not see that the laws are faithfully executed unless he possesses the power of removal. . . . It will be a sufficient security against the abuses of subordinate officers, that the eye of the president is upon them, and that he can communicate their delinquency. . . . It may be said, that there are certain great officers, heads of departments and foreign ministers, between whom and the president entire confidence should exist. That is admitted. But, surely, if the president remove any of them, the people ought to know the cause.

The angry Senate debate over the censure of Jackson dragged on for three months; Clay's resolution that the President had overextended his authority eventually passed by a 26-to-20 vote. Each year thereafter the Democrats tried to get the resolution expunged from the Senate Journal. In 1837 they finally succeeded in accomplishing what they wanted and the unhappy phrases were struck out (see page 57). But Clay himself continued to condemn Jackson at every opportunity. In 1836, for example, he wrote a revealing letter to Francis Brooke.

■ If a President may name his successor, and bring the whole machinery of the Government, including its one hundred thousand dependents, into the canvass; and if by such means he achieves a victory, such a fatal precedent as this must be rebuked and reversed, or there is an end of the freedom of election. No one doubts that this has been done. And no reflecting man can doubt that, having been once done, it will be again attempted, and unless corrected by the people, it will become, in time, the established practice of the country.

Clay was extremely upset by congressional behavior during the last years of Jackson's Administration, when the new Whig party was slowly emerging (see pages 54–55). He felt that the members' lack of courage in the face of Jackson's continued provocations was unforgivable, and stated as much in a letter to Francis Brooke on February 10, 1837. Returned to the Senate by his ever-faithful Kentucky supporters, he confided to his long-time friend that he probably would not complete his term.

Van Buren, the eighth President, was a frequent adversary of Clay, but their relationship was sprinkled with spiked banter. On one occasion, goaded by Clay during a speech in 1834 attacking the Jackson Administration, Van Buren (then Vice-President) left his chair as presiding officer, sauntered across the Senate chamber, and stopped before his tormentor. "Mr. Clay," he asked, "may I borrow a pinch of your excellent snuff?" Stymied, Clay handed over his snuffbox, Van Buren thanked him, bowed, and proceeded out of the room. Another instance occurred during a dinner at the White House. Clay and other guests were seated at the table when a servant reported that the kitchen was in flames. Clay turned to Van Buren and remarked: "Mr. President, I am doing all I can to get you out of this house, but I assure you I do not want to burn you out." Just prior to the election of 1840, Clay encountered Van Buren in the latter's political bailiwick—upstate New York. "I hope I do not obstruct your way," Van Buren said. "Not here, certainly," retorted his opponent.

■ The majority [of the Senate] was reminded that they alone possessed the power to vindicate the privileges of the Senate against the Executive encroachments. But they all remained mute; not one venturing to offer any motion. Such is the degradation to which Congress is reduced! You congratulate me on my acceptance of the new appointment recently conferred on me to the Senate. I think you ought to have condoled and sympathized with me, because, by the force of circumstances, I was constrained to remain in a body, in the humiliated condition in which the Senate now is. I shall escape from it as soon as I decently can, with the same pleasure that one would fly from a charnel-house.

While Clay often refused to pit himself against Jackson's heir apparent, Martin Van Buren, he did not remove himself from a possible candidacy opposing the Little Magician in 1840. His intimations are clear in a letter he wrote to a "Committee of Gentlemen in New York" on August 6, 1837. This is careful wording by a prospective presidential candidate.

■ I have not, for several years, looked to the event of my being placed in the chair of Chief Magistrate, as one that was probable. . . . While I am not insensible to the exalted honor of filling the highest office within the gift of this great people, I have desired retirement from the cares of public life; and although I have not been able fully to gratify this wish, I am in the enjoyment of comparative repose, and looking anxiously forward to more. I should be extremely unwilling, without very strong reasons, to be thrown into the turmoil of a presidential canvass. . . . If I were persuaded that a majority of my fellow-citizens desired to place me in their highest executive office, that sense of duty by which I have been ever guided would exact obedience to their will. Candor obliges me, however, to say that I have not seen sufficient evidence that they entertain such a desire. Entertaining these feelings and sentiments, I think it best for the present to adhere to the passive position which I have prescribed to myself.

Relatively few of Clay's personal letters to his wife and children survive, yet those that are available provide a real glimpse of his devotion to his family. On his way to Washington in November 1835, Clay wrote a concerned letter to Lucretia from Maysville, where he often boarded a boat for the trip upstream on the Ohio. His wife had not come with him because she was so worried about the critical illness of their daughter (see page 59). Thomas Metcalfe, Governor of Kentucky from 1828 to 1832, lived about midway between Lexington and Maysville and Clay often spent the night at his home. Aaron Dupuy was a household slave who long served as Clay's personal body servant. His wife Charlotte was emancipated in 1840.

■ I got to Governor Metcalfe's, last night, in good time, and reached here to-day, at two o'clock. The weather has been very fine, and my ride was a very good one. They tell me that a steamboat will be here this evening, in which, when it arrives, I shall embark. I have directed Aaron to go to

Governor Metcalfe's to-morrow night, and the next day home. I feel very uneasy about our dear daughter, Anne. I sincerely hope that she may get well, and that all my apprehensions may prove groundless. I feel too, my dear wife, most sincerely and excessively alive respecting your lonely situation. I regret it extremely, and whatever you may think to the contrary, I should have preferred, greatly, your accompanying me. But I hope and believe that this is the last separation, upon earth, that will take place, for any length of time, between us. And I hope that you will make every effort in your power to be cheerful, contented, and happy.

Because of his indecisive nature, James Brown Clay, one of the youngest members of a large family, was a constant source of concern to his father. After attending Transylvania University and serving as a clerk for two years in a Boston firm, at nineteen the young man went to Missouri, where he became interested in agriculture. It was there that Clay addressed this letter to him on May 26, 1837.

■ Just as I was making preparations for my trip to St. Louis, and had resolved to start in a few days, the proclamation of the President arrived, calling Congress on the first of September. I shall be obliged to leave home, to reach Washington in time, about the middle of August. Consequently I have only two months and a half to attend to my private affairs. . . . I am compelled, therefore, to abandon my contemplated journey for the present. I assure you, my dear son, that I do it with great regret; for I wanted much to see you, and to see your place and the improvements you have made upon it.

As I can not go to see you, you must come to see me. You will yourself judge of the most convenient time for you to leave home, and come here. . . . Should you want money to bring you home, you must inform me, or if there be not time to inform me, draw upon me.

On returning from Congress in the fall of 1837, Clay wrote another letter to James. Obviously his son's venture in Missouri was not a great success.

Clay was adhering to the custom of his times when he signed this earliest surviving letter to his wife: "H. Clay." Even the most loving letters of that era normally closed with a formal signature instead of a "Henry"—much less a "Harry." He wrote this to Lucretia from Liverpool in 1815, when a sea voyage was still an extremely hazardous undertaking that required precautions not usually accompanying other modes of travel. About to embark for America, Clay was careful to send this missive by another ship and enclose with it a copy of a power of attorney and an accounting of financial transactions he had entered upon while in Europe. He thus hoped "to guard against any accidents which may attend me." The "outfit" mentioned was a payment given by the State Department to each representative of the American government. It was intended to defray expenses incurred by entertaining, traveling, and living abroad.

The 1835 letter to his wife printed on these pages also indicates the geographical distances that often separated the couple. She had little desire for public life; besides, Ashland badly needed her attention. Clay's biographer Joseph Rogers states: "The estate was large and the slaves numerous. She superintended every operation. She arose first in the morning and was the last to retire."

money. On the other side is a memorandum of charges agt. the U. States which are to be brought forward on Settlement of my account, besides my outfit and Salary

Yr. affectionate husband
H. Clay

Lexington was Clay's hometown for fifty-five years. During the first three decades of the nineteenth century, it was the nation's leading cultural center west of the Appalachians, as well as the economic center of that area until the depression of 1819, from which the town only slowly recovered. This vista of the city in its early years confirms the favorable impression recorded by travelers. In 1810 the ornithologist Alexander Wilson wrote happily: "The numerous shops piled with goods, and the many well-dressed females I passed in the streets; the sound of social industry, and the gay scenery of 'the busy haunts of men,' had a most exhilarating effect on my spirits. . . . It has numerous excellent institutions for the education of the youth, a public library, and a well-endowed University. . . . Lexington at present can boast of men who do honor to science, and of females whose beauty and amiable manners would grace the first circles of society." In 1816 another observer, Samuel R. Brown, reported with satisfaction: "Main street presents to the traveler as much wealth and more beauty than can be found in most of the Atlantic cities. . . . The inhabitants are as polished, and . . . as luxurious as those of Boston, New York, or Baltimore; and their assemblies and parties are conducted with as much ease and grace, as in the oldest towns in the union."

■ I have been quite uneasy about you, but hope that you have escaped sickness. You ought to be very careful with yourself, for your Missouri fevers are very dangerous. I am sorry to hear of the great loss you have sustained in sheep; and I am now convinced more than ever that it is unwise for you to keep them. . . . I think you had better fatten what remain and sell them for mutton. I expect to remain at home until late in November, and then proceed again to Washington, although I am very tired of so frequently crossing the mountains.

By the end of 1837, James had decided to study history and then law. His delighted father promptly forwarded a bibliography for commencing his studies in history, as well as providing some cogent advice about study hours.

■ Your resolution to study, and to begin with history, is a good one, and I hope you will persevere in it. Gillie's Greece, with Plutarch's Lives; Gibbon's Rise and Fall of the Roman Empire; Tacitus; Hume, with the continuation; Russell's Modern Europe; Hallam's Middle Ages; Robertson's Charles V., Indies, etc.; Marshall's Life of Washington; Botta's History of the American Revolution. These books, and others, may be read with advantage; and you should adopt some systematic course as to time, that is, to read so many hours out of the twenty-four.

Less than three weeks after the previous missive, Clay wrote James a letter filled with parental concern. The father here expresses his anxiety over the son's solitude, and fears the temptations that could arise.

■ You complain of not hearing from me. I have written to you several times since I have been here, and would have written oftener, if I had had any thing to communicate. . . . You must not suppose that I feel any want

of affection toward you. Far otherwise. You are constantly in my thoughts, and in my hopes. I feel that you must be very lonesome, and regret to hear that you are not happy. You know, my dear son, that I feared you would not be, separated as you are from all who love you, and that I reluctantly consented to your going to Missouri. I hope that you will endeavor to cultivate feelings of contentment, and I shall be most happy, on my return home, if we can make any arrangement by which you can come back to Kentucky, and live in the midst of your friends. The account you give me of your affairs is encouraging, and the account of you which I receive from others also gives me high satisfaction. What I would especially guard you against, is, every species of dissipation; and I own to you that I have feared your solitary condition might tempt you into it. But I sincerely hope that may not prove to be the case.

In 1838, Clay was "looking out for a wife" for his son, though conceding that James would "have to select for yourself." Later James returned to Kentucky to study law; however, he continued to be gloomy. In 1848, Clay admonished him: "I am sorry that you indulge in bad spirits. You are wrong to do so, and I think you have no occasion to do so. You have much to cheer and animate you. More by far than most persons." Nevertheless, Clay was pleased with James, and when he was appointed American chargé d'affaires at Lisbon in 1849, at the age of thirty-one, the father wrote a letter filled with paternal pride to his friend Thomas B. Stevenson of Maysville.

■ The mission to Portugal has been tendered to my son James in a handsome manner, and very creditably to the President. James's situation, in a pecuniary point of view, is one of perfect independence, and he has no need of any office as a means of support; but he has determined to accept the appointment, which he could not well decline, being unoccupied at present, and there existing no impediment to his going abroad.

Fatherly advice still followed James to the Portuguese capital. This letter is dated December 4, 1849:

■ I am glad that you entertain confidence in your competency to discharge the duties of your official position. That is a very proper feeling, within legitimate bounds; but it should not lead to any relaxation of exertions to obtain all information within your reach, and to qualify yourself by all means in your power to fulfill all your official obligations. How do you get along without a knowledge of the French language? Are you acquiring it? . . . I hope you will adhere to your good resolution of living within your salary. From what you state about your large establishment, I am afraid that you will exceed that prudent limit.

By early 1850, the restless James began to tire of his diplomatic duties. His father did not try to dissuade him from returning to the United States, and again warned him about living above his salary.

With the possible exception of Henry Clay, Chief Justice John Marshall may well have been Andrew Jackson's strongest opponent. Even with the authority of the Supreme Court behind him, however, Marshall fared little if any better against Jackson than did Clay himself. When the Court rendered a judgment for the Indians that the President opposed, Jackson was quoted as saying defiantly: "John Marshall has made his decision; now let him enforce it." Of course Jackson triumphed, as Marshall had no physical means to enforce his ruling. In 1832, Marshall vainly hoped that Clay's campaign would oust Jackson from the White House. Marshall's five-volume biography of George Washington (recommended by Clay, opposite page) caused him several years of auctorial anguish —and even so, Marshall later admitted: "That work was hurried into the world with too much precipitation."

Refused an engagement by the Grand Opera of Paris, Jenny Lind began her professional singing career with a tour of Northern Europe during 1844-1845 at the age of twenty-four. By 1847 she had enchanted London. P. T. Barnum, the most memorable American promoter of all time, contracted with Miss Lind for a concert tour of America in 1850 that was preceded by one of Barnum's spectacular outbursts of publicity. Miss Lind lived up to expectations. Her voice, according to many, possessed excellent range, power, and flexibility. Her looks were satisfactory too. George Templeton Strong, the contemporary commentator, said: "None of her portraits do her any justice. She is not pretty nor handsome, nor exactly fine-looking, but there's an air about her of dignity, self-possession, modesty, and goodness that is extremely attractive."

■ I have no doubt that you may return at the end of the year, if you wish it. Whether you do so or not ought to depend on your estimate of what will most conduce to the health and happiness of your family and yourself. I should be sorry if you allowed your expenses to exceed your salary. Public functionaries are too apt to think themselves more bound than they really are to dispense hospitality. He acts wisest who limits himself to his salary.

James resigned his position as chargé d'affaires at Lisbon on July 19, 1850. Resuming residence in Missouri, he became once more the object of parental worry. Clay wrote to his son December 23, 1850, about a conversation he had with Daniel Webster, then Secretary of State, concerning James. Jenny Lind, "the Swedish nightingale," had recently arrived in America.

■ I have not yet had a good opportunity of conversing with either the President or Mr. Webster about you or your late mission; but the other night at Jenny Lind's concert, sitting by Mr. Webster, he broke forth in extravagant praises of you. . . .

I should regret deeply to see you set down doing nothing. You must engage in some occupation or you will be miserable. The law, farming, or the public service, are the only pursuits which I suppose present themselves to you. You don't like the first, which is moreover nowhere in Kentucky profitable; and your decision must be between the two others. I had inferred that you were tired of diplomacy, unless you could get a higher grade than that which you lately held. At present there is none that I know of; but perhaps some vacancy may occur. . . . You did not say whether you were satisfied or not with my sale of your house and lot. I would not have sold it but for your great anxiety to sell. It was a good house, but I never liked its external appearance. The situation was one of the finest in Lexington.

STRADDLING THE SLAVERY ISSUE

The following selection of documents, ranging in date from a speech in 1827 to his last will and testament of 1851, convey vividly that Clay assumed a position of almost complete ambivalence—in a nation polarized between slaveholders and abolitionists. The historian Clement Eaton has neatly summarized Clay's attitude as "a practical acceptance of the institution and a theoretical opposition to it." A member of Kentucky's well-to-do landowning group, Clay was virtually forced to own slaves in order to operate his property; in 1846 there were about sixty slaves at Ashland. He treated them well, causing a visitor to remark: "The houses of his slaves are all very neat, and surrounded by better gardens, and more flowers and shrubbery than one-half of the farmhouses in the country."

Opposed to immediate emancipation, Clay believed that in the states where whites greatly outnumbered blacks, freedom could be obtained gradually. On the other hand, he regarded slaves as mere property, and if a runaway slave was captured, he defended the right of the owner to claim him. According to Clay, the answer to the slave problem in the United States was to ship emancipated Negroes to settlements in Africa. He belonged to the American Colonization Society in Washington, and on January 20, 1827, gave his views in an address to that organization, while he was Secretary of State. Freed Negroes from the United States established the colony of Liberia on the west coast of Africa in 1822.

■ The Society . . . now protests, that it entertains no purpose, on its own authority or by its own means, to attempt emancipation, partial or general; that it knows the general government has no constitutional power to achieve such an object; that it believes that the States, and the States only, which tolerate slavery, can accomplish the work of emancipation. . . .

The object of the Society was the colonization of the free colored people, not the slaves, of the country. Voluntary in its institution, voluntary in its continuance, voluntary in all its ramifications, all its means, purposes, and instruments, are also voluntary. But it was said that no free colored persons could be prevailed upon to abandon the comforts of civilized life and expose themselves to all the perils of a settlement in a distant, inhospitable, and savage country; that, if they could be induced to go on such a quixotic expedition, no territory could be procured for their establishment as a colony; that the plan was altogether incompetent to effectuate its professed object; and that it ought to be rejected as the idle dream

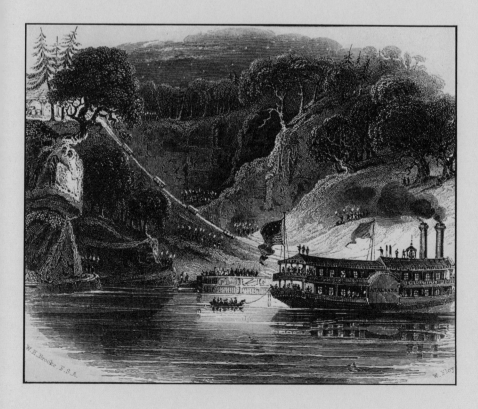

This illustration of an Alabaman river scene, "Slaves shipping cotton by torchlight," appeared in an 1842 book by J. S. Buckingham. Although slavery was neither "romantic" nor "picturesque" to those entrapped by the institution, this British author wrote a glowing panorama: "We made several halts at the landing-places of estates. One of these halts was rendered peculiarly interesting, from the romantic and picturesque scene which it exhibited. . . . The negroes from the plantation above . . . added to the crew, made the whole number employed, from fifty to sixty persons. . . . The night was cloudy and dark . . . strong torchlight was therefore necessary, to enable the laborers to do their work. . . . The glare of torches moving from spot to spot, without any visible agent . . . occasional flashes of forked lightning, rolling of thunder, and shouting of the men, when they hailed from . . . the bluff above, or responded from the beach . . . formed a moving scene."

Sojourner Truth was a slave in New York till that state abolished slavery within its boundaries in 1827, when she was about thirty. Like most slaves, who were considered mere property and whose births were seldom recorded, she never knew her exact age. Originally named Isabella Baumfree, she adopted her symbolic name in 1843, became a fiery speaker at antislavery meetings, and did much to help fugitive slaves who escaped to the North. Clay supported the Fugitive Slave Act, which empowered local authorities throughout America to return such runaways to their owners. But his personal hatred of slavery is thought to have sprung from an experience in his Virginia boyhood. Joseph Rogers, a biographer, tells it: "A negro who had run away from some distance had made his home in the swamps near by, and was a great favorite with all the boys in the neighborhood because he knew where the best fish were to be found, the first berries, and the finest 'fox-grapes.' News of his location coming to his master, a constable was sent to bring him back. The negro gave battle, in which he was accidentally killed. Clay never forgot this. He never forgot that the love of liberty is inherent in human nature, regardless of the color of the skin, though he was often doubtful as to what should be done with the institution."

of visionary enthusiasts. The Society has outlived, thank God, all these disastrous predictions. It has survived to swell the list of false prophets. It is no longer a question of speculation whether a colony can or can not be planted from the United States of free persons of color on the shores of Africa. It is a matter demonstrated; such a colony, in fact, exists, prospers, has made successful war, and honorable peace, and transacts all the multiplied business of a civilized and Christian community. It now has about five hundred souls, disciplined troops, forts, and other means of defense, sovereignty over an extensive territory, and exerts a powerful and salutory influence over the neighboring clans.

Numbers of the free African race among us are willing to go to Africa. The Society has never experienced any difficulty on that subject, except that its means of comfortable transportation have been inadequate to accommodate all who have been anxious to migrate. Why should they not go? Here they are in the lowest state of social gradation; aliens—political, moral, social aliens—strangers, though natives. There, they would be in the midst of their friends, and their kindred, at home, though born in a foreign land, and elevated above the natives of the country, as much as they are degraded here below the other classes of the community. . . .

The Colonization Society has never imagined it to be practicable, or within the reach of any means which the several governments of the Union could bring to bear on the subject, to transport the whole of the African race within the limits of the United States. Nor is that necessary to accomplish the desirable objects of domestic tranquillity, and render us one homogeneous people. . . . Let us suppose . . . that the whole population at present of the United States, is twelve millions, of which ten may be estimated of the Anglo-Saxon, and two of the African race. If there could be annually transported from the United States an amount of the African portion equal to the annual increase of the whole of that caste, while the European race should be left to multiply, we should find at the termination of the period of duplication . . . that the relative proportions would be as twenty to two. [After] a second term of duplication, the proportion would be as forty to two—one which would eradicate every cause of alarm or solicitude from the breasts of the most timid. But the transportation of Africans . . . would tend to accelerate the duplication of the European race, who . . . would fill up the void space.

If I could be instrumental in eradicating this deepest stain upon the character of our country, and removing all cause of reproach on account of it, by foreign nations; if I could only be instrumental in ridding of this foul blot that revered State that gave me birth, or that not less beloved State which kindly adopted me as her son; I would not exchange the proud satisfaction which I should enjoy, for the honor of all the triumphs ever decreed to the most successful conqueror. . . .

There is a moral fitness in the idea of returning to Africa her children, whose ancestors have been torn from her by the ruthless hand of fraud and violence. Transplanted in a foreign land, they will carry back to their soil the rich fruits of religion, civilization, law, and liberty. May it not be one of the great designs of the Ruler of the universe (whose ways are often inscrutable by short-sighted mortals) thus to transform an original crime into a signal blessing, to that most unfortunate portion of the globe. . . .

Every emigrant to Africa is a missionary carrying with him credentials in the holy cause of civilization, religion, and free institutions. Why is it that the degree of success of missionary exertions is so limited, and so discouraging to those whose piety and benevolence prompt them? Is it not because the missionary is generally an alien and a stranger, perhaps of a different color, and from a different tribe? There is a sort of instinctive feeling of jealousy and distrust toward foreigners which repels and rejects them in all countries; and this feeling is in proportion to the degree of ignorance and barbarism which prevail. But the African colonists, whom we send to convert the heathen, are of the same color, the same family, the same physical constitution. When the purposes of the colony shall be fully understood, they will be received as long-lost brethren restored to the embraces of their friends and their kindred by the dispensations of a wise Providence. . . .

It is not this Society which has produced the great moral revolution which the age exhibits. What would they, who thus reproach us, have done? If they would repress all tendencies toward liberty and ultimate emancipation, they must do more than put down the benevolent efforts of this Society. They must go back to the era of our liberty and independence, and muzzle the cannon which thunder its annual joyous return. They must revive the slave-trade, with all its train of atrocities. They must suppress the workings of British philanthropy, seeking to meliorate the condition of the unfortunate West Indian slaves. They must arrest the career of South American deliverance from thralldom. They must blow

Clay devoted much of the speech cited here to an overly optimistic account of how well the freed American slaves were already faring in their new African home in Liberia. That country has maintained its independence since its foundation and is now a member of the United Nations, but its progress has been neither easy nor automatic. This engraving of Negroes arriving in Liberia appeared in *The National Magazine* of March 1854, accompanying an article that was also rather too sanguine: "Americans successfully planted free negroes on the coast of Africa. Slaves from the United States, made freemen, have become citizens of the Republic of Liberia, enjoy all of its immunities, vote for their own officers and legislators, and are themselves eligible to the highest honors and stations. Every immigrant is entitled to five acres of land on his arrival; if he has a family he receives a larger quantity, according to its numbers, and can purchase as much as he wishes for a dollar an acre. If he is a mechanic, merchant or professional man, instead of a farm he can select a building lot in some of the villages."

William Lloyd Garrison (above), like many other abolitionists, began his opposition to slavery as a believer in African colonization. Finding this position ineffectual since the method was so slow and costly, he soon started to attack speeches such as Clay's (see pages 201–204): "But no where do I see the claims of justice enforced with becoming fearlessness or candor—no personal application—no direct allusion to the awful guilt of debasing the physical, and defiling the moral workmanship of the great God . . . not a word—Therefore my dissatisfaction."

out the moral lights around us, and extinguish that greatest torch of all which America presents to a benighted world, pointing the way to their rights, their liberties, and their happiness. And when they have achieved all these purposes, their work will be yet incomplete. They must penetrate the human soul, and eradicate the light of reason and the love of liberty. Then, and not till then, when universal darkness and despair prevail, can you perpetuate slavery, and repress all sympathies, and all humane and benevolent efforts among freemen, in behalf of the unhappy portion of our race doomed to bondage.

As a political figure, Clay could not afford to offend any great numbers of potential voters. Consequently, his temporizings often brought him abuse from both abolitionists and slaveholders. Expecting to be nominated by the Whigs as a presidential candidate in 1840, Clay wrote of his dilemma to Francis Brooke in November 1838:

■ You think I have too good an opinion of mankind. I confess that I have, throughout life, striven to think well of them, but the last thirteen years have shaken my faith very much. I yet, however, believe the mass to be honest, although very liable to deception. . . . The introduction of this new element of Abolition into our elections can not fail to excite, with all reflecting men, the deepest solicitude. It is, I believe, the first time it has been done. Although their numbers are not very great, they are sufficiently numerous, in several States, to turn the scale. I have now before me a letter from the Secretary of the American Anti-Slavery Society, in New York, in which he says: "I should consider (as in all candor I acknowledge I would) the election of any slaveholder to the Presidency a great calamity to the country."

This music-spangled picture from the 1840 presidential campaign shows the Whig candidate, William Henry Harrison, standing by a log cabin alleged to be his and offering a wooden-legged voter a drink of cider from the keg alongside him. In actuality, Harrison—who had won the battle of Tippecanoe nearly thirty years before and had done nothing notable since—occupied a sixteen-room mansion on an estate of 3,000 acres. But the common-man trappings undoubtedly helped Harrison defeat Van Buren. One campaign jingle summed up most of the Whig propaganda:
"He lives in a cabin built
   of logs,
Drinks nothing but hard cider
   too,
He plows his own ground and
   feeds his own hogs,
This fellow of Tippecanoe."

By the bye, is it possible that two of the Judges of the Court of Appeals attended and took part in the proceedings of the recent Convention and that Judge Tucker presided? If it be true I regard the fact as a strong mark of the degeneracy of the times

I have not enjoyed good health since my return home, from severe colds, but I am getting better and we have the prospect of an early and fine Spring. I found Mrs Clay in her usual good

The danger is that the contagion may spread until it reaches all the free States; and if it ever comes to be acted on as a rule among them, to proscribe slaveholders, they have the numbers to enforce it. . . . My own position, touching slavery, at the present time, is singular enough. The Abolitionists are denouncing me as a slaveholder, and slaveholders as an Abolitionist, while they both unite on Mr. Van Buren.

I should be extremely happy to visit Richmond and see you and the many other friends I have there, but I can not do it while I remain a *quasi* candidate for the Presidency. A candidate in fact I can not say, and have not said to any human being I would be. I am strongly inclined to promulgate that I will not be, under any circumstances. . . . They would say that I saw the grapes were sour. But then, what need I care for any thing they may say?

Clay's vitriol often fell on the abolitionists. He felt that their inflexibility was hindering any gradual movement toward emancipation by causing the Southern states to adopt more severe measures for controlling slaves. More than ever he feared a division between the states. When Clay was warned that such an attitude might be attacked by the extremists of both political parties, he remarked: "I had rather be right than be President." In July 1842, Clay reiterated his middle-of-the-road sentiments:

■ I regard the existence of slavery as an evil. I regret it, and wish that there was not one slave in the United States. But it is an evil which, while it affects the States only, or principally, where it abounds, each State within which it is situated is the exclusive judge of what is best to be done with it, and no other State has a right to interfere in it. . . . Congress possesses no power or authority to abolish it. Congress is invested with no power relating to it, except that which assumes its legitimate and continued existence. . . .

Although I believe slavery to be an evil, I regard it as a far less evil than would arise out of an immediate emancipation of the slaves of the United States, and their remaining here mixed up in our communities. In such a contingency, I believe that a bloody civil war would ensue, which would terminate only by the extinction of the black race.

Nine months prior to the Whig national convention in December 1839, Clay was prodding such stalwart friends as Francis Brooke in Virginia to further his cause as a presidential candidate. In this letter written at Ashland on April 2, 1839, he recounts to Brooke the history of the 1832 convention from which he learned the value of strong local political organization on the state and county level. According to Clay, the young men that year "held a convention in Lexington. It was well attended...They made many stirring and eloquent speeches, published an address to the State, put it into complete organization, by the appointment in all the Counties of large Committees of Vigilance & Correspondence, and returned home full of enthusiasm. The result was that Jackson was beaten by upwards of 7,000 votes. If you could get a similar convention . . . at Charlottesville or Staunton just before the election, I believe that it would be attended with a similar result." In the part of the letter here excerpted, Clay questions the propriety of federal judges attending a political convention. "If it be true," he states, "I regard the fact as a strong mark of the degeneracy of the times."

It results, from these opinions which I entertain, that I consider the movements of the Abolitionists as altogether unauthorized and most unfortunate. I believe them productive of no good whatever, but attended with positive mischief to both the white and the black races. . . . I have regretted extremely the agitation of abolition in the free States. . . . The great body of Abolitionists, like the great mass of every party, I have no doubt, is honest, sincere, and humane. Their leaders deceive them, and will endeavor to profit by them. . . .

Abolition is a delusion which can not last. It is impossible it should endure. What is it? In pursuit of a principle—a great principle, if you please—it undertakes to tread down and trample in the dust all opposing principles, however sacred. It sets up the right of the people of one State to dictate to the people of other States. It arrays State against State. To make the black man free, it would virtually enslave the white man. With a single idea some of its partisans rush on blindly, regardless of all consequences. They have dared even to threaten our glorious Union with dissolution. And suppose that unhallowed object achieved, would it emancipate the slaves? What is their next step? Is it to light up a war between the dissevered parts of the Union, and through blood, devastation, and conflagration, to march forward to emancipation? Are they at all sure that through such diabolical means they would be able finally to arrive at their object? No . . . let each State, and the people of each State, take care of their own interests. . . . We have enough to do in our respective and legitimate spheres of action—enough for the exercise of all the charities and sympathies of our nature. . . .

The generation that established our independence achieved a great and glorious work. Succeeding generations have accomplished much in advancing the growth, the power, and the greatness of this nation. We must leave some things to posterity, and among others the task of making adequate provision for the institution of Slavery. . . . Let us cease to agitate a topic which divides, distracts, and inflames the community. . . . Let us, in place of discord and dissension, cultivate peace, harmony, and good will among the people and the States of this Confederacy. And let us recollect that we have other duties—far higher duties—to perform toward our country, toward posterity, and toward the world, than even the extirpation of African slavery, however much its original introduction among us is to be deplored.

Clay often brought up the subject of slavery in his correspondence. In the following letter of September 1843, he wrote Calvin Colton (later Clay's biographer and the editor of several collections of his papers), urging him to prepare an article on abolition and giving him a suggested outline. An Episcopal clergyman and author, Colton also served as a professor of political economy at Trinity College, Hartford, Connecticut.

■ Allow me to suggest a subject for one of your Tracts which, treated in your popular and condensed way, I think would be attended with great

Only thirty-seven when he piloted the Compromise of 1850 through the shoals of the Senate, Senator Stephen A. Douglas felt that Clay's connection with the Compromise had hindered its passage, even though he had contributed mightily to its formulation. "If Mr. Clay's name had not been associated with the bills," said Douglas, "they would have passed long ago. The Administration was jealous of him and hated him, and some Democrats were weak enough to fear that the success of his bill would make him President. But let it always be said of Old Hal that he fought a glorious and patriotic battle. No man was ever governed by higher and purer motives." Like Clay, Douglas himself was an unsuccessful contender for President (losing to Lincoln in 1860). Like Clay, he gambled, made enemies, and attracted a devoted following. Later he even adopted Clay's middle-of-the-road position, trying to tread the path of compromise between North and South.

and good effect, I mean Abolition. It is manifest that the ultras of that party are extremely mischievous, and are hurrying on the country to fearful consequences. . . .

I will give you an outline. . . . Show the origin of slavery. Trace its introduction to the British Government. Show how it is disposed of by the Federal Constitution. That it is left exclusively to the States, except in regard to fugitives, direct taxes and representation. Show that the agitation of the question in the free States, will first destroy all harmony, and finally lead to disunion. That the consequences of disunion [are] perpetual war—the extinction of the African race—ultimate military despotism.

But the great aim and object of your Tract should be to arouse the laboring classes in the free States against Abolition. Depict the consequences to them of immediate abolition. The slaves being free, would be dispersed throughout the Union; they would enter into competition with the free laborer; with the American, the Irish, the German; reduce his wages; be confounded with him, and affect his moral and social standing. And as the ultras go for both abolition and amalgamation, show that their object is to unite, in marriage, the laboring white man, and the laboring black man, and to reduce the white laboring man to the despised and degraded condition of the black man.

Clay's last act concerning slaves was contained in his personal will, dated July 10, 1851. A moderate document for its day, it portrays as well as any other the cautious policy that characterized Clay's thinking on slavery.

■ In the sale of any of my slaves, I direct that members of families shall not be separated without their consent. My will is, and I accordingly direct, that the issue of all my female slaves, which may be born after the first day of January, 1850, shall be free at the respective ages, of the males at twenty-eight, and of the females at twenty-five; and that the three years next preceding their arrival at the age of freedom, they shall be entitled to their hire or wages for those years, or of the fair value of their services, to defray the expense of transporting them to one of the African colonies, and of furnishing them with an outfit on their arrival there. And I further direct, that they be taught to read, to write, and to cipher, and that they be sent to Africa. I further will and direct, that the issue of any of the females, who are so to be entitled to their freedom, at the age of twenty-five, shall be deemed free from their birth, and that they be bound out as apprentices to learn farming, or some useful trade, upon the condition also, of being taught to read, to write, and to cipher. And I direct, also, that the age of twenty-one having been attained, they shall be sent to one of the African colonies, to raise the necessary funds for which purpose, if they shall not have previously earned them, they must be hired out a sufficient length of time.

I require and enjoin my executors and descendants to pay particular attention to the execution of this provision of my will. And if they should sell any of the females who or whose issue are to be free, I especially desire

From the presidential election of 1824 until the start of the campaign of 1848, John J. Crittenden remained a loyal and devoted supporter of Henry Clay. At the same time he pursued a varied career of public service in Congress, the Cabinet, and as Governor of Kentucky. In 1848, however, Crittenden's allegiance went to Taylor. He explained: "I prefer Mr. Clay to all men for the Presidency; but my conviction . . . is that he cannot be elected. . . . Mr. Clay, I trust, is of too noble a nature . . . to doubt the sincerity of my friendship because of my regard for truth and candor. I should consider myself as dishonored—I should consider myself a false and treacherous friend—if I should advise or say that Mr. Clay could be elected when I believe the contrary. Such a course might suit a flatterer, not a friend." Despite this, Clay did find it hard to forgive him. But ten days before his death Clay said: "Mr. Crittenden and myself are cordial friends."

them to guard carefully the rights of such issue by all suitable stipulations and sanctions in the contract of sale. But I hope that it may not be necessary to sell any such persons who are to be entitled to their freedom, but that they may be retained in the possession of some of my descendants.

DISPUTES, DEFEAT, AND DECLINE

Even after his rejection as the Whig presidential candidate in 1840, Clay was determined to continue as the chief Whig representative in Congress. William Henry Harrison, the Whig nominee, defeated Van Buren—and recognizing that peace between the executive and the legislative branches of government would be abetted by conversations with the ruffled Clay, the President-elect visited him in Kentucky. After his arrival in Washington early in December 1840, Clay summarized these talks in a letter to Francis Brooke. Two of Clay's friends, John J. Crittenden and Thomas Ewing, entered the Cabinet; Webster was named Secretary of State.

■ I left General Harrison at Lexington, and I have seen and conversed a good deal with him. . . . I communicated to him that, during the short time I expected to remain in public life, I had no desire to change my position in the Senate. He professed, and I have no doubt now entertains, sentiments of warm regard and attachment to me. I do not believe that he had then made up his mind as to the members of his Cabinet. I think it probable, although he did not say so, that he will invite Crittenden and Ewing to take places in it. Beyond that I will not venture even a conjecture. I thought it right to explain frankly to him my feelings and relations toward Mr. Webster, and I stated to him that, although my confidence in that gentleman had been somewhat shaken, during the last eight years, I did not see how any Whig President could overlook him; that if I had been elected, I should have felt myself constrained to offer him some distinguished station; and that if he chose to appoint him to office, it would not diminish the interest I felt in the success of his Administration, nor my zeal in its support, if it were conducted in the principles I hoped it would be. I added an expression of my opinion that he was not suited to the office of Secretary of the Treasury, which I had understood some of his friends wished him to fill.

The ways of reconciliation were not smooth; a few days after Harrison's inauguration Clay was at loggerheads with Tippecanoe over his accusation that Clay had attempted to dictate presidential appointments. He sent a blistering reply to Harrison:

■ I was mortified by the suggestion you made to me on Saturday, that I had been represented as dictating to you, or to the new Administration—mortified, because it is unfounded in fact, and because there is danger of the fears, that I intimated to you at Frankfort, of my enemies poisoning

Horace Greeley, founder of the New York *Tribune* in 1841, believed strongly in equality. His aim was to launch a journal "removed alike from servile partisanship on the one hand, and from gagged, mincing neutrality on the other." Thomas McElrath, his partner, a more practical man, gave the paper stability and organization. By 1846, the *Tribune* was regarded as the best newspaper in New York. Essentially a Whig, Greeley actively supported Clay in 1844 and, when he lost, wrote: "I loved him for his generous nature, his gallant bearing, his thrilling eloquence, and his life-long devotion to what I deemed our country's unity, prosperity, and just renown. Hence, from the day of his nomination in May to that of his defeat in November, I gave every hour, every effort, every thought, to his election."

208

your mind toward me. . . . If to express freely my opinion, as a citizen and as a Senator, in regard to public matters, be dictation, then I have dictated, and not otherwise. There is but one alternative which I could embrace, to prevent the exercise of this common right of freedom of opinion, and that is retirement to private life. That I am most desirous of, and if I do not promptly indulge the feeling, it is because I entertain the hope—perhaps vain hope—that by remaining a little longer in the Senate, I may possibly render some service to a country to whose interest my life has been dedicated.

I do not wish to trouble you with answering this note. I could not reconcile it to my feelings to abstain from writing it. Your heart, in which I have the greatest confidence, will justly appreciate the motives of, whatever others may say or insinuate, your true and faithful friend.

Harrison died after only a month as President. John Tyler succeeded him, and when Clay failed to gain any ground against Tyler over the chartering of a new national bank (see page 68), he decided in 1842 to resign from the Senate. In a world-weary letter to Francis Brooke, he complimented his friend on refusing to take a more active position. There is evidence, however, that at this very time Clay himself was already planning another major effort to begin that unceasing round of activities no presidential aspirant can avoid.

■ I was glad to learn that you had it in your power to accept the office of President of the Court of Appeals, and that you were right to decline it. As we advance in years, our labors ought to lighten. With the view to lessen mine, and in contemplation of the unhappy and disturbed state of our public councils, arising out of the course of Mr. Tyler, I mean to

The struggle between John Tyler (above) and Clay to control the Whig party had far-reaching results for politics in America. Northerners gradually took over Whig leadership. Democrats, on the other hand, found Southerners inclined to accept their philosophy. Some critics also envisioned difficulties in Tyler's personal life, as well as his public future, when he married Julia Gardiner in 1844. A widower, he was fifty-four, while she was only twenty-four. Julia was a sometime mannequin who had appeared in New York advertisements such as the one at left, where her gown bears the notice: "I'll Purchase at Bogart & Mecamly—No. 86, 9th Avenue. Their goods are Beautiful & Astonishingly Cheap." Tyler's marriage with the "fleshy" Miss Gardiner (as one wag described her) actually turned out rather well, and they had seven children. *209*

resign my seat in the Senate, during this session. I want rest, and my private affairs want attention. Nevertheless, I would make any personal sacrifice, if, by remaining here, I could do any good, but my belief is I can effect nothing, and perhaps my absence may remove an obstacle to something being done by others. I shall therefore go home in the spring.

Judging from Clay's bellicosity before the War of 1812, it might be thought he would have joined wholeheartedly in the outcry for war with Mexico when the opportunity arose for expanding toward the southwest. Such was not the case. While he believed in fighting to uphold the nation's interests, by 1844 he did not think it a justifiable means for acquiring additional territory. During the early months of the year, Clay traveled through the South, electioneering in the region that he considered his weakest source of support. Because the annexation of Texas was so closely linked to the expansion of slavery, Clay and his party hoped to eliminate the topic as a campaign issue. But by April, finding the South engrossed by the Texas question, he finally decided a statement was needed. In Raleigh, North Carolina, he wrote a significant letter:

■ Texas . . . revolted against the government of Mexico, flew to arms, and finally fought and won the memorable battle of San Jacinto, annihilating a Mexican army, and making a captive of the Mexican President. The signal success of that revolution was greatly aided, if not wholly achieved, by citizens of the United States, who had migrated to Texas. These successes . . . impose on us the obligation of scrupulously avoiding the imputation of having instigated and aided the revolution, with the ultimate view of territorial aggrandizement. After the battle of San Jacinto, the United States recognized the independence of Texas . . . *de facto*, without regarding the question *de jure*. That recognition did not affect or impair the

In 1842, Mexico had twice tried to retake Texas but succeeded only in doing considerable damage and looting in the San Antonio area. Some Texans under Colonel William Fisher decided to raid Mexico in retaliation. Without any authorization from the government of Texas, they pounced on the Mexican town of Meir, where 176 of them were trapped by a larger Mexican force. The Texans surrendered after being told they would be treated with "consideration"—and Mexican General Antonio Santa Anna then promptly ordered the execution of one man out of ten. Each captive decided his own fate by drawing a bean from a large pot containing 176 black and white beans (see illustration). The seventeen who drew black beans were marched into an adjoining courtyard and shot.

rights of Mexico, [which] still asserts her right to reduce Texas to obedience, as a part of the republic of Mexico. . . .

If the government of the United States were to acquire Texas, it would acquire along with it all the incumbrances which Texas is under, and among them the actual or suspended war between Mexico and Texas. . . . Annexation and war with Mexico are identical. Now, for one, I certainly am not willing to involve this country in a foreign war for the object of acquiring Texas. I know there are those who regard such a war with indifference, and as a trifling affair, on account of the weakness of Mexico. . . . But I do not look upon it thus lightly. I regard all wars as great calamities, to be avoided, if possible, and honorable peace as the wisest and truest policy of this country. What the United States most need, are union, peace, and patience. Nor do I think that the weakness of a power should form a motive, in any case, for inducing us to engage in or to depreciate the evils of war. Honor and good faith and justice are equally due from this country toward the weak as toward the strong. . . .

We have been seriously charged with an inordinate spirit of territorial aggrandizement; and, without admitting the justice of the charge, it must be owned that we have made vast acquisitions of territory within the last forty years. Suppose Great Britain and France, or one of them, were to take part with Mexico, and by a manifesto, were to proclaim that their objects were to assist a weak and helpless ally to check the spirit of encroachment and ambition of an already overgrown Republic, seeking still further acquisitions of territory, to maintain the independence of Texas, disconnected with the United States, and to prevent the further propagation of slavery from the United States, what would be the effect of such allegations upon the judgment of an impartial and enlightened world? . . .

I do not think that Texas ought to be received into the Union, as an integral part of it, in decided opposition to the wishes of a considerable and respectable portion of the Confederacy. I think it far more wise and important to compose and harmonize the present Confederacy, than to introduce a new element of discord and distraction into it. In my humble opinion, it should be the constant and earnest endeavor of American statesmen to eradicate prejudices, to cultivate and foster concord, and to produce general contentment among all parts. . . . And true wisdom . . . points to the duty of rendering its present members happy, prosperous, and satisfied with each other, rather than to attempt to introduce alien members, against the common consent.

Leader of the rebellion against the Mexicans for Texas independence, and commander in chief of the forces that defeated Santa Anna at San Jacinto, Sam Houston was active in United States politics before he migrated west to the Indian country of Cherokee Nation, now Oklahoma, and then to Texas. Houston had been a member of the House of Representatives and Governor of Tennessee. While in Washington as a congressman, he defined what he regarded as a perfect combination for 1824: "What a splendid administration it would make with Old Hickory as President and Mr. Clay as Secretary of State." Although Clay and Houston were on opposing sides with regard to the annexation of Texas, they did agree on preservation of the Union. When Houston refused to take the oath of allegiance to the Confederacy in 1861, he was ousted from his post as Governor of Texas.

Calhoun—who had become Secretary of State once President Tyler showed himself far more in tune with the Democrats than with the Whigs—negotiated a treaty to annex Texas. The Whigs defeated its ratification in the Senate. But realizing that his political support in the South was slipping away, Clay qualified his position. On July 1, 1844, he wrote the first of two public letters he hoped would mollify Southern voters while not antagonizing those in the North—an attempted compromise that helped Clay lose in November (see pages 71–73):

■ I consider the Union a great political partnership; and that new members ought not to be admitted into the concern at the imminent hazard of its dissolution. Personally I could have no objection to the annexation of Texas; but I certainly would be unwilling to see the existing Union dissolved or seriously jeoparded for the sake of acquiring Texas.

In a region where adult baptism was widely practiced, Clay's baptism at the age of seventy (see pages 74 and 75) was not unique. While he had long attended services and been a pewholder in Lexington's Episcopal church, he took decades to mull over his formal acceptance of a faith. Three years before he decided to be baptized, and shortly after his agonizingly narrow defeat of 1844, he wrote to a minister:

■ I am greatly obliged by the desire you manifest that I should seek, in the resources of religion, consolation for all the vexations and disappointments of life. I hope you will continue your prayers for me. . . . I have long been convinced of the paramount importance of the Christian religion. I have, for many years, fervently sought its blessings. I shall persevere in seeking them, and I hope, ultimately, to attain a firm faith and confidence in its promises. There is nothing for which I feel so anxious. May God, in his infinite mercy, grant what I so ardently desire.

James K. Polk's election as President soon brought the nation to war with Mexico. Still opposed to a military chieftain for President, Clay wrote a friend in May 1847, concerning General Zachary Taylor and echoing his earlier sentiments on Jackson. At the end of this excerpt, he intimates that he might, after all, run once more himself.

■ Thank you for the friendly expression of your regret and sympathy, on account of the great and irreparable loss which I have sustained, in the death of my beloved son, on the bloody field of Buena Vista. . . . Although I feel some consolation in the gallant manner of my son's death in the service of his country, and in the general sympathy which the public has so generously displayed on account of it, the deep wound which I have received can only be effectually healed by Him whose dispensations have produced it. . . .

The war with Mexico is yet in progress. We do not certainly know how it will terminate, nor how General Taylor himself may finally come out of it. In the mean time, it would be very embarrassing to him to be a recognized candidate for the Presidency in opposition to the very party, to the orders of whose Administration he is subject. Then there is General Scott. Perhaps, while I am now writing, he is in possession of the city of Mexico. Will he create no competition with General Taylor? May we not have two Whig generals in the field of politics? And as the other party may desire the *éclat* of military deeds, may they not bring forward some third. . . .

If it were highly probable or certain that we must take General Taylor, or submit to the continuance in power of the present dominant party, that would present a different state of things. The question then would be between the perpetuation and increase of corruption, leading certainly to the destruction of the Government, on the one hand, and the ultimate danger of military despotism, on the other. In such a painful dilemma, it might be expedient, as an only resort, to select the General as the Whig candidate. But this ought not to be done but upon the strongest necessity; and at this early day no such necessity is manifest. On the contrary, there is much reason to hope that the Whig party may be able to elect any fair and honorable man they may choose to nominate.

Clay sounded even more like a candidate in a speech on November 13, 1847, when he assailed the American policy of aggression against Mexico. It was not an unpatriotic speech but one that pointed out the dangerous similarities of power politics in Europe and in the Western Hemisphere. He had changed decidedly from his firebreathing days as a War Hawk.

■ The day is dark and gloomy, unsettled and uncertain, like the condition of our country in regard to the unnatural war with Mexico. The public mind is agitated and anxious, and is filled with serious apprehensions as to its indefinite continuance, and especially as to the consequences which its termination may bring forth, menacing the harmony, if not the existence, of our Union. . . .

War, pestilence, famine, by the common consent of mankind, are the three greatest calamities which can befall our species; and war, as the most

The two most successful American generals in the Mexican War both thirsted for the Presidency as a sort of added bonus for their military achievements. Zachary Taylor (above), victor at Buena Vista, beat out Clay for the 1848 Whig nomination and went on to the White House. Winfield Scott (on horse, below) captured Mexico City after a dangerous campaign and then received the 1852 Whig nomination. Unluckily for Scott, one of his subordinates in Mexico—Brigadier General Franklin Pierce of New Hampshire—was the Democratic candidate and trounced his old commander by an electoral vote of 254 to 42.

I have been excessively overrun with Company at the Tavern (the U.S. Hotel) at which I slept, and have been very much jaded. To get a little rest, and to catch some breath, I have accepted an invitation from Mr. Gales to remain at his house, during the few days which I shall continue here I have just removed into it, and find my quarters both quiet and elegant. It is Mr. St. C. Clarke house on the Square of the Presidents. I dined at the Presidents the day before yesterday, and was entertained with the greatest civility.

Early in 1848, Clay wrote to his wife, Lucretia, of his plans for resting a few days in Washington before beginning his homeward journey to Ashland via Philadelphia, Baltimore, and Pittsburgh. Fatigued by the bevy of supporters who were entreating him to run for the Presidency again, he needed a few days' respite. Undecided about the advisability of another campaign, however, he assured his wife that he should "suspend the execution of the resolution in regard to the P[residency] and may not take any decisive step until I get home. This is the course strongly urged by many friends." Although Clay had opposed Polk in the election of 1844 and the two had conflicting views on the war with Mexico, he was still welcome at the White House and invited there on occasion, as is evidenced by this excerpted paragraph.

direful, justly stands in front. Pestilence and famine, no doubt for wise although inscrutable purposes, are inflictions of Providence. . . . Their duration is not long, and their ravages are limited. . . . War is the voluntary work of our own hands, and whatever reproaches it may deserve should be directed to ourselves. When it breaks out, its duration is indefinite and unknown—its vicissitudes are hidden from our view. In the sacrifice of human life, and in the waste of human treasure, in its losses and its burdens, it affects both belligerent nations; and its sad effects of mangled bodies, of death and of desolation, endure long after its thunders are hushed in peace. War unhinges society, disturbs its peaceful and regular industry, and scatters poisonous seeds of disease and immorality, which continue to germinate and diffuse . . . long after it has ceased. . . .

Of all the abominable transactions which sully the pages of history, none exceed in enormity that of the dismemberment and partition of Poland by the three great continental powers, Russia, Austria, and Prussia. . . . That the power of the United States is competent to the conquest of Mexico, is quite probable. But let us avoid affixing to our name and national character a similar, if not a worse stigma than that involved in the partition of Poland. I am afraid that we do not now stand well in the opinion of other parts of Christendom. . . . All the nations, I apprehend, look upon us, in the prosecution of the present war, as being actuated by a spirit of rapacity, and an inordinate desire for territorial aggrandizement.

Torn between his insatiable desire to be President and the sound advice of good friends who tried to dissuade him, Clay nevertheless hankered for another campaign. In this letter of February 1848 to Leslie Combs, a dedicated Whig who had made speeches for him during the election of 1844, Clay justifies his temporary passivity but exudes confidence.

■ I remain in my passive position in regard to the Presidency. To this course I have been strongly urged. It is generally approved. Whether and when I may change it, depends on circumstances. There is no occasion for precipitate action. Mine at least shall be deliberate; having due regard to country, party, friends. If I were to credit all I hear and see, there would be no doubt of my election, if nominated by the National Convention, with my consent; but experience has brought diffidence, and I do not lend too ready an ear to even agreeable things. I learn from New York that there is not a particle of doubt that, if I were a candidate, the vote of that State would be given me by an immense majority.... Our Kentucky and other friends ought to know what an up-hill business that is of supporting [General Taylor] in the free States; and yet I lose no suitable occasion to impress on all union, harmony and concord. I am fully convinced that no preference will be expressed next week in Virginia, at Richmond, for General Taylor.

Despite this determination to remain inactive in any presidential candidacy, Clay did have one final fling at his goal in 1848. Passed over at the Whig national convention in favor of Zachary Taylor, Clay refused to take part in the campaign and even declined the offer of a seat in the Senate. An embittered letter to a Kentucky politician, James Harlan, dated June 22, 1848, is descriptive of Clay's disappointment. Lewis Cass was the Democratic nominee for President in 1848.

■ I shall take no active or partisan part in the canvass, but remain quiet, submitting to what has been done so far as relates to myself. I think this is the course prompted by self-respect and personal dignity.... Of course I can never vote for Cass. It is too soon to form any satisfactory opinion as to the issue of the contest. Neither candidate seems to be entirely ac-

Inconsistent in his basic political attitudes, Lewis Cass—for whom Clay here states he "can never vote"—was a prime example of the philosophy that the end justifies the means. A nationalist first, he avidly supported the Mexican War and even hoped that the United States would send an invading force into Yucatan: "We must continue our occupation of Mexico and push the invasion still farther." Yet he favored revolutions in other nations. In domestic politics, he was somewhat conservative, though liberal whenever it suited his purpose.

Clay's comparison of the American partition of Mexico with the Russian-Austrian-Prussian partition of Poland (see opposite page) was harsh but just. Both actions, in Clay's phrase, were "actuated by a spirit of rapacity, and an inordinate desire for territorial aggrandizement." Here King Stanislav of Poland is seen clutching desperately at his crown, hoping to retain it and at least a shred of his kingdom, as Catherine II of Russia, Joseph II of Austria, and Frederick II of Prussia mark out the areas they are seizing. By 1795 the three nations had grabbed all of Poland, and it vanished from the map of Europe until 1919. During the first partition in 1772, Maria Theresa, then the Empress of Austria, conceded that her deed was evil. In Frederick's contemptuous words: "She wept, but she kept on taking."

ceptable to the party which supports him. And I suppose that party will probably succeed between whose members there will be ultimately the least division and the greatest intermediate reconciliation. . . .

P. S. The Governor very handsomely tendered me the Executive appointment to the Senate, which I this day declined accepting.

True to his word, Clay stayed in retirement at Ashland during the Taylor campaign. However, it was not a silent retreat from the world of politics, and his pronouncements about the Whig nominee were made publicly and in private. The first two paragraphs of this excerpt were part of a message to the Louisville Committee dated June 26, 1848. The last paragraph is from a letter to Thomas Stevenson in September of that year.

■ I have been much importuned from various quarters to endorse General Taylor as a good Whig, who will, if elected, act on Whig principles, and carry out Whig measures. But how can I do that? Can I say that in his hands Whig measures will be safe and secure, when he refuses to pledge himself to their support? when some of his most active friends say they are obsolete? when he is presented as a No-party candidate? when the Whig Convention at Philadelphia refused to recognize or proclaim its attachment to any principles or measures, and actually laid on the table resolutions having that object in view?

Ought I to come out as a warm and partisan supporter of a candidate, who, in a reversal of our conditions, announced his purpose to remain as a candidate, and consequently to oppose me, so far as it depended upon himself? Tell me what reciprocity is in this? Magnanimity is a noble virtue, and I have always endeavored to practice it; but it has its limits, and the line of demarcation between it and meanness is not always clearly discernible. . . .

I may be constrained to vote for [Taylor] as I can vote for nobody else now before the public. But if I do, I shall do it quietly. I wish to lead or mislead no one. Should he be elected, and disappoint the Whigs, I desire to be spared any reproaches for having induced any of them to vote for him. Besides, I could not, in justice to myself, come out in any speech or letter, in his support, without assigning such reasons for my course as would operate, perhaps, as much against him as for him.

Some disgruntled elements wanted Clay to run on a separate ticket, but in a letter of September 20, 1848, he emphatically rejected any such notion. While Taylor again received short shrift, Millard Fillmore, who became President on Taylor's death in 1850, was given Clay's blessing.

■ I would not accept a nomination if it were tendered to me, and it is my unaffected desire that no further use be made of my name in connection with that office. . . . Movements in various quarters having for their object to present me as their candidate to the American people . . . have been made without any approbation from me. In the present complicated state

A former Anti-Mason, active in western New York politics, Millard Fillmore did not always reciprocate Clay's praise cited here. As early as 1834, he was certain Clay would not be a winning candidate for the Whigs in 1836. Fillmore wrote of his concern to Thurlow Weed: "Clay and his friends cling to the last hope. They are doing everything to keep him on the course. It is not for you or me to calculate the extent of this pernicious influence. We regard him as a hackneyed politician, possessed of talent . . . but so strongly suspected of a want of integrity that he might be regarded as a dead weight. . . . But here we are—no help for us. I think after all Clay will not decline." Clay lost that nomination and Van Buren won the election easily. In Congress later, Fillmore was a Clay Whig with some reservations—and Clay was delighted with Fillmore's zeal in raising protective tariffs in 1842. By 1850, Fillmore deeply appreciated Clay's political moves, and in the months before his death Fillmore paid several visits to the ailing statesman at the National Hotel.

of the Presidential election they can not, in my opinion, be attended with any public good. . . . I entertain with you the strongest apprehension from the election of General Cass, but I do not see enough of hope and confidence in that of General Taylor to stimulate my exertions and animate my zeal. . . .

I have great pleasure in bearing my humble testimony in favor of Mr. Fillmore. I believe him to be able, indefatigable, industrious and patriotic. He served in the extra session of 1841 as Chairman of the committees of the two houses of Congress, and I had many opportunities of witnessing his rare merits.

Millard Fillmore remained in Clay's good graces. In 1850, Clay wrote to his son Thomas of the new President's continuing friendliness. John J. Crittenden, Clay's old Kentucky ally, had fallen in Clay's esteem, however, when he supported Taylor in 1848.

■ My relations with Mr. Fillmore are perfectly friendly and confidential. In the appointment of Mr. Crittenden I acquiesced. Mr. F. asked me how we stood? I told him that the same degree of intimacy between us which once existed, no longer prevailed; but that we were on terms of civility. I added that, if he thought of introducing him into his Cabinet, I hoped that no considerations of my present relations to him would form any obstacle.

Once more, in 1851, Clay had to decline the reintroduction of his name as a possible presidential candidate. In a letter to Daniel Ullman, a New York supporter, he stipulated his reasons.

■ You will recollect that the last time but one that I was in the city of New York, I had the pleasure of dining with you and a number of other friends. . . . We then had a frank, full, and confidential conversation on the connection of my name with the next Presidency; and that I then declared that I did not wish ever again to be brought forward as a candidate. From that declaration, I have never since deviated in thought, word, or deed. . . . On a review and reconsideration of the whole matter, I adhere to that declaration. Considering my age, the delicate state of my health, the frequency and the unsuccessful presentation of my name on former occasions, I feel an unconquerable repugnance to such a use of it again.

Clay did have a preference for the Whig candidate in 1852, however. Daniel Ullman was the recipient of this letter—dated March 6, 1852, just three months before Clay's death—which underlines the Kentuckian's faith in Fillmore and gives quietly eloquent testimony of his concern for his party. General Winfield Scott and Daniel Webster were the "competitors" mentioned.

■ You rightly understood me in expressing a preference for Mr. Fillmore as the Whig candidate for the Presidency. This I did before I left home,

While he favored the eight resolutions proposed by Clay in 1850, Alexander Hamilton Stephens, then a representative from Georgia, was sure that there would never be "harmony and peace between the two great sections of the Union." Slight—he seldom weighed more than ninety pounds —but vigorous, Stephens worked for Clay's election in 1844, yet by 1852 thought so little of the Whig candidate for President (Scott) that he cast his ballot for Daniel Webster, who had died nine days earlier.

Attending an 1845 Colonization Society meeting in Washington, Stephens overheard a classic remark by a congressman from North Carolina: "Clay could get more men to run after him to hear him speak, and fewer to vote for him, than any man in America." In 1860–1861, Stephens tried to keep his home state of Georgia in the Union, but when this failed he willingly became Vice-President of the Confederacy. In 1866 he was elected to the United States Senate, which refused to seat "a rebel." After tempers had cooled, he served in the House.

and have frequently here in private intercourse, since my arrival at Washington. . . . Mr. Fillmore has administered the Executive Government with signal success and ability. He has been tried and found true, faithful, honest, and conscientious. I wish to say nothing in derogation from his eminent competitors, they have both rendered great services to their country; the one in the field, the other in the Cabinet. They might possibly administer the Government as well as Mr. Fillmore has done. But then neither of them has been tried; he has been tried in the elevated position he now holds, and I think that prudence and wisdom had better restrain us from making any change without a necessity for it, the existence of which I do not perceive.

THE COMPROMISE OF 1850

Clay had not held public office since he resigned from the Senate in 1842, though he had nearly been elected President in 1844 and mustered considerable strength for the nomination in 1848. Meanwhile, he had spent most of his time at Ashland and much of his effort on the law practice he now shared with his son James. Yet he could not decently decline his state's obvious desire to have him back in the Senate; his fellow Kentuckians knew that another grave national crisis was imminent, and that their best possible contribution toward resolving it would be to send the Great Compromiser to the scene of action. In the following letter of January 31, 1849, to Thomas B. Stevenson, Clay accurately predicted Kentucky's choice. He was less accurate, however, in what he wrote Stevenson after the election: "I shall not place myself in any leading

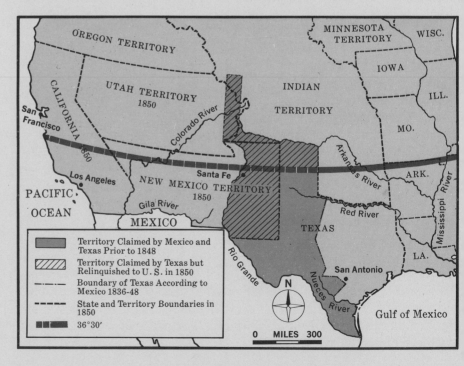

The Texas boundary was disputed at the time that region won its independence from Mexico, as well as after it became a state in the Union. From 1836 to 1845, while Texas was a separate republic, the boundary quarrel was with Mexico. After the annexation of Texas and the Mexican War, the argument over what areas should be part of Texas became a domestic affair. It was finally resolved by the Compromise of 1850 (see pages 79–81). The 36° 30′ line on this map indicates where the nation would have been separated between slave and free states had the Southern recommendation, which advocated extending the Missouri Compromise line to the Pacific, been accepted.

position. . . . I shall rather seek to be a calm and quiet looker on, rarely speaking, and when I do, endeavoring to throw oil on the troubled waters."

■ I suppose that I shall be elected to the Senate by the General Assembly of Kentucky, in which case I shall hardly feel myself at liberty to decline, conferred as the office will be without any solicitation from me, without my being a candidate, and with the knowledge of a strong disinclination on my part to return to that body. Deference to the will of the General Assembly, a sense of duty, and the possibility of my being able to do some good, overcome my repugnance. If I go to Washington, it will be with an anxious desire that I shall be able to support the measures of the new Administration, in consequence of their conformity with Whig policy.

Far from "rarely speaking" or being "a calm and quiet looker on," the elderly and ailing Clay probably spoke more and worked harder in 1850 than during any session of Congress in his vigorous prime. Southerners were threatening to secede unless slavery was permitted in the territory newly taken over from Mexico; the Wilmot Proviso (see page 74) was being pressed again; California was demanding admission as a free state. The first paragraph excerpted below (from a letter to his son James) shows that Clay was already feeling his way toward a solution. The second paragraph is from a letter to Leslie Combs, urging him to organize a movement against "disunion" in the state of Kentucky.

A determined Whig, as well as a prominent Kentucky lawyer and legislator, Leslie Combs possessed qualities that endeared him to Clay. He willingly fought for his beliefs, having served valorously in the War of 1812; in 1836, with his own money, he raised an entire regiment to help Texas achieve independence from Mexico. As one of Clay's trusted friends and political allies, he made numerous speeches during Clay's unsuccessful bid for the Presidency in 1844. Two years later Combs became Speaker of the Kentucky legislature, and in 1860, at the climax of his career, was elected clerk of the Court of Appeals by a huge majority. An avowed unionist, Combs carried out Clay's request to him here for "salutary action." When the Civil War began, he applied his energy and influence toward preventing Kentucky's secession.

■ No certain developments are yet made of what Congress may do on the subject of slavery. I think there is a considerable majority in the House, and probably one in the Senate, in favor of the Wilmot proviso. I have been thinking much of proposing some comprehensive scheme of settling amicably the whole question, in all its bearings; but I have not yet positively determined to do so. Meantime some of the Hotspurs of the South are openly declaring themselves for a dissolution of the Union, if the Wilmot proviso be adopted. This sentiment of disunion is more extensive than I had hoped, but I do not regard it as yet alarming. It does not reach many of the Slave States. . . .

The feeling for disunion among some intemperate Southern politicians, is stronger than I hoped or supposed it could be. The masses generally, even at the South, are, I believe, yet sound; but they may become influenced and perverted. The best counter-action of that feeling is to be derived from popular expressions of public meetings of the people. Now, what I should be glad to see, is such meetings held throughout Kentucky. . . . Can't you get up a large powerful meeting of both parties, if possible, at Lexington, at Louisville, etc., to express, in strong language, their determination to stand by the Union? . . . Now is the time for salutary action, and you are the man to act. I inclose some resolutions, which, or some similar to them, I should be happy to see adopted. Prudence and propriety will suggest to you, that too free a use of my name should not be made in getting up this movement.

A compromise had to be offered, and the old statesman was the logical choice to make it. Early in February 1850, arguing for the set of resolutions he had proposed, Clay made what has become a highly regarded appeal to reason and an historic argument for the preservation of the Union.

■ What vicissitudes do we not pass through in this short mortal career of ours? Eight years, or nearly eight years ago, I took my leave finally, and, as I supposed, forever, from this body. At that time I did not conceive of the possibility of ever again returning to it. . . . I have come here . . . in obedience to a sense of stern duty, with no personal objects, no private views, now or hereafter, to gratify. . . .

I must take occasion here to say that in my opinion there is no right on the part of any one or more of the States to secede from the Union. . . .

The Constitution of the United States was made not merely for the generation that then existed, but for posterity—unlimited, undefined, endless, perpetual posterity. And every State that then came into the Union, and every State that has since come into the Union, came into it binding itself, by indissoluble bands, to remain within the Union itself, and to remain within it by its posterity forever. . . . Let me say to the North and to the South, what husband and wife say to each other. We have mutual faults; neither of us is perfect; nothing in the form of humanity is perfect; let us, then, be kind to each other—forbearing, forgiving each other's faults—and above all, let us live in happiness and peace together. . . . I have said, what I solemnly believe, that dissolution of the Union and war are identical and inevitable; and they are convertible terms; and such a war as it would be, following a dissolution of the Union! . . . We may search the pages of history, and none so ferocious, so bloody, so implacable, so exterminating—not even the wars of Greece, including

On July 28, 1848, a carpenter at work on a sawmill in California excitedly showed his employer, John Sutter, some gold he had found in the millrace. There was more, he told Sutter—much, much more—where this had come from! Sutter tried to conceal the discovery, but word trickled out and the California Gold Rush began. Within a year 80,000 "Forty-Niners," like those shown at right, came to seek their fortune. "We are on the brink of an Age of Gold," crowed Horace Greeley. But the "age" had its dark side, for earlier settlers like Sutter were bankrupted by prospectors squatting on their land, ravaging their streams, and stealing their cattle. California, in dire need of organized status to end mounting lawlessness, achieved statehood as one of the segments composing the Compromise of 1850.

those of the Commoners of England and the revolutions of France—none, none of them all would rage with such violence, or be characterized with such bloodshed and enormities as would the war which must succeed, if that event ever happens, the dissolution of the Union. . . . In conclusion, I implore, as the best blessing which Heaven can bestow upon me, upon earth, that if the direful event of the dissolution of this Union is to happen, I shall not survive to behold the sad and heart rending spectacle.

While the debate blistered in Washington, Clay confidently wrote his son James, then still in Lisbon, the first paragraph below. The second paragraph is from his letter of March 16, 1850, to James Harlan; in it Clay gave vent to his scorn for the lack of cooperation between the White House and the Capitol. On March 11, Senator William H. Seward of New York (later to become one of the greatest of all Secretaries of State) had made an extremist speech for which Clay had little respect.

■ On . . . the Slavery subject . . . I made a speech, and offered a plan of compromise, of which I send you a copy. The speech has produced a powerful and salutary effect in the country and in Congress. Whether the plan will be adopted or not remains to be seen. I think if any is finally adopted it will be substantially mine. . . .

I have never before seen such an Administration. There is very little co-operation or concord between the two ends of the avenue. There is not, I believe, a prominent Whig in either House that has any confidential intercourse with the Executive. Mr. Seward, it is said, had; but his late Abolition speech has, I presume, cut him off from any such intercourse, as it has eradicated the respect of almost all men for him.

At the height of the wrangling over the Compromise, the great voice of the South, John Calhoun, was silenced on March 31, 1850, and his death was announced in the Senate. Although the contention between the two men was often bitter (see page 62), Clay's seconding speech for the Senate's order for the South Carolinian's funeral is indicative of the respect they shared mutually:

■ My personal acquaintance with him . . . commenced upward of thirty years ago. We entered at the same time the House of Representatives at the other end of this building. . . . Such . . . was the high estimate I formed of his transcendent talents, that, if at the end of his service in the executive department under Mr. Monroe, he had been called to the highest office in the government, I should have felt perfectly assured that, under his auspices, the honor, the prosperity, and the glory of our country would have been safely placed. But . . . he is gone! No more shall we witness from yonder seat the flashes of that keen and penetrating eye, darting through this chamber. No more shall we witness that torrent of clear, concise, and compact logic, poured out from his lips, which, if it did not always carry conviction to our judgment, commanded our great admiration. Those eyes and those lips are closed forever! . . .

Although short and not an accomplished orator, William H. Seward still gave the impression of being a courageous, earnest person, convinced he was right. Opposed to slavery, he did not wait long after his arrival in the nation's capital to express decided views on the controversial subject. A senator from New York, he rose on March 11, 1850, to deliver an address, soon to become famous, that aroused Clay's contempt. Attacking the Compromise measures, Seward argued: "The national domain is ours. . . . It was acquired by the valor and with the wealth of the whole nation. We hold, nevertheless, no arbitrary power over it. . . . The Constitution regulates our stewardship. . . . But there is a higher law than the Constitution. . . . Whether, therefore, I regard the welfare of the future inhabitants of these new territories, or the security and welfare of the whole people of the United States, I cannot consent to introduce slavery into any part of this continent, which is now exempt from what seems to me so great an evil . . . or to compromise the questions relating to slavery, as a condition of the admission of California."

A cool, shrewd man, John Caldwell Calhoun was the leading apostle of state sovereignty. Harriet Martineau described him as "the cast-iron man, who looks as if he had never been born." Calhoun's daily life was organized into careful routines whether he was on his plantation or in Washington. Oliver Dyer, amazed by his lucidity, declared: "His ideas were so clear and his language so plain that he made a path of light through any subject he discussed." Honest, frank, and convinced of the justice of his argument, Calhoun wrote toward the end of his life: "In looking back, I see nothing to regret, and little to correct." He even expressed a desire to have "Nullification" etched on his tombstone.

He possessed a genius of the highest order. In felicity of generalization of the subject of which his mind treated, I have seen him surpassed by no one, and the charm and captivating influence of his colloquial powers have been felt by all who have conversed with him. I was his senior . . . in years—in nothing else. According to the course of nature, I ought to have preceded him. It has been decreed otherwise. I know that I shall linger here only a short time, and shall soon follow him. And how brief, how short is the period allotted even to the youngest among us! . . . Ought we not to profit by the contemplation of this melancholy occasion? Ought we not to draw from it the conclusion how unwise it is to indulge in the acerbity of unbridled debate? How unbecoming, if not presumptuous, in us who are the tenants of an hour in this earthly abode, to wrestle and struggle together with a violence which would not be justifiable even if it were our perpetual home. . . . I trust we shall all be instructed by the eminent virtues and merits of his exalted character, and be taught by his bright example to fulfill our great public duties by the lights of our own judgment and by the dictates of our own consciences, as he did, according to his honest and best conceptions of those duties, faithfully and to the last.

The successful enactment of the various parts of the Compromise of 1850 owed much to Henry Clay (see pages 79–85 and 118–120). A year after the passage of these resolutions, he wrote a committee of New Yorkers—summarizing in flowing style his definition of state sovereignty and his deep satisfaction that the Compromise had achieved its purpose of preventing a breaking-up of the United States. But he warned that, if civil war should come, the national government would have no choice but to use force to maintain the Union.

■ The sovereignty of the States, prior to the adoption of the present Constitution, was limited and qualified by the articles of confederation. They had agreed among themselves to create a *perpetual* Union. When, therefore, the thirteen original States passed from under those articles, to the Constitution, they passed from a less to a more perfect Union, and agreed to further limitations upon their sovereignty. . . .

It may be affirmed, with entire truth, that all the attributes of sovereignty which relate to peace and war, commerce, navigation, friendship and intercourse with, and, in short, all that relate to foreign powers, and several of those attributes which relate to the internal administration of the States themselves, are voluntarily surrendered to the general government, and can not be exercised by the States. The performance of any of the forbidden acts would be null and void, no matter in what solemn and authentic form, nor by what State authority, the legislature, a convention, or the people themselves of the State, in an aggregate mass, it might be performed. The Constitution of the United States would instantly intervene, vacate the act, and proclaim the overruling, supreme and paramount authority of the Constitution, laws and treaties of the United States. . . . No State can do any thing repugnant to the Constitution, laws and treaties

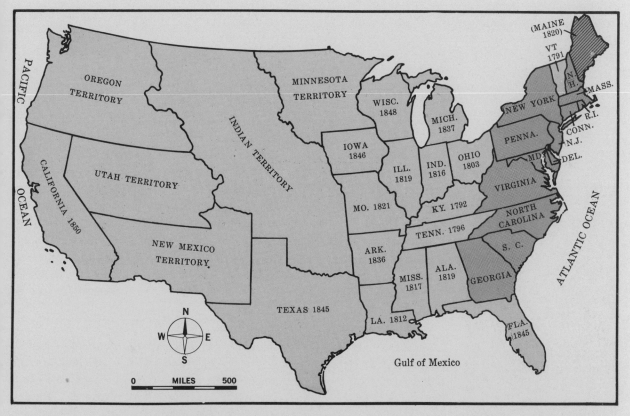

of the United States. . . . The alleged right of secession is, I apprehend, sometimes confounded with a right of revolution. But its partisans mean a totally different thing. They contend that it is a peaceful, lawful, and, if not constitutional remedy, that it is not forbidden by the Constitution. They insist that it is a State right, to be recognized and respected; and, that whenever exercised by a State, if necessary, is entitled to the co-operation of other States. The prudent valor of these partisans, in imitation of the previous example of the friends of nullification, disclaims the purpose of using themselves, and protests against the application to them of any physical force. . . .

It is incumbent upon wise and considerate men, before they hastily engage in a revolution, deliberately to consider the motives and causes of revolt, and carefully to calculate the probable consequences of forcible resistance. If unsuccessful, they know that they will be guilty of treason, and incur the penalty inflicted upon traitors. . . . If there are local exceptions at the North and at the South, of rash and misguided men, who would madly resist the Constitution and laws of the United States, let us not despair of their return, in seasonable time, to reason and to duty. But suppose we should be disappointed, and that the standard should be raised of open resistance to the Union, the Constitution and the laws, what is to be done? There can be but one possible answer. The power, the authority and dignity of the government ought to be maintained, and resistance put down at every hazard. Government . . . would lose all respect, and fall into disgrace and contempt, if it did not . . . exercise the right of employing force. . . .

The duty of executing the laws and suppressing insurrections, is without limitation or qualification; it is co-extensive with the jurisdiction of the United States, and it comprehends every species of resistance to the execution of the laws, and every form of insurrection, no matter under what auspices or sanction it is made. Individuals, public meetings, States, may resolve, as often as their tastes or passion may prompt them to resolve, that they will forcibly oppose the execution of the laws, and secede from the Union. While these resolutions remain on paper, they are harmless; but the moment a daring hand is raised to resist, by force, the execution of the laws, the duty of enforcing them arises, and if the conflict which may ensue should lead to civil war, the resisting party, having begun it, will be responsible for all the consequences.

HONORS—AND TUBERCULOSIS

Toward the end of his long life, Henry Clay was the recipient of various honors bestowed by his admirers. The most lasting of these is the biography that Calvin Colton was then preparing. The work took several years to compile and write before the earliest edition of it was published in 1845. The first paragraph here excerpted concerns Clay's reaction to Colton's original outline; the second paragraph, written nearly a year later, indicates that Clay was fully prepared to cooperate with Colton in this endeavor. And when, in 1845, Colton queried the Kentuckian about a possible coat of arms to use as an illustration in the biography, he evoked the response contained in the third paragraph.

■ Do not imagine that I am forgetful of you, or insensible to your exertions for the public, and for me. I have been absent from home, my correspondence is excessively oppressive, and not until this afternoon have I been able to read your life of me. In the main, its facts are correct. It is a good outline, well-adapted to its purpose. There are a few inaccuracies, and too much commendation and panegyric. . . .

Such a work, truly and faithfully written, might be made very interesting. But every thing will depend upon its execution. I believe you possess sufficient ability to perform the task, if you have sufficient time and sufficient materials. However, this is a moment of too great interest and excitement either to decide definitely upon the propriety of such a work, or for me to make now any contributions toward its composition. I hope we shall both live some years yet, and have many opportunities of seeing and conferring with each other upon the subject, after which we can come to a satisfactory conclusion. . . .

I have really no coat of arms, and if I had, I should doubt the propriety of the use of it suggested by you. In lieu of it, would it not be better to

Edwin Forrest, whose amusing encounter with Clay is described on page 86, was a robust performer who thrived on romantic roles. From playing odd parts in roving stock companies, he rose to eminence as the first native American to rival in brilliance Britain's foremost players. He was also the first American actor to offer playwrights financial incentives, awarding prizes to the writers of significant new plays. A prizewinning work, *The Gladiator* (by Robert M. Bird), gave Forrest one of his most famous and durable parts, that of the Roman slave Spartacus, whose costume he wears here.

employ some object drawn from those interests which I have sought to promote in the National Councils? A loom, shuttle, anvil, plow, or any other article connected with manufactures, agriculture, or commerce.

Daniel Ullman and other New Yorkers told Clay in 1851 that they wanted to present him with a large gold medal and sought his advice on what details to include. He answered:

■ I have looked at the list of events and subjects which are proposed to be inscribed on the medal. I have made out and sent herewith a more comprehensive list, embracing most of the important matters, as to which I had any agency, during my service in the National Councils. As to the Cumberland Road, no year can be properly fixed. Appropriations for it were made from year to year, for a series of years, which were violently opposed, and the support of which chiefly devolved on me. So in regard to Spanish America, the first movement was made by me in 1818, and my exertions were continued from year to year, until the measure of recognition was finally completed in 1822.

The list now sent may be too large for inscription on the medal. Of course it is my wish that it should be dealt with, by abridgment, or omission as may be thought proper. The two reports, made by me in the Senate, which gave me much credit and reputation were, 1st. That which proposed an equal distribution among the States of the proceeds of the public domain; and 2d. That which averted General Jackson's meditated war against France, on account of her failure to pay the indemnity. I carried both measures against the whole weight of Jackson; but he pock-

Clay enjoyed visiting Saratoga Springs, where he not only drank the mineral waters but also promenaded along high-pillared, vine-clad piazzas such as this one at Congress Hall. In his book *Such was Saratoga*, Hugh Bradley states: "Calhoun, Clay, and Webster came during several seasons. . . . It was mamma, the girls, and the traveling celebrities who ruled at Saratoga Springs. . . . The main hotels were built for habitation only during the mildest weather. Nevertheless they did provide an outward impression of size and grandeur such as never will be equaled by the skyscraper hotels of modern great cities. . . . From 1820 almost until the Civil War, politicians of all degrees . . . found Saratoga Springs a pleasant place for consultation and divertissement." In 1839, a ball was given there in Clay's honor, and eight hundred people applauded when he entered, as the band played "Hail, Columbia!"

Despite his frequent absences from Kentucky, Henry Clay's marriage to Lucretia Hart endured a lifetime. At first Lucretia shared the trips to Washington, but she preferred the farm in Lexington. Clay's biographer Joseph Rogers observes: "She made the farm pay when her husband did not use up all the surplus in entertaining. On leaving for Washington, he always gave her a generous check for expenses, which she as regularly gave back to him on his return. She was said to be the best farmer in Fayette County; he the next best." The warmth between the two did not lessen with the years. When Clay returned to Lexington in 1850, after his triumph at compromise, a welcoming crowd insisted on a speech. He expressed his appreciation but added: "I must ask you to excuse me, for, strange as it may seem, there is an old lady at Ashland whom I would rather see than all of you." The couple are here portrayed in old age.

eted the Land Distribution bill, which was not finally passed until 1841. He could not, however, make war against France, without the concurrence of Congress, and my report preserved the peace of the two countries. My Panama instructions were the most elaborate (and if I may be allowed to speak of them), the ablest State paper that I composed while I was in the Department of State. They contain an exposition of liberal principles, regulating Maritime War, Neutral Rights, etc., which will command the approbation of enlightened men and of posterity.

The gold medal, duly struck, was formally presented to Clay in his rooms at Washington's National Hotel on February 9, 1852. One side showed his head in bas-relief, with his nose jutting out impressively. The reverse had a long list of his achievements. Soon afterward, the medal was lost in transit; it was never recovered. On March 18, 1852, Clay twitted Ullman:

■ I received your kind letter informing me of the loss of the medal. I am truly sorry for the occurrence, and the more so because I ought to have followed your directions to send it by Adams' Express. . . . The fact of its presentation, and even the representations upon the medal have been so widely diffused as to render the presentation of it historical. You will recollect that I jocosely remarked while you were here that some Goth, when I was laid low in the grave, might be tempted to break off my nose and use the valuable medal which it contains! I did not then, however, anticipate the possibility of such an incident occurring so quickly.

Ill health stalked Henry Clay during the last decade of his life. Occasional visits to Newport, Saratoga Springs, and Cape May relaxed the man and relieved the sickness for a time, but these were vacations, not cures. Exhausted by the winter session of Congress in 1850–1851, and apparently already suffering from the tuberculosis that would cause his death, Clay informed his wife that he would return to Ashland via a southern route. One of the few letters to Lucretia that survives, it exemplifies Clay's steadfast devotion to her.

■ MY DEAR WIFE.—I have finally concluded to return by Cuba and New Orleans. The greatest difficulty I felt in coming to this conclusion, has been my long absence from you, and my desire to be with you. But my cough continues. Although I do not [have to stay in bed] my health is bad, and the weather has been the worst of March weather. The road, too, by Cumberland, I am told, is almost impassable. I hope that I may be benefited by the softer climate of Cuba. I expect to go on the 11th, from New York, in the steamer Georgia; and I think my absence from home will not be prolonged beyond a month, that is, the middle of April.

Clay did get home that spring, and on May 9 wrote his son James: "A troublesome and inconvenient cough has hung by me for six months past; it has reduced and enfeebled me very much. Dr. Dudley thinks that my lungs are unaffected, and that it proceeds from some derangement in the functions of the stomach. . . . My hopes rest upon the effects of warm weather." The summer sun did not stop the tuberculosis; nevertheless, Clay was determined to attend the session of Congress that began in December 1851. Shortly after his return to Washington, he must have realized that what was wracking his body would be fatal. On December 17 he resigned from his seat in the Senate with the resignation to take effect on September 1, 1852. On Christmas Day, he wrote to his daughter-in-law Mary, the wife of Thomas Clay, reassuring his son and family about the state of his health and the care he was receiving:

■ I am under very great obligations to you and to Thomas for the kind offer which you have made, to come either one or both of you to Washington, to attend me during my present illness. If there were the least occasion for it, I should with pleasure accept the offer; but there is not. Every want, every wish, every attention which I need, is supplied. The hotel at which I stay has a bill of fare of some thirty or forty articles every day, from which I can select any for which I have a relish, and if I want any thing which is not on the bill of fare, it is promptly procured for me. The

The sickness that finally consumed Henry Clay was taking its toll by February 1852. Four months before his death, he wrote to his daughter-in-law Susan, the wife of James: "The winter has been exceptionally rigorous, and I have not been out of the house for eight weeks." Although his writing was perhaps a trifle less steady than in earlier years, it was still easily read. His mind continued to be alert, and he was extremely interested in everything that concerned his large family.

My dear Susan   Washn. 12th Feb. 1852

I recd. your letter of the 27th Ult°, and I had recd. that of James of the 1st. I write now so uncomfortably and so slow that I take up my pen with great repugnance. I was very glad to receive both of your letters, and was delighted to contemplate the picture of your domestic happiness with your husband and children. As the world recedes from me, I feel my affections more than ever concentrated on my children, and theirs.

My health has improved a little within the last few weeks, but the cough still hangs on, and unless I can get rid of it or greatly diminish it, I cannot look for a radical cure. The winter has been excessively rigorous, and I have not been out of the house for eight weeks. You must not believe all you see in the news papers, favorable or unfavorable about my health.

John Cabell Breckinridge, who delivered the most expressive eulogy on Clay, was in some ways his true successor both in Lexington and in Kentucky. Grandson of Clay's old patron (see pages 125–126), the younger Breckinridge was a Democrat who ran for Congress against Clay's close colleague Leslie Combs, and upset him in a normally Whig district. The Lexington lawyer's funeral oration on Clay consolidated his own high place in the affections of the area's people: "As a leader in a deliberative body Mr. Clay had no equal in America. In him, intellect, person, eloquence, and courage united to form a character fit to command. He fired with his own enthusiasm, and controlled by his amazing will, individuals and masses. No reverse could crush his spirit, no defeat reduce him to despair. Equally erect and dauntless in prosperity and adversity, when successful he moved to the accomplishment of his purposes with severe resolution; when defeated he rallied his broken bands around him, and from his eagle eye shot along their ranks the contagion of his own courage. Destined for a leader, he everywhere asserted his destiny. In his long and eventful life, he came in contact with men of all ranks and professions, but he never felt that he was in the presence of a man superior to himself. . . . He assumed and maintained a position of preeminence." Later Breckinridge was Vice-President under Buchanan; he was also a United States Senator, a notable Confederate general, and Jefferson Davis' Secretary of War. In 1865 he went into exile, but returned in 1869 to resume his law practice.

state of my case may be told in a few words. If I can get rid of this distressing cough, or can materially reduce it, I may yet be restored to a comfortable condition. That is the present aim of my physicians, and I have some hope that it has abated a little within the last few days. But if the cough can not be stopped or considerably reduced, it will go on until it accomplishes its work. When that may be, it is impossible to say, with any sort of certainty. I may linger for some months, long enough possibly to reach home once more. At all events, there is no prospect at present of immediate dissolution. Under these circumstances, I have no desire to bring any member of my family from home, when there is not the least necessity for it. With regard to the rumors which reach you from time to time, and afflict you, you must bear with them, and rest assured of what I have already communicated to your mother, that if my case should take a fatal turn, the telegraph shall communicate the fact.

By February 1852, the situation was so much worse that Clay began to prepare himself and his family for the eventuality of death. His interest in his family never flagged, however, as his letter to James on February 24 reveals:

■ I should have written you oftener, but I am so feeble, and write with so little comfort, that I take up the pen reluctantly. I hope that you and Susan, notwithstanding my apparent delinquency, will write me frequently, giving me full details of all your plans, improvements, and business. There is nothing now that interests me so much as to receive full accounts from the members of my family frequently. Although you have got more in debt than I could have wished, you ought to be very happy. In dear Susan you have an excellent wife, and you have a fine parcel of promising children, and you have ample means of support. . . .

My health continues very delicate. I have not been out of the house for upward of two months. I can not recognize any encouraging change. My cough still hangs on, although I sometimes hope that it is a little abated. If I can not get rid of it, or at least greatly diminish it, I think it must prove fatal. But I may linger for months to come. I should be glad to get home once more.

My love to Susan, and kisses for all the children. I would be glad to write more, but you can not conceive how this little letter has exhausted me.

The next two paragraphs are from letters to James dated March 14 and April 10. Clay was clearly aware that the end was near, while the general optimism emanating from his doctors reflects a medical psychology that is evidently timeless.

■ My health continues nearly stationary, not getting better nor worse, except in one particular, and that is sleep. Although I take an opiate every night, and lie in bed fourteen hours, I can get no sound, refreshing sleep. A man whose flesh, strength, appetite and sleep have been greatly reduced, must be in a bad way, but that is my condition. I have taken immense quantities of drugs; but with little if any effect on my cough, the disease which threatens me. I may linger on some months, but if there be no speedy improvement, I must finally sink under it. . . .

What will be the issue of my illness it is impossible to predict. My own opinion of the case is less favorable than that of my physicians. If my strength continues to fail me, I think I can not last a great while. I feel perfectly composed and resigned to my fate, whatever it may be.

Later in April, Clay knew he would never again see his beloved Ashland. On April 27, he summoned his son Thomas by telegraph, a device only a few years old. The son remained until Clay died on June 29; that afternoon, Thomas wrote his wife:

■ Shortly after I wrote to you this morning I was summoned by James to my father's bedside. "Sit near me, my dear son," he said; "I do not wish you to leave me for any time to-day." In about an hour after, he said, "Give me some water." I gave him about half a glassful, which he drank, and still retained the tube in his mouth. In a few moments he released the tube, and said, "I believe, my son, I am going." Five minutes after, he told me "to button his shirt collar," which I did. He then caught my hand, and retained it in his pressure for some time. When he relinquished it, I discovered he was dying. I summoned Governor Jones, of Tennessee, who occupied the room above him, and in five or ten minutes after, he had ceased to breathe. May my mother, and all of you, be prepared for it. A nation mourns, but it is his gain. He is free from pain, and I thank God. Oh! how sickening is the splendid pageantry I have to go through from this to Lexington.

Clay's funeral procession was as lengthy and elaborate as his son Thomas reluctantly predicted it would be in this closing excerpt. Between June 29 and July 9, the cortege slowly wound from Washington via Baltimore, Wilmington, Philadelphia, New York, Albany, Buffalo, Cleveland, and Cincinnati, finally to arrive in Lexington. Then his body lay in state at Ashland for a night, with only his widow permitted in the chamber that contained his coffin. Kentucky erected a massive monument over his grave, surmounted by a tall Corinthian column on which was a heroic statue of the Great Compromiser. Still other ceremonies followed the funeral itself. This contemporary engraving depicts the memorial procession held in New York City on July 20. At the left is the Astor House, most famous New York hotel of the period. George Templeton Strong recorded the event in his diary entry of Thursday, July 22: "Henry Clay's sham funeral Tuesday very imposing. Streets very generally draped in mourning, specially Broadway. The Astor House shrouded in black bombazine from cornice to sidewalk. Only the windows left unveiled."

CHRONOLOGY

PERSONAL LIFE   PUBLIC LIFE

Virginia and Kentucky

1777 Born on April 12 in Hanover County, Virginia.
1781 Father dies; Clay home sacked by British troops.
1791 Works as clerk in store.
1792 Mother and stepfather move to Kentucky.
1793 Begins to study law.
1797 Migrates to Kentucky.
1799 Marries Lucretia Hart.
1808 Serves as titleholder for 13,000 acres in Kentucky.

1797 Admitted to Virginia bar.
1798 Starts Kentucky law practic gains reputation as orator in Junto d bating society.
1799 Active at convention to revi Kentucky constitution.
1803 Elected to state legislature.
1806 Defends Aaron Burr in court; se to U.S. Senate.
1807 Reelected state legislator.
1809 Slightly wounded in duel wi Humphrey Marshall.
1810 Returns to U.S. Senate.

"Harry of the West"

1811 Wife and six children accompany him to Washington.
1816 Ashland includes 513 acres and mansion.
1817 Imports Hereford cattle.
1820 Friend's financial failure leaves him pressed for money.
1822 LL.D. from Transylvania University; his death reported during bout with fever; daughter Susan marries.

1811 Opposes national bank; elect Speaker of the House.
1811–12 Leads the "War Hawks."
1814 Peace commissioner in Ghent.
1816 Supports the Bank.
1818 Urges recognition of Latin Ame ican republics.
1819 Lawyer for the Bank.
1820 Guides Missouri Compromise.
1824 Runs for President and form lates American System.

Whigs and Jacksonians

1825 Daughters Susan and Eliza both die within a month.
1828 Son Thomas sent to jail for wild behavior.
1829 Mother, stepfather, and brother all die.
1831 Son Henry graduates from West Point; son Theodore goes insane; Ashland enlarged by 300 additional acres.
1836 Borrows $20,000 from John Jacob Astor.
1840 Visits Virginia birthplace.

1825 Backs Adams over Jackson; a pointed Secretary of State; deni charge of "corrupt bargain."
1826 Fights duel with Randolph.
1831 Elected to Senate.
1832 Defeated for President.
1833 Introduces Compromise Tariff.
1834 Promotes Senate vote of censu of Jackson.
1836 Heads Colonization Society.
1839 Loses presidential nomination Harrison.

The Great Compromiser

1842–45 Mortgages Ashland after son Thomas' financial failures.
1845 Contributions from anonymous supporters save Ashland.
1847 Son Henry killed at battle of Buena Vista; is baptized by an Episcopal clergyman.
1851 Makes will providing for eventual liberation of his slaves.
1852 Receives Hungarian patriot, Louis Kossuth; dies on June 29 in Washington.

1841 Struggles for Whig leadershi with President Tyler; introduces publ lands bill.
1842 Resigns from Senate; speaks ou against abolitionism.
1844 Tours the South; straddles Texa issue; defeated for President.
1847 Condemns Mexican War.
1848 Loses presidential nomination.
1849 Elected to Senate.
1850 Engineers the Compromise.

POLITICAL—MILITARY EVENTS IN AMERICA	CULTURAL—ECONOMIC EVENTS IN AMERICA	WORLD EVENTS

POLITICAL—MILITARY EVENTS IN AMERICA

777 Battle of Saratoga.
781 Battle of Yorktown.
787 Slavery prohibited in Northwest Territory.
789 Federal government begins.
791 Indians trounce General St. Clair.
792 Kentucky statehood.
796 Tennessee statehood.
798 Alien and Sedition Acts.
803 Louisiana Purchase.
807 Jefferson's Embargo.
809–17 Madison is President.

CULTURAL—ECONOMIC EVENTS IN AMERICA

1782 Crèvecoeur publishes *Letters from an American Farmer*.
1784 Iroquois cede land.
1784–87 Economic depression.
1787 First national coinage.
1791 First United States bank.
1796 Public lands up for sale.
1800 Library of Congress founded.
1804–06 Lewis & Clark Expedition.
1806 Webster's *Dictionary*.
1807 Fulton's *Clermont* on Hudson.
1809 Irving's *Knickerbocker History*.

WORLD EVENTS

1779–82 British victories in India.
1781 Kant's *Critique of Pure Reason*.
1783 First balloon ascent.
1789 French Revolution begins.
1791 Canadian government revised.
1794 Kosciusko leads Polish revolt.
1798 British suppress Irish revolt.
1804 Napoleon becomes Emperor.
1808 Goethe's *Faust* (Part One); Beethoven's *Fifth Symphony*.

1812–15 War of 1812.
1814 British burn Washington; Hartford Convention.
1817–25 Monroe is President.
1818 Jackson's raid into Florida; U.S.-Canada boundary to the Rockies is determined.
1819 Annexation of Florida.
1823 Monroe Doctrine proclaimed.
1824 Boundary agreement with Russia in Pacific Northwest.

1811 First steamboat on Ohio; Astoria founded in Oregon.
1812 Rush's *Diseases of the Mind*.
1814 Key's "Star-Spangled Banner."
1815 Boat steams upstream for first time, New Orleans to Louisville.
1816 First protective tariff.
1817 American Colonization Society.
1819 Major economic crisis.
1820 American missionaries embark for Hawaii.
1822 Ex-slaves found Liberia.
1824 Owen founds New Harmony.

1812 Napoleon invades Russia; Peninsular Campaign.
1813 Bolivar leads revolts.
1814 Stephenson displays locomotive.
1815 Battle of Waterloo; Holy Alliance formed; Macadam builds British roads.
1817 Ricardo's *Political Economy*.
1819 First steamer crosses Atlantic; British occupy Singapore.
1821 Greek Revolution begins.
1822 Brazilian autonomy.

1825 New parties: National Republican and Democratic Republican.
1829–37 Jackson is President.
1830 Webster-Hayne debate.
1831 Nat Turner's Rebellion.
1832 Black Hawk War; Bank renewal is vetoed.
1832–33 Nullification crisis.
1835–36 Texas wins independence.
1836 Gag Rule halts antislavery petitions in Congress.
1837–41 Van Buren is President.

1825 Erie Canal is opened; Eastern Indians are moved west.
1828 "Tariff of Abominations."
1830 Smith founds Mormon Church.
1831 Garrison starts the *Liberator*.
1833 Anti-Slavery Society begun.
1834 McCormick patents reaper.
1836 Temperance Union founded; McGuffey's first *Reader*.
1837 Morse displays telegraph; Emerson's "The American Scholar."
1837–43 A major depression.

1825 British unions legalized.
1826 First Pan-American convention.
1829 Britain's Catholic Emancipation.
1830–39 French conquest of Algeria.
1831 Faraday's electromagnetics.
1833 British abolish slavery.
1834 English Poor Law passed.
1835–37 Great Trek of the Boers.
1837–1901 Queen Victoria reigns.
1838 Dickens' *Oliver Twist*.
1840 Canadian provinces united.

1841 President Harrison dies; Tyler succeeds him.
1842 Dorr Rebellion in Rhode Island; U.S. recognizes Hawaii.
1845 Annexation of Texas; the term "manifest destiny" is coined.
1845–49 Polk is President.
1846 Wilmot Proviso defeated.
1846–48 Mexican War.
1849–50 Taylor is President.
1850 Death of Calhoun.
1850–53 Fillmore is President.

1841 Greeley founds *Tribune;* Cooper's *The Deerslayer*.
1841–47 Brook Farm.
1843–44 Slavery splits churches.
1844 Brigham Young heads Mormons after lynching of Smith.
1845 Poe's "The Raven."
1846 Howe patents sewing machine; Smithsonian Institution.
1849 Thoreau's *Civil Disobedience*.
1850 Jenny Lind's American debut.
1851 Melville's *Moby Dick*.
1852 Stowe's *Uncle Tom's Cabin*.

1842 Opium War in China ends.
1845 Irish Famine begins.
1846 British repeal Corn Laws.
1848 Revolts rock Europe; Marx and Engels issue *Communist Manifesto;* Macaulay's *History of England;* Thackeray's *Vanity Fair*.
1849 British repeal Navigation Laws.
1850 Dickens' *David Copperfield*.
1851 First world's fair at Crystal Palace in London.
1852–70 Napoleon III rules France.

ANNOTATED BIBLIOGRAPHY

The following titles, divided into three major categories, have been selected for their usefulness to the reader.

WORKS ABOUT CLAY'S LIFE

Mayo, Bernard. *Henry Clay: Spokesman of the New West.* Houghton Mifflin, 1937.

Mayo's biography, which covers only the first thirty-five years of Clay's life, is a colorful and perceptive account of his career in Virginia, Kentucky, and Washington until the War of 1812. It is especially helpful for its clear depiction of the political, economic, and social conditions in Kentucky between 1797 and 1812. There are several remarkably sensitive pen portraits of Clay's associates and friends.

Eaton, Clement. *Henry Clay and the Art of American Politics.* Little, Brown, 1957.

This is a concise examination of Clay's public and personal aspirations, triumphs, and defeats. Eaton contends that Clay did not significantly contribute to American political theory and that he believed any social changes must come very gradually. However, Eaton concedes that the conservative elements in Clay's character were accompanied by his somewhat radical ideas on such vital issues as slavery and the right of citizens to petition and dissent. This divergence, according to Eaton, was responsible for Clay's ability to hammer out compromises— while at the same time it contributed to his intolerance of those who would not readily adjust to differences of opinion.

Van Deusen, Glyndon G. *The Life of Henry Clay.* Little, Brown, 1937.

The most authoritative full-scale biography published to date focuses on Clay against the background of his period. The author effectively introduces the drama of Clay's personal life into the detailed narrative of his public career. The judgments, though usually favorable to the subject, are always objective within the historical context.

Schurz, Carl. *Henry Clay* (2 vols.). Houghton Mifflin, 1887.

The German immigrant who became an outspoken advocate of slave emancipation in America—and one of his adopted land's distinguished Cabinet officers—portrays Clay with feelings of both admiration and contempt. Himself a practical politician who was also an idealist, Schurz could respect and at the same time deplore a man like Clay who disliked slavery but temporized on it for pressing political reasons. Schurz's own deep commitment to the "higher principles" of life, as well as his fine use of a language not native to him, suffuse his long, penetrating book with distinct qualities of eloquence and permanency.

Colton, Calvin. *The Life of Henry Clay, the Great American Statesman* (2 vols.). Barnes, 1856.

The author did much of his research for this massive work while he was a guest at Ashland. Too much of a panegyric by an enthusiastic admirer, it nevertheless remains a primary source of information about Clay.

Rogers, Joseph M. *The True Henry Clay.* Lippincott, 1904.

The Kentuckian who wrote this biography intended to draw a definitive picture of Clay before the last personal memories of him faded. Rogers makes him a hero without denying his faults. Clay is depicted as the leader of America's "real democracy"—the middle class.

The following specialized studies are useful for advanced reading or research on Clay:

Poage, George Rawlings. *Henry Clay and the Whig Party.* University of North Carolina Press, 1936.

The manner in which splinter groups came together to oppose Jackson is the starting point of this detailed monograph. It follows Clay's rise to leadership of the Whigs, and credits him with molding the party that finally nominated him.

Mooney, Booth. *Mr. Speaker: Four Men Who Shaped the United States House of Representatives.* Follett, 1964.

The "Four Men"—all notable Speakers of the House—were: Henry Clay, Thomas B. Reed, Joseph G. Cannon, and Sam Rayburn. Clay appears as the greatest of these Speakers, and the prime creator of the office as it is known today.

Alexander, Holmes. *The Famous Five.* The Bookmailer, 1958.

The "Famous Five" were the men selected as the Senate's outstanding members of all time: Henry Clay, Daniel Webster, John C. Calhoun, Robert La Follette, and Robert Taft. The author treats Clay as the foremost Senator of them all, but denies that he was qualified for the Presidency. John F. Kennedy, then a Senator himself, contributed the foreword.

EDITIONS OF CLAY'S WRITINGS

Hopkins, James F. (ed.) *The Papers of Henry Clay*, Vols. I–IV. University of Kentucky Press, 1959–1967.

The correspondence, speeches, and writings of Henry Clay are here presented in their most complete and exact form. Unfortunately, the collection extends only to 1828. Six more volumes now in the process of being researched and edited are projected. Alongside the major pieces, this expertly footnoted collection includes such minutiae as bills, promissory notes, and receipts, which give it authenticity and flavor. In addition to what Clay wrote, it also contains significant documents addressed to him. Until later volumes appear, those who want to consult the original papers covering Clay's wide range of significant activities during his last twenty-four years must resort to the earlier works listed below.

Colton, Calvin (ed.). *The Works of Henry Clay* (10 vols., Federal edition). Putnam, 1904. ———. (7 vols.). Henry Clay Publishing Co., 1897. ———. (6 vols.). Barnes, 1857.

———. *The Private Correspondence of Henry Clay.* Barnes, 1856.

These various editions of Clay's writings, while not marked by careful modern scholarship, were unusually full for their times and will continue to be invaluable until the volumes edited by James Hopkins are finished. Colton not only knew Clay in person, but also was diligent in rounding up his scattered papers. The collections of 1897 and 1904 cited above are, in effect, merely republications of Colton's original broad surveys.

BOOKS ABOUT EVENTS AND PEOPLE CONTEMPORARY WITH CLAY

De Tocqueville, Alexis. *Democracy in America* (2 vols.). Knopf, 1945.

Written by an astute French viewer of America in the early 1830's, this classic abounds in penetrating observations on the character of American democracy. While it is not easy reading, it is essential for any serious student of the period. De Tocqueville throws much light on the strengths and weaknesses of the democratic process.

Dangerfield, George. *The Era of Good Feelings.* Harcourt, 1952.
Although he has a tendency toward questionable generalizations, Dangerfield writes perceptively and with great facility. Concentrating on the period when the Federalist party succumbed and the Jefferson-Republican party split, he substantially covers the political developments of that era.

Johnson, Gerald W. *America's Silver Age: The Statecraft of Clay-Webster-Calhoun.* Harper, 1939.
Three political biographies are here combined to present an overall view of the party warfare of the period. The author—a lively writer who sometimes prefers to be stimulating rather than precise—depicts Clay as the champion of peace and compromise. But Andrew Jackson emerges with more resoundingly heroic qualities.

Van Deusen, Glyndon G. *The Jacksonian Era, 1828–1848.* Harper, 1959.
In this general survey of the twenty-year period indicated by the title, the political leaders of the time are all shrewdly yet objectively treated on their individual merits. Clay is woven in and out of the story as a major opponent of Jackson.

Schlesinger, Arthur M., Jr. *The Age of Jackson.* Little, Brown, 1945.
Writing brilliantly, Schlesinger is opinionated—and decidedly biased in favor of Jackson over the Whigs. Later scholarship has modified his contentions about Jacksonian economic policies. His portrayal of Jacksonian democracy as a forerunner of the New Deal has come under severe fire. Nonetheless, this book remains an important—and most readable—interpretation of the Jacksonian period.

Binkley, Wilfred E. *American Political Parties: Their Natural History.* Knopf, 1962.
In this large treatise, there is a spirited account of the rise and fall of political parties during Clay's long period at center stage. It is thoughtfully done, and very useful in providing a political party background for Clay's activities.

Pratt, Julius W. *Expansionists of 1812.* Macmillan, 1925.
This scholarly work discusses the background and the causes of the War of 1812. It emphasizes the influence of the frontier and the supposed agreements between Southern and Western expansionists. Pratt's interpretation, however, should be balanced against that of the next volume below.

Perkins, Bradford. *Prologue to War: England and the United States, 1805–1812.* University of California Press, 1961.
The most recent, and best, analysis of the Anglo-American diplomacy that underlay the War of 1812, this book reads well. The subject matter is clearly presented, and the judgments are backed by evidence.

——— (ed.). *The Causes of the War of 1812.* Holt, 1962.
Perkins here presents selections from the works of more than a dozen authorities on the period. He successfully brings out the varied points of view as to the origins of "the second war for independence." In addition, his introduction offers a judicious summary.

Eaton, Clement. *The Growth of Southern Civilization, 1790–1860.* Harper, 1961.
Political, economic, social, and cultural factors are included in this illuminating survey of life in the South before the Civil War. This book presents a useful background for Clay's political career.

Cash, Wilbur J. *The Mind of the South.* Knopf, 1941.
The author provides a fine analysis of Southern ideas and attitudes in the antebellum period. His volume is a "must" for anyone who wishes to understand the subject. Much of it is remarkably pertinent today.

Taylor, William R. *Cavalier and Yankee.* Doubleday, 1963.
An apt use of literary sources makes this a stimulating and perceptive account of the search for a national character prior to the Civil War. The author is most concerned with the South's quest for inclusion in the national framework, although the Northern and Western regional elements are not excluded from his panorama.

Abernethy, Thomas P. *From Frontier to Plantation in Tennessee.* University of North Carolina Press, 1932.
This study in early pioneer democracy is particularly valuable for its disclosure of the beliefs and motives of the Southern frontiersman. It gives an interesting picture of Andrew Jackson, Clay's great opponent, during the first part of his career.

Dumond, Dwight L. *Antislavery Origins of the Civil War in the United States.* University of Michigan Press, 1939.
This analysis reviews the various ways in which both the abolitionist indictment of slavery and the Southern defense of the "peculiar institution" contributed to the coming of the Civil War. It helps to explain why national political leaders, such as Clay, dreaded the rising tumult over slavery.

Barnes, Gilbert Hobbs. *The Antislavery Impulse, 1830–1844.* Appleton, 1933.
Special emphasis is placed here on the moral aspects of the antislavery movement. Critical of William Lloyd Garrison, Barnes ascribes more importance to other leaders, chiefly Western, in the movement to free the slaves.

Nye, Russell B. *Fettered Freedom.* Michigan State College Press, 1949.
Slavery's assault on the right of petition and freedom of the press provoked a popular reaction. This volume provides an important examination of the entire question in relation to the democratic process.

Cole, Arthur C. *The Whig Party in the South.* American Historical Association, 1913.
This fundamental study investigates the aspirations, aims, and influence of the Southern Whigs. Although written more than fifty years ago, it has not been superseded by any later work.

Hamilton, Holman. *Prologue to Conflict.* University of Kentucky Press, 1964.
The Compromise of 1850 is discussed authoritatively in this volume. The author shows that passage of the component parts of the Compromise was due largely to Democratic support, and especially to the efforts and canny parliamentary maneuvers of Stephen A. Douglas.

Nevins, Allan. *Ordeal of the Union,* Vol. I. Scribner's, 1947.
Introducing vivid characterizations in his customary dramatic style, Nevins describes America during the last five years of Clay's life. First-rate historical writing, it brings the period to life.

Hammond, Bray. *Banks and Politics in America, from the Revolution to the Civil War.* Princeton University Press, 1957.
Hammond provides the best treatment extant of the interaction between finance and politics during the antebellum period. He is favorable to Nicholas Biddle and critical of Jackson. While the subject is formidable, this book makes it easily comprehensible.

Wellington, Raynor G. *The Political and Sectional Influence of the Public Lands, 1828-1842.* Riverside Press, 1914.
Thorough but far from easy reading, this work is basic to a full understanding of the problems and policies resulting from the controversies over the public lands.

Taylor, George R. *The Transportation Revolution, 1815-1860.* Rinehart, 1951.
This excellent book gives the reader a good understanding of the rapid development of economic life in America. It explains why Clay's American System had such an appeal for the business class.

Bemis, Samuel F. *John Quincy Adams and the Foundations of American Foreign Policy. John Quincy Adams and the Union.* Knopf, 1949, 1956.
These two volumes constitute the most recent, and best, full-scale biography of Adams. Both are based on sound research, and are enlivened by a skillful use of imaginary conversation—a device most unusual in books by a professional historian.

Bassett, John Spencer. *The Life of Andrew Jackson* (2 vols. in one). Macmillan, 1928.
Written by an eminent scholar, this is a balanced and judicious study of Old Hickory. Bassett is generally favorable to Jackson, but his partiality is always restrained by his respect for the facts.

James, Marquis. *The Life of Andrew Jackson* (2 vols. in one). Bobbs-Merrill, 1938.
Eminently readable, owing to a dash and charm superior to the workmanlike prose of Bassett, this biography contains a vast amount of research—and an almost equally vast prejudice in favor of Jackson.

Van Deusen, Glyndon G. *Thurlow Weed: Wizard of the Lobby.* Little, Brown, 1947.
The political boss par excellence in New York history undergoes a penetrating scrutiny in this book. There is a fine description of the Whig convention, when Weed was instrumental in denying Clay the 1840 presidential nomination.

———. *Horace Greeley, Nineteenth Century Crusader.* University of Pennsylvania Press, 1953.
One of the highlights in this searching biography is its account of how the editor of the New York *Tribune* threw his personal and journalistic influence behind Clay in 1844, and was emotionally crushed by the Whig leader's defeat.

Wiltse, Charles M. *John C. Calhoun* (3 vols.). Bobbs-Merrill, 1944-1951.
Painstaking research in primary sources makes this an exhaustive though pedestrian biography. It remains the most thorough portrayal of Calhoun, despite its bias in his favor.

Fuess, Claude M. *Daniel Webster* (2 vols.). Little, Brown, 1930.
This work cannot be rated as more than adequate—the judgments on Webster are simply too generous. Still, much scholarship went into it, and no subsequent biography has replaced it.

Sellers, Charles G., Jr. *James K. Polk: Jacksonian, 1795-1843. James K. Polk: Continentalist, 1843-1846.* Princeton University Press, 1957, 1966.
Polk was not a wholly attractive figure, but he played an important role at a crucial time in American history. These are the first two volumes of a trilogy that should be the definitive study of an unusually successful President of the United States.

Hamilton, Holman. *Zachary Taylor* (2 vols.). Bobbs-Merrill, 1941-1951.
Hamilton's work is the most authoritative Taylor biography with regard to both content and style. He presents the essential facts about the Mexican War General who was President during part of the struggle over the 1850 Compromise.

Rayback, Robert J. *Millard Fillmore: Biography of a President.* Henry Stewart, Inc., 1959.
The only available biography of the nation's thirteenth President—and the man Clay wanted to see reelected in 1852—this work did not appear until eighty-five years after Fillmore's death. Negating the belief that Fillmore was an ineffective and self-important man, the author has written a lively corrective, emphasizing that his subject achieved his ends in both local and national politics.

INDEX

(* indicates an illustration; † indicates a map reference; pages 7–88 are in the Biography; pages 89–120 are in the Picture Portfolio; pages 121–229 are in His Own Words.)

PICTURE CREDITS

The sources for the illustrations are listed below. Some have been abbreviated as follows: BA—Bettmann Archive; Columbia —Columbia University Library; Culver—Culver Pictures; Granger—The Granger Collection; HCMF—Henry Clay Memorial Foundation, Lexington; Kentucky—University of Kentucky, Lexington; LC—Library of Congress; LIFE—Life Picture Collection; NYHS—New-York Historical Society; NYPL—New York Public Library; Pennsylvania—Historical Society of Pennsylvania.

The maps on pages 218 and 223 are by Rafael Palacios. The drawings on page 230 are by Bette J. Davis. Photographers are credited after source and —.

Cover: NYHS. 2 NYHS. 4-5 (left to right) Harry Shaw Newman, The Old Print Shop, New York—Frank Lerner; HCMF—Frank Lerner; Kentucky—Frank Lerner.

BIOGRAPHY: 7 Harry Shaw Newman, The Old Print Shop, New York—Frank Lerner. 8 Kiplinger Collection. 10 Abby Aldrich Rockefeller Folk Art Collection, Williamsburg. 11 Culver. 12 Colonial Williamsburg. 13 M.W. Anderson, Lexington, Kentucky—Frank Lerner. 15, 16-17 Columbia. 19 NYPL. 21 Franklin D. Roosevelt Library, Hyde Park. 23 Culver. 24 NYHS. 25 Columbia. 27 Culver. 29 I.N. Phelps Stokes Collection, NYPL. 30 Culver. 35 Pennsylvania. 38 NYHS. 42 BA. 44, 46 NYPL. 49 Culver. 50 NYHS. 53 Culver. 54 Pennsylvania. 55 I.N. Phelps Stokes Collection, NYPL. 56 American Antiquarian Society, Worcester, Massachusetts. 57 National Archives. 60, 61 Culver. 63 NYPL. 65, 66 LC. 68 New York State Historical Association. 70, 71 NYPL. 73 Year, Inc. 76 LC. 78 NYPL. 80, 81, LC. 83 BA. 85 Tim Gidal. 87 LC.

PICTURE PORTFOLIO: 89 The Capitol, Washington D.C., American Heritage Publishing Co. 90 LC—Henry Beville. 91 (top) anonymous owner; (bottom) detail of "The Start of the Hunt," artist unknown, gift of Edgar William and Bernice Chrysler Garbisch, National Gallery of Art. 92 (top) Museum of Art, Rhode Island School of Design, Providence; (bottom) Shelburne Museum, Vermont. 93 LC—Henry Beville. 94-95 (top) Gjon Mili; (bottom) I.N. Phelps Stokes Collection, NYPL, American Heritage Publishing Co. 96-97 (left to right) NYHS; National Portrait Gallery, Smithsonian Institution—Jay Levitan; Mrs. Edward R.C. Haskell, Charleston, South Carolina; Tennessee Historical Society, Nashville; Buffalo and Erie County Historical Society; Miss Katherine Turner, Lexington, Kentucky—Frank Lerner; (bottom) U.S. Naval Academy Museum, Annapolis—Henry Beville. 98 Ann S.K. Brown Military Collection. 99 (top) The Peale Museum, Baltimore; (bottom) Smithsonian Institution—Herbert Orth. 100 (top) Peabody Museum, Harvard University; (bottom) City Art Museum of Saint Louis; 101 Jahn & Ollier Engraving Co., collection of The Boatmen's National Bank of Saint Louis. 102-103 (all) Kentucky—Frank Lerner. 104 NYHS. 105 (top to bottom) Chicago Historical Society; Pennsylvania; North Carolina Museum of Art. 106-107 NYHS; Du Pont Museum, Winterthur, Delaware. 108-109 The Jockey Club, New York—Frank Lerner; Museum of Fine Arts, Boston; (bottom right) HCMF—Frank Lerner. 110 (top) NYHS—T. Fernand Bourges; (bottom) U.S. Military Academy Museum, West Point. 111 NYPL—Frank Lerner. 112-113 Maryland Historical Society; (top right) NYHS; (bottom) NYPL—Frank Lerner. 114-115 (top and right) LC; (bottom left) BA. 116 HCMF. 117 (bottom) HCMF—Frank Lerner; (right) HCMF. 118-119 (top left) Smithsonian Institution—Eric Schaal; (bottom left) Herbert Gehr; (right) LC. 120 Pontalba House, Louisiana State Museum—Eric Schaal.

HIS OWN WORDS: 121 Kentucky—Frank Lerner. 123 (top) NYHS; (bottom) Culver. 124 LC—Henry Beville. 126 Granger. 127 (top) BA; (bottom) NYPL. 129 (top) Granger; (bottom) BA. 130 LC—Henry Beville. 131 NYPL. 132 BA. 133 Columbia. 134 (both) Granger. 136 Columbia. 137 BA. 138 (top) Brown Brothers; (bottom) BA. 141 LC—Henry Beville. 143 Columbia. 144 Elizabeth H. Evans. 146 Columbia. 147 Harris & Ewing. 148 NYHS. 149, 150 BA. 151 LC—Henry Beville. 152 Du Pont Photo Library. 154 Columbia. 157 LC. 158, 159 Culver. 160 BA. 164 NYPL. 165 Kentucky—Frank Lerner. 166 American Antiquarian Society, Worcester, Massachusetts. 167, 168 Columbia. 170 LC—Henry Beville. 173 Culver. 174 BA. 176 NYPL. 179 Culver. 180 NYPL. 181 BA. 183 Colonial Williamsburg. 185, 187 BA. 188 Culver. 191 NYPL. 192 BA. 193 NYPL. 194 LC. 196 Culver. 197 LC—Henry Beville. 198 Granger. 199 LC. 200 Culver. 201, 202, 203 NYPL. 204 (top) Culver; (bottom) BA. 205 LC—Henry Beville. 206 Culver. 207 BA. 208 Culver. 209 (top) BA; (bottom) Museum of the City of New York. 210 NYPL. 211 BA. 213 (both) NYPL. 214 LC—Henry Beville. 215 (top) Culver; (bottom) BA. 216, 217 BA. 219 Columbia. 220, 221 BA. 222, 224, 225 Culver. 226 (both) NYPL. 227 LC—Henry Beville. 228 Granger. 229 BA.